GALACTIC
FEDERATIONS
COUNCILS
& SECRET SPACE PROGRAMS

GALACTIC FEDERATIONS COUNCILS

& Secret Space Programs

MICHAEL E. SALLA, PH.D.

BOOK SEVEN OF THE SECRET SPACE PROGRAM SERIES

TENNESSEE, USA

GALACTIC FEDERATIONS, COUNCILS
& SECRET SPACE PROGRAMS

Exopolitics Consultants
PO Box 946
Dandridge, TN 37725 USA

Printed in the United States of America

Cover Design: Rene McCann & Angelika Whitecliff
Cover images by Christine Kesara Dennett

ISBN 978-0-9986038-8-9
Library of Congress Control Number: 2022909967

Dedication

For all those brave contactees who faced ridicule, censorship, and retaliation for revealing the truth about face-to-face encounters with extraterrestrial visitors.

Table of Contents

Table of Figures

Preface

In 2013, I wrote *Galactic Diplomacy: Getting to Yes with ET Civilizations*, where I analyzed nineteen extraterrestrial and 'intraterrestrial' civilizations that had been described by different contactees and whistleblowers who had firsthand experiences with these technologically advanced entities. I examined each of these civilizations in terms of eyewitness encounters, key activities, and overall impact upon human civilization. While my list was not exhaustive, I felt confident that the extraterrestrial civilizations examined were the most important for humanity to understand at that point in our history. What I did not do at the time was investigate what organizations these and other extraterrestrial civilizations belonged to. I simply did not have enough reliable data back then to reach any conclusive understanding of what the principle extraterrestrial organizations interacting with humanity were. That situation has recently changed.

There has been a significant increase in reliable information showing that extraterrestrial visitors are organized into distinct associations, which are not necessarily aligned with one another. While some of these organizations are friendly and cooperate with each other, other organizations are not. Indeed, some of these associations are antagonistic towards one another and have been involved in galactic wars that have spanned years, decades, or even longer. Importantly, there is significant evidence that this hostility between the different extraterrestrial organizations has carried over to Earth, and many nation states have been historically used in a proxy war between these alien groups.

To make matters even more confusing and complex, this proxy war, which can be traced back at least to the World War II era, has an important temporal component. Extraterrestrial visitors possess exotic technologies that enable them to travel backward and forward in time as easily as it is for humans to currently commute between different locations on the Earth's surface. Based on eyewitness testimonies to be presented, this temporal war has led to different extraterrestrial organizations developing a strong incentive to intervene in human affairs to prevent a future galactic tyranny that can be traced back to Earth at this very point in our historical evolution.

This book is divided into two parts. In Part One, I analyze the principle extraterrestrial organizations that are interacting with humanity. My list is not exhaustive. It is intended to focus on those organizations that are the most relevant and best supported in terms of eyewitness and insider accounts. Most importantly, I focus on off-world organizations that have had the most positive impact on humanity's long-term interests and are generally considered to be friendly or neutral. I have left future researchers the more challenging task of discerning the principal characteristics of 'unfriendly' extraterrestrial organizations, whose histories and activities are far more difficult to understand. My esteemed colleague Richard Hoagland once said that when it comes to government entities managing the UFO and extraterrestrial issue, the "lie is different at every level." This is especially true when it comes to unfriendly extraterrestrial organizations, but thankfully less so when it comes to friendly or neutral groups.

Consequently, I have only described the proverbial tip of the iceberg when it comes to the different extraterrestrial organizations interacting with or monitoring Earth. There is far more beneath the surface that future investigators will have to fathom. What follows in Part One will provide the reader with a sufficient foundation to understand the principle extraterrestrial organizations that are most relevant to humanity's evolution at this point in our history.

In Part Two, I describe how secret space programs have responded to the intervention of the friendly extraterrestrial organizations, which have had a profound impact on human affairs both on Earth and in our solar system. This has led to a still-unfolding planetary liberation process, while secret space programs have assumed primary responsibility for managing affairs in our solar system. Put simply, the intervention of friendly extraterrestrial organizations, the departure of unfriendly groups, all watched by more neutral alien associations—acting as a kind of galactic umpire—have led to a profound change in human affairs. A Star Trek future is finally within humanity's grasp, and nothing will stop us from entering our bold new future.

Michael Salla, Ph.D.
March 5, 2022

CHAPTER 1

The Ashtar Command

You know now that we are here, and that there are more beings on and around your Earth than your scientists admit. We are deeply concerned about you and your path towards the light and will do all we can to help you. Have no fear, seek only to know yourselves, and live in harmony with the ways of your planet Earth.

—Vrillon, Ashtar Galactic Command

George Van Tassel

The first public references to an extraterrestrial organization visiting Earth were made in 1952 by the famous contactee George Van Tassel. Today that space-based organization is widely known as the "Ashtar Command", eponymously named after its alleged leader, Commander Ashtar. Ashtar, along with numerous subordinates and other extraterrestrials of unspecified affiliation, established a direct telepathic communication link with Van Tassel. At the time, Van Tassel was the owner of a private airport at Giant Rock, California. Earlier in his career, he had worked as a mechanic for 22 years in the aviation industry for major companies such as Douglas Aircraft, Howard Hughes, and Lockheed Aircraft. His contact experiences began in the early 1950s with telepathic messages, and he later had his first physical contact in 1953 with an extraterrestrial called Solganda. Van Tassel is best known for organizing the Giant Rock conventions that began in 1954 and continued until 1977. These were huge UFO conventions, the largest UFO meetings ever held, which took place at Van Tassel's airport home in the Mojave Desert. Impressively, he would get up to 11,000 people coming to each of his Giant Rock conventions.

All the leading UFO researchers and contactees of the time went to these groundbreaking conventions, whose rapid growth in popularity greatly disturbed public authorities. The FBI in particular went to great lengths to tarnish Van Tassel and Giant Rock Convention supporters, branding them as communist sympathizers plotting to overthrow the US government. Freedom of Information Act documents confirm the FBI's involvement. An August 4, 1954 report by an unnamed FBI Special Agent declared:

> The saucer groups appear to be another means of raising funds for the Communist Party. When chosen by the communist screening group, members would be given further indoctrination. A very conceivable place to clear them would be through such a place as Giant Rock Airport, located approximately 15 miles northwest of Joshua Tree, California.
>
> The Giant Rock group, which now has under construction a so-called "College of Universal Wisdom" to be located at Giant Rock Airport, is in my opinion teaching and advocating the overthrow of the U.S. government by publishing literature, which subtly aids in Communist indoctrination, and could provide a substantial amount of revenue as a fundraising "front" group for the Communist Party.[1]

Despite unfounded accusations made public in the FBI efforts to tarnish the flying saucer movement, the conventions were an enormous success and marked a notable accomplishment by Van Tassel, who organized them due to his own contact experiences. He knew how important the extraterrestrial information was for the general public to hear and wanted to create a public forum for other contactees to share what they had experienced and learned.

Figure 1. First Giant Rock Convention

Van Tassel had amazing information to share about a new technology he was developing called the Integratron, housed in a two-story hemisphere-shaped structure. The Integratron was designed with the help of extraterrestrials and had multiple functions, including healing and age rejuvenation. The Integratron was designed for people to experience healing, restorative effects, and other benefits by utilizing sound vibrations. Unfortunately, Van Tassel never got to finish the Integratron. He died under mysterious circumstances taking with him the secrets for finalizing it and making it operational. Nevertheless, it is still partly operational and continues to draw people to its location near Giant Rock.

Later in 1952, after several contacts took place, Van Tassel went public by releasing a small book titled *I Rode a Flying Saucer*. He wrote about his communications with the extraterrestrials belonging to the Ashtar Command, and explained the process by which he was vibrationally attuned to receive the initial telepathic communications:

Each vibration or transmission has to be tuned in, to receive it intelligently. In the process of "dialing" these "wave-lengths," I seem to have one that persisted in attuning itself to my "receiver." I had become cautious, through experience, because I found many of the vibrations could "burn up my cabinet," my physical body. This particular vibration is exceptionally powerful, and the cooperation I received from its source assisted me in many ways to gradually become accustomed to its power. After I could receive this intelligence, in attunement, without physical discomfort, the beings of the vibration gave me the following information.[2]

Figure 2. George Van Tassel & Integratron Model

Van Tassel says he received telepathic communications from entities claiming to be extraterrestrials residing in a space base. What made his alleged telepathic communications worthy of attention were the stunning accuracy of several predictions that were relayed.

His book begins with a communication he received on January 6, 1952, introducing several beings who claimed they resided in the alleged spacebase called 'Schare', located 72,000 miles above Earth, from which smaller flying saucer craft would visit our planet. On March 7, 1952, Van Tassell received the following message: "Greetings from the realms of Schare. Watch your skies in your months of May to Aug."[3] The extraterrestrials were predicting much UFO activity during the coming summer.

A month later, on April 6, Van Tassel received another message: "Your Pentagon will soon have much to muddle over. We are going to give this globe a buzz. I hope they do not intercept us from in front."[4] What the extraterrestrials were alluding to from their space base—72,000 miles above the Earth—is that they were going to conduct overflights of sensitive US military facilities and give the whole planet a wake-up call to the existence of alien life. Furthermore, they were giving the US military/Pentagon a veiled warning not to attempt to intercept the craft. After Van Tassel received these warnings of future events, what exactly happened in the summer of 1952 for which Van Tassel had received an advanced warning about?

1952 Washington Flyover

The famous Washington DC UFO flyovers occurred over three successive weekends beginning on July 12/13, followed by more sightings on July 19/20, and finally on July 26/27. These overflights were not just above Washington DC airspace, but over other East Coast cities and rural areas. The sighted UFOs flew in formation and created a major international buzz, just as predicted a few months earlier by Van Tassel's contacts. However, a question emerges of how many of the flying saucer craft were part of the group communicating with George Van Tassel and came from the space base Schare, and how many were part of a negative group of alien visitors that the Ashtar Command had given warnings about. In an April 27, 1952 message, the Ashtar Command representative said:

> Do not be confused between what you call fireballs, flying saucers and cigar shaped objects all seen by your people. Those cigar shaped ships are spaceships from a neighboring planet, and as you know the fireballs are ships from Blaau [galactic sector our solar system is moving into]. Our so-called saucers are from Schare.... Some of the cigar-shaped ships are not investigating with peaceful intent and our investigation concerns them as much as this globe. We shall keep a close watch upon them and they know it.[5]

Van Tassel's acknowledgment that there were two competing groups of extraterrestrials visiting Earth and conducting overflights of major population centers is critical to keep in mind.

In my book, *Antarctica's Hidden History* (book three of the Secret Space Programs series), I wrote about a German secret space program (SSP) that had been established in Antarctica during World War II.[6] In short, the German Antarctic base was created in collaboration with a group of very aggressive non-human Reptilian-looking extraterrestrials called "Draconians," who had helped the Germans develop their breakaway colony and fleets of flying saucers. According to William Tompkins, an "insider" who was part of a covert US Navy espionage program that had infiltrated Nazi Germany's top aerospace companies through its spy network, the extraterrestrial visitors helping Nazi Germany were part of a Draconian Empire, later revealed to be an interstellar organization that sought galactic domination.[7]

There were also human-looking extraterrestrials allied with the Draconian Empire with even more advanced flying saucers than the Germans had. This group helped the Germans defeat the US Navy's Operation Highjump expedition led by Admiral Richard Byrd in February 1947. Recently, in 2021, the Farsight Institute conducted a remote viewing experiment with five world-class remote viewers who, for the first time, gave insights into this human-looking group of extraterrestrials working with the

Draconians to defeat Admiral Byrd's naval task force.[8] According to the remote viewers, the human-looking group allegedly came from the Alcyone star system and was opposed to the Ashtar Command, as I will soon explain. Later in 1947, the Antarctic German SSP conducted flights over US territory, causing great concern amongst US political and military leaders. This resulted in the Eisenhower administration making agreements with the Germans and their extraterrestrial allies in the mid-1950s, as I discussed at length in *Antarctica's Hidden History*.

It is reasonable to assume that the flying saucer craft witnessed over the three successive weekends in July 1952 came from at least two distinct sources that were at odds with one another and even in competition over who would be first to reach an agreement with US leaders. In short, the formations of flying saucers over successive weekends may have been some combination of positive extraterrestrial craft from the Ashtar Command, and German Antarctic spacecraft and their negative alien allies who had their own separate agenda, as explained in *Antarctica's Hidden History*. How these disparate groups of spacecraft coordinated with one another in these flyovers over Washington DC and other US and global cities is a crucial question to explore.

What we do know, according to Van Tassel's communications, is that some of these crafts belonged to an organization he called the "Ashtar Command." Here is a message Van Tassel received on July 18, 1952, one day before the second of the Washington DC flyovers:

> Hail to you beings of Shan [aka Earth], I greet you in love and peace, my identity is Ashtar, commandant quadra sector, patrol station Schare, all projections, all waves. Greetings ... The purpose of this organization is, in a sense, to save mankind from himself. Some years ago your time, your nuclear physicists penetrated the "Book of Knowledge"; they discovered how to explode the atom.... We

> have not been concerned with their explosion of plutonium and UR 235, the Uranium mother element; this atom is an inert element.
>
> We are concerned, however, with their attempt to explode the hydrogen element.... We are not concerned with man's desire to continue war on this planet, Shan. We are concerned with their deliberate determination to extinguish humanity and turn this planet into a cinder... this condition occurred before in this solar system and the planet Lucifer was torn to bits.[9]

It is worth emphasizing that Van Tassel sent Ashtar's message to the US Air Force one day before the two most publicized of the Washington flyovers began on the evening of July 19, 1952. We do not know which group conducted the first, less publicized flyover on July 12. The main flyover, or at least the one that the Ashtar Command conducted, began on July 26. Afterward, Van Tassel linked the July 26 flyover as the "buzz" referred to by the Ashtar Command:

> Is it coincidence that a letter mailed by me to Air Forces Intelligence Command, at the request of the Saucer beings in the July 18th message, was in their hands when the "buzz" occurred? I do not comprehend how the letter's arrival, the "buzz", the reference to the Pentagon, and the expected interception, can all be coincidence. My belief is that the saucer beings timed it that way to let the Air Force know that this information was authentic. The return receipt showed they received the letter July 22nd, 1952. The "buzz" was on July 26, 27 and 28th.[10]

Van Tassel's correspondence was confirmed through the Freedom of Information Act, where the Air Force Office of Special

Investigations (OSI) acknowledged receiving a letter from Van Tassel on July 31, 1952 (see figure below).[11]

105-445-39, dated July 31, 1952, re individuals
and G. W. VAN TASSEL, reflects that the Detachment Commander
of OSI, March Air Force Base, California, received a letter
from captioned individual entitled, "Brotherhood of Cosmic
Christ", which attempts to explain flying saucers and
indicates contacts had been received by captioned individual
from the beings of another world, who operate them.

Figure 3. FBI record of Air Force Office of Special Investigations receiving a letter from George Van Tassel

Van Tassel's correspondence with the US Air Force clearly points to the last of the three weekends of the Washington DC flying saucer flyovers involving the Ashtar Command. Therefore, it can be deduced that the two preceding weekends (July 12/13 and 19/20) involved flying saucer-shaped craft from other groups, one of which was the German Antarctic colony (aka the Dark Fleet) and their extraterrestrial allies. The spacecraft of the Dark Fleet and its allies were sent to intimidate the Truman Administration into making an agreement on unfavorable terms (essentially a surrender). On the other hand, the Ashtar Command fleet was presumably sent to reassure the Truman administration that there was an alternative option available, rather than capitulating to the Antarctic Germans' demands.

Ashtar Command, Robert Oppenheimer & Nuclear Weapons

Van Tassel's July 18, 1952, message clearly shows that officials from the Ashtar Command were greatly concerned about the Truman administration's development of thermonuclear weapons, which represented a quantum leap on destructiveness over the fission bombs dropped on Hiroshima and Nagasaki to end World War II. It is very significant that the relationship between extraterrestrial visitors and humanity's development of nuclear weapons had been earlier discussed in a leaked June 1947 draft policy paper intended for President Truman that was written by Dr.

9

Robert Oppenheimer, the father of the atomic bomb, and Albert Einstein. The draft paper—classified Top Secret—was titled "Relationships with Inhabitants of Celestial Bodies." In it, Oppenheimer and Einstein stated:

> And now to the final question of whether the presence of celestial astroplanes in our atmosphere is the direct result of our testing atomic weapons?
>
> The presence of unidentified spacecraft flying in our atmosphere (and possibly maintaining orbits about our planet) is now, however, as a fact accepted by our military.
>
> On every question of whether the United States will continue testing of fission bombs and develop fusion devices (hydrogen bombs), or reach an agreement to disarm and the exclusion of weapons that are too destructive ... the lamentations of philosophers, the efforts of politicians, and the conferences of diplomats have been doomed to failure and have accomplished nothing.[12]

The Oppenheimer- Einstein paper is documentary evidence that as early as 1947, the US military had known unidentified spacecraft (aka flying saucers) were descending from high in Earth's orbit. This makes it very likely that one or more large motherships had been detected in Earth's orbit—including the large Ashtar Command mothership Schare, hovering at 72,000 miles.

Importantly, the Ashtar Command associated thermonuclear weapons with the destruction of a planet, Lucifer (aka Maldek, Tiamat), whose remnants now occupy the asteroid belt. At the time, there was no scientific data suggesting that the asteroid belt was all that remained of an exploded planet. It would be decades later, in 2000, that Dr. Thomas Van Flandern, an astronomer with the US Naval Observatory in Washington DC, would write a scientific paper on "The Exploded Planet Hypothesis."[13] Essentially, Van Flandern found ample scientific data to support the hypothesis that a planet once occupied the asteroid belt where all that is left of it now is asteroid debris. Van Flandern's research is powerful corroboration for the accuracy of Van Tassel's communications from the Ashtar Command.

In the late 1940s, a raging debate began within the US administration over the wisdom of developing thermonuclear weapons. On October 28, 1949, the General Advisory Committee to the Atomic Energy Commission delivered a report opposing a crash program to build a hydrogen bomb on both moral and technical grounds.[14] The Advisory Committee's chair, Dr. Robert Oppenheimer, as already seen in the draft Oppenheimer and Einstein paper, was an outright opponent of hydrogen bomb development. A 1949 report from Oppenheimer's General Advisory Committee condemned further research on developing hydrogen bombs on moral grounds:

> The fact that no limits exist to the destructiveness of this weapon makes its very existence and the knowledge of its construction a danger to humanity as a whole. It is necessarily an evil thing considered in any light. For these reasons, we believe it important for the President of the United States to tell the American public and the world that we think it's wrong on fundamental ethical principles to initiate the development such a weapon.[15]

As the 1949 report makes clear, there was a raging debate over developing thermonuclear weapons, dividing the US scientific community and policy advisors. There was, however, a key world event that would play a critical role in settling the debate—the death of the Soviet dictator, Joseph Stalin, on March 5, 1953.

Stalin's death appears to have been another accurate prediction from the Ashtar Command that was relayed through Van Tassel. In an April 11, 1952 message, he was told: "Your globe will be affected by the death of one of the highest leaders causing great strife."[16] Stalin's death indeed caused confusion in the Soviet Union and around the globe since there was no designated successor, and senior Soviet leaders competed with one another for the top leadership position. This impacted crucial decisions such as moving forward with the development of thermonuclear weapons and whether the Soviets should collaborate with the United States in managing such weapons.

Vrillon Message

A major development in 1977 caused the Ashtar Command to be known throughout the planet. A television broadcast on November 26, 1977, was interrupted or hacked by an external third party. A purported communication from the Ashtar Command was transmitted to an independent television network in Great Britain called ITV, interrupting the normal news feed. What was heard by the audience was the following:

> This is the voice of [Vrillon] a representative of the Ashtar Galactic [Command] speaking to you. For many years you have seen us as lights in the skies. We speak to you now in peace and wisdom as we have done to your brothers and sisters all over this, your planet Earth. We come to warn you of the destiny of your race and your world so that you may communicate to your fellow beings the course you must take to avoid the disasters which threaten your world, and the beings on our worlds around you.
>
> This is in order that you may share in the great awakening, as the planet passes into the New Age of Aquarius. The New Age can be a time of great peace and evolution for your race, but only if your rulers

are made aware of the evil forces that can overshadow their judgments. Be still now and listen, for your chance may not come again. For many years your scientists, government and generals have not heeded our warnings; they have continued to experiment with the evil forces of what you call nuclear energy. Atomic bombs can destroy the Earth, and the beings of your sister worlds, in a moment. The wastes from atomic power systems will poison your planet for many thousands of your years to come. We, who have followed the path of evolution for far longer than you, have long since realized this - that atomic energy is always directed against life. It has no peaceful application. Its use, and research into its use, must be ceased at once, or you all risk destruction. All weapons of evil must be removed.

The time of conflict is now past. The race of which you are a part may proceed to the highest planes of evolution if you show yourselves worthy to do this. You have but a short time to learn to live together in peace and goodwill. Small groups all over the planet are learning this, and exist to pass on the light of the dawning New Age to you all. You are free to accept or reject their teachings, but only those who learn to live in peace will pass to the higher realms of spiritual evolution.

Hear now the voice of Vrillon, a representative of the Ashtar Galactic Command, speaking to you. Be aware also that there are many false prophets and guides operating in your world. They will suck your energy from you - the energy you call money and will put it to evil ends giving you worthless dross in return. Your inner divine self will protect you from this. You must learn to be sensitive to the voice within that can tell you what is truth, and what is confusion, chaos and untruth. Learn to listen to the voice of truth which is within you and you will lead yourselves on to the path of evolution. This is our message to our dear friends. We have watched you growing for many years as you too have watched our lights in your skies.

You know now that we are here, and that there are more beings on and around your Earth than your scientists admit. We are deeply concerned about you and your path towards the light and will do all we can to help you. Have no fear, seek only to know yourselves and live in harmony with the ways of your planet Earth. We of the Ashtar Galactic Command thank you for your attention. We are now leaving the plane of your existence. May you be blessed by the supreme love and truth of the cosmos.[17]

The message was striking in its content and consistency with what Van Tassel had communicated over 20 years earlier. The reference to Ashtar Command ships being seen in the skies, the dawning of a new age for humanity, and the great danger posed by nuclear weapons were all topics Van Tassel had previously discussed at length in his books and lectures.

The Vrillon message's assertion that an organization called the Ashtar Command had been sending its spacecraft over Earth's skies and warning national leaders about the dangers of nuclear weapons but had been ignored, was new information to the vast majority of ITV's British viewers. Van Tassel's prior communications with the Ashtar Command were only known to a relative few in Britain that had either attended the Giant Rock conventions, read his books, or attended UFO events. Here's a brief summary of what subsequently happened:

The TV station apologized to its viewers for the inconvenience and publicly dismissed the whole matter as a hoax. Soon, all British media outlets published the news about this incident, and then it grabbed the attention of international media. The ITV company, whose broadcast was interrupted by this message, long and carefully searched for the culprit of the incident, a possible prankster or ingenious technician who managed to hack their equipment. Unfortunately, they failed to trace the culprit. They only managed to find out that the signal was sent to the Hannington transmitter antenna located on Connington Hill and broadcasting to Berkshire and North Hampshire. And the signal source was quite small, located somewhere near the antenna.[18]

It is very clear that the mysterious third party that hijacked the ITV broadcast—the Ashtar Galactic Command—did so to test how listeners would react. Of course, the official reaction was very predictable. It was covered up by senior national security officials— what is generally called the 'Cabal', 'the Illuminati', or the 'Deep State'—who ensured that the mass media would dismiss the incident as a hoax.

One famous British researcher, John Reppion, pointed out that the Vrillon message was fundamentally different from earlier pranks played out on US television networks, and he thought this supported the message's authenticity.[19] Despite the wide-ranging debate over its authenticity, the most plausible scenario is that the Vrillon message was a test designed to see how humanity would react to direct communication from an extraterrestrial organization—the Ashtar Command. The reaction from the mainstream media conclusively showed that the Deep State was very capable of neutralizing the effect of any communications from the Ashtar Command that went directly to Earth's population. The entire Vrillon incident showed that alternative means to direct communications had to be developed if humanity was to learn the truth about extraterrestrial visitors and the decades-long cover-up by national security leaders.

Elena Danaan on the Ashtar Command

A more recent credible source on the Ashtar Command is Elena Danaan, who, like Van Tassel, is an extraterrestrial contactee. Danaan worked for 20 years as a professional archeologist before leaving her career to develop her psychic, shamanic, and intuitive abilities. In 2019, she began having regular physical encounters with human-looking extraterrestrials who had earlier rescued her in an abduction incident involving Gray extraterrestrials when she was nine years old. She wrote about her contact experiences in her best-selling book, *A Gift from the Stars* (2020). In it, she describes the origins of the Ashtar Command and its relationship with two other extraterrestrial organizations called the "Draconia [aka Ciakahrr] Empire" and the "Galactic Federation of Worlds," which I will discuss in the next chapter.

Importantly, Danaan gives a clear idea of the extraterrestrial factions that the Ashtar Command was competing against in attempting to influence human affairs.

> Due to significant infiltration and corruption by agents of the Ciakahrr Empire, a rebel faction, mainly humanoids, separated from the Ashtar Collective and took side with the Galactic Federation of Worlds. Skilled in military procedures, the Ashtar separatists were offered by the Galactic Federation of Worlds to help with the operations in the Terran system. The outpost was set up on the planet Jupiter. To differentiate from the Ashtar Collective … the Ashtar separatists took the name of Ashtar Galactic Command. They are not based in a

particular system but in a large moving mothership.[20]

Danaan's information gives us a clear idea that the origins of the Ashtar Command come from it being a splinter group from another larger organization—the "Ashtar Collective"—established in a different solar system. Apparently, the Ashtar Command disagreed with the Ashtar Collective working alongside the Draconian Empire. The Ashtar separatists subsequently came to our solar system and worked alongside another large extraterrestrial organization—the Galactic Federation of Worlds—to perform military oriented functions from a space base established above Jupiter.

In the original George Van Tassel messages from 1952, the spacebase "Schare" was operating 72,000 miles above the Earth. Given that this was five years prior to the launch of Sputnik, which officially kicked off the satellite era, it would make sense that the Schare spacebase would have had to relocate back to Jupiter to escape detection. In addition, agreements reached between major Earth governments and different extraterrestrial factions in the 1950s may have also been a factor in the relocation of Schare back to Jupiter.

What makes Danaan's claims stand out from others that have been in communication with the Ashtar Command is that she says she was physically taken to their floating mothership suspended high in Jupiter's atmosphere in October 2020.

> As I stood beside Thor Han, watching our descent into the Jovian atmosphere, a cold shiver ran through my body. From now on my thoughts would be monitored by the Ashtar Command's security system ... The descent seemed endless and although we were traversing terrifying storms, violent winds and threatening titanic clouds, the ship was sliding smoothly, with ease. The structures of the Ashtar outpost started to appear through the thick ochre fog ... it was very intimidating. I knew it was just a

military facility but yet, its reputation was well known.

Protected under a gigantic dome the Jovian city extended with its glistening roads, bridges and buildings, across a vast surface. It was in fact the ship, which landed a very long time ago when the Galactic Federation of Worlds requested help to protect our solar system…. We descended at the level of the high buildings, our ship sliding in between the silvery towers until reaching the entrance of a tunnel … Moving a great speed along a corridor leading to lower levels, we finally emerged into a great and amazing hall filled with light. The high buildings were made of glass and metallic structures.

This place was gigantic! A real city! I felt Thor Han's hand tightening over mine. Come on he said in a hasty tone, the commander is waiting for me. … I followed him as if wandering through a dream. The hall included different modules of graceful buildings defying the laws of gravity.[21]

Danaan's visit to the Ashtar Command floating base was the first time anyone described being inside it. Her experience corroborated Van Tassel and other contactee reports that the Ashtar Command existed and had an enormous mothership from which it could monitor and interact with Earth.

Remote Viewing the Ashtar Command Base above Jupiter

Danaan's experience and claims regarding the Ashtar Command came to the attention of Dr. Courtney Brown, who founded the Farsight Institute, which specializes in remote viewing.

Farsight organizes regular remote viewing projects on specific 'blind' targets using teams of skilled remote viewers. On December 17, 2021, Dr. Brown released the results of one of these remote viewing "Celestial Projects" that investigated the alleged existence of an "Ashtar Command," and whether it had a floating base hidden in the clouds of Jupiter.[22] The results of the remote viewing sessions, conducted using blind scientific protocols, directly support Elena's key claims about the Ashtar Command.

Dr. Brown released a press and video statement introducing the goals of the remote viewing sessions, and the targets being investigated. He explained why he chose the target for Part 1 of the project:

> More recent information suggested by some authors not connected with Farsight seems to suggest that there was a planetary collective called the Ashtar Collective that was made up of various species, and it said that this Collective was infiltrated by the Reptilians. The same Reptilians that we here at Farsight have found plaguing modern day Earth. The Ashtar Command is said to have broken off from that Collective to form a very capable military group that has facilities that are currently based inside the clouds of Jupiter. These are some of the claims made by others relating to the Ashtar Command.
>
> If such a facility does exist in the clouds of Jupiter, then they obviously would have the technological ability to survive safely in this environment, and the extremely hostile environment would offer benefits, such as significant levels of protection that a military facility would enjoy. It would be hard to find the facility without help. Any approach to the facility would be noticed and the ships of many species might not even be able to survive the atmospheric

conditions at all, in order to mount an attack. So, from our perspective it sort of makes sense that such a facility in the clouds of Jupiter might exist.[23]

Figure 4. Drawing by Elena Danaan of her inside the Ashtar Command Base. We Will Never Let You Down (2021) p.40.

While Dr. Brown did not specify who the authors were discussing the Ashtar Command facility, these almost certainly included Elena

Danaan and myself in our respective coverage of this facility and its involvement in alleged secret agreements that occurred in July 2021. I will discuss the Jupiter agreements in a later chapter.

In his press statement/video, Dr. Brown explained the remote viewing sessions were conducted using blind scientific protocols, where the viewers were told nothing about the project or the specific target. They were only told there is a numerical target (e.g., T1) or an alphanumeric subject (e.g., SA), and they should remote view it. This scientific protocol prevents the problem of frontloading whereby remote viewers insert their own biases and judgments into the sessions when they know about the targets in advance.

In the sessions themselves, one of the remote viewers, Aziz Brown (Courtney Brown's son), illustrated the importance of the blind scientific protocols when he explained how he had formed a judgment about the target and found this immediately influenced the session until he consciously withdrew his assumption. This exemplified the necessity of blind scientific conditions for remote viewing sessions, so viewers do not allow their biases and preconceptions to creep in and influence the session.[24] Unfortunately, far too many individuals, some with significant public followings, claim to remote view targets without using any blind scientific protocols. This leads to a lot of 'frontloading', thereby significantly impacting the accuracy of their results and the overall credibility of remote viewing as an intelligence-gathering tool.

After the sessions involving up to four trained and very experienced remote viewers associated with the Farsight Institute were completed, Dr. Brown released his conclusion about the project. He said:

> Regarding the first target, we simply wanted to know if such a thing as the Ashtar Command actually exists in the clouds of Jupiter. As far as our data indicate, it does. It seems to be a secretive facility, and it does not seem to be involved in

communicating with the Earth population. I personally highly doubt that anyone in the Ashtar Command is channeling information to human receivers on Earth. It makes no sense for them to try to compete with Orion and Reptilian efforts to manipulate the human population through the spread of disinformation. If they were interested in interacting with humanity on a more personal level, they would be located closer to Earth and not hidden inside the clouds of Jupiter. As best as we can discern, they are primarily a military organization.[25]

There are some important takeaways from Dr. Brown's conclusions. First, the Ashtar Command does exist and has a base in the upper atmosphere of Jupiter. Second, he is skeptical that members of the Ashtar Command are directly communicating with humans on Earth. Third, the Ashtar Command is primarily a military organization.

Regarding his first conclusion, this is highly significant. It means that in addition to other extraterrestrial organizations identified by Dr. Brown and his remote viewing teams in earlier "Celestial Projects"—the Galactic Federation of Worlds, the Draconian (Reptilian) Empire, the Orion (Gray) Alliance, and the 'Dominion'—there is another extraterrestrial organization monitoring human affairs and our solar system.[26]

Even more significantly, the findings of the remote viewing sessions confirm claims first made by Elena Danaan that the Ashtar Command has a giant floating city/base suspended high in Jupiter's atmosphere.[27] As Dr. Brown reasoned, this would provide a stealthy base of operations for activities throughout our solar system and the Earth itself.

Second, Dr. Brown is very skeptical about claims of individuals claiming to be in telepathic communications with members of the Ashtar Command. As discussed earlier, the first individual claiming to communicate telepathically with the Ashtar Command was George Van Tassel (1952), who was followed by

Trevor James Constable (1958) and many others.[28] Today there are several individuals claiming to be in telepathic communication with the Ashtar Command, and Dr. Brown rightly points out that many of these are simply ruses by service-to-self extraterrestrials masquerading as the Ashtar Command.

Does his skepticism also apply to the contact experiences and telepathic communications of Elena Danaan? To answer this question, it is helpful to point out that Danaan says that she was actually taken to the Ashtar Command base and witnessed it first-hand and met personnel there. Second, Danaan has been in telepathic communications with representatives of the Galactic Federation of Worlds who have shared information about the Ashtar facility. She does not claim to be in touch with the Ashtar Command itself, let alone channeling information from base personnel.

Third, Dr. Brown reveals that the Ashtar Command is a military organization. This is consistent with George Van Tassel's original channelings from different Ashtar Command personnel, including Ashtar himself. In her two books, *A Gift From the Stars* and *We Will Never Let You Down*, Danaan described the origins of the Ashtar Command and its military functions in our solar system today.

In conclusion, the Farsight remote viewing project confirms the accuracy of recent claims made by Danaan about the existence of an Ashtar Command, which has been known to be intervening in human affairs since the early 1950s. This provides great confidence that the Ashtar Command is a very real extraterrestrial organization, currently located high in Jupiter's atmosphere, and that it is an important part of what lies ahead for humanity as we enter our galactic awakening.

CHAPTER 2

Galactic Federation of Worlds

The UFOs have asked not to publish that they are here, humanity is not ready yet. Trump was on the verge of revealing, but the aliens in the Galactic Federation are saying: Wait, let people calm down first.

—Prof Haim Eshed

O n December 4, 2020, Professor Haim Eshed generated worldwide headlines when in an interview published by the Israeli national newspaper, Yedioth Aharonot, he revealed the existence of a Galactic Federation monitoring human affairs.[29] Eshed had served from 1981 to 2010 as the head of Israel's satellite program and had a rank of brigadier general in military intelligence. He is widely considered to be the father of Israel's military space program, so his Galactic Federation comments were difficult to dismiss. After boldly asserting President Donald Trump was ready to make an extraterrestrial disclosure announcement, Professor Eshed explained why the truth was not revealed, according to an extract of the interview translated into English:

> They [Galactic Federation] don't want to start mass hysteria. They want to first make us sane and understanding. They have been waiting for humanity to evolve and reach a stage where we will generally understand what space and spaceships are.[30]

The possibility that President Trump was contemplating disclosure of a Galactic Federation and extraterrestrial life caught many off guard. Could an American President genuinely be having secret liaisons with an off-planet organization without the mass media and general public being aware of this? There is evidence that several of Trump's predecessors both communicated and met with representatives of a Galactic Federation wanting to assist humanity's evolution. To understand this untold history and what it means today, we need to begin with the first historical references to a Galactic Federation monitoring human affairs.

Daniel Fry and the Galactic Federation

Another famous contactee from the George Van Tassel era was Daniel Fry who worked as a rocket scientist for Aerojet at White Sands Missile Range in the late 1940s. This is the location where most Nazi German scientists had been taken under Operation Paperclip to develop the first rockets for the US military. Fry's specialty was propulsion systems which meant he had the ability to travel anywhere within the very large White Sands complex to investigate debris from rocket tests. On July 4, 1949, Fry had an encounter with a remotely controlled flying saucer that landed at the White Sands. He went inside of it to investigate. Once inside the craft, he spoke remotely with an extraterrestrial who controlled the craft through its radio communications system. Fry didn't actually see the extraterrestrial who called himself 'Alan' but was nevertheless asked if he wanted to go on a quick ride and back to New York City, an offer he immediately accepted. Five years later, he wrote a book about the White Sands incident where he went into detail about events and what he was told.

Fry was given a lot of information about advanced physics, propulsion systems, and the pre-history of our solar system, which he presented in a short booklet called, *To Men of Earth*, published in 1954. It was a fiction based on fact account about the philosophy and pre-history of extraterrestrial visits to Earth. In it he wrote:

> The planet itself [Earth], has been under occasional
> observation, by passing ships of the Galactic
> Federation, for more than a hundred generations,
> and there are a few records which were made much
> earlier.[31]

This is the first recorded reference to a "Galactic Federation" observing Earth from a distance over the course of many thousands of years as they passed in the vicinity.

Fry's information is very similar to what was found much later in the recollections of individuals undergoing past-life regressions, according to a famed hypnotherapist and best-selling book author, Dolores Cannon. In her book series, *The Convoluted Universe*, Cannon spoke about different extraterrestrial groups monitoring Earth and how they would secretly interact with open-minded individuals in different historical eras to pass on advanced knowledge.[32] The goal was to organically assist human evolution without openly intervening and impacting humanity's evolution by the extraterrestrials being viewed as gods. It can be presumed that Alan, Fry's extraterrestrial contact, was a member of the Galactic Federation passing on information to an individual who was ready for such contact.

What is significant in Fry's reference to a Galactic Federation is that it didn't show any willingness to intervene in human affairs until the dawn of the atomic age—when things changed dramatically. According to Alan, extraterrestrials began to pay closer attention as nuclear weapons were developed, especially regarding thermonuclear weapons and the threat they posed to humanity:

> [Alan] Most of the thinkers of your race are well
> aware of the danger inherent in the use of nuclear
> weapons, but there is another aspect of the
> problem which is not generally recognized. That is
> the fact that unless unity is achieved between your
> nations, the very existence of such weapons will

eventually bring about the downfall of your civilization, even though they are never used.[33]

As already mentioned, the dangers of nuclear weapons were something that Van Tassel also described as of great concern to the Ashtar Command. What's different with Fry's account is that this concern is for the first time linked to a "Galactic Federation" that he mentions in his *To Men of Earth* booklet.

This takes me to the hydrogen bomb's development, which represented a quantum leap in terms of the destructiveness of nuclear weapons technologies. On November 1, 1952, the first test of a thermonuclear device, called 'Ivy Mike', was conducted in the US. This nuclear test occurred only three days before the election of President Dwight D. Eisenhower. Why would the Truman administration move forward with a test only days before a new President was elected? The answer is very interesting. Eisenhower was highly popular and polls showed he was certain to win. It appears that influential people within the Truman administration wanted to lock the future President Eisenhower into a policy of thermonuclear weapons development regardless of the dangers they posed.

The powerful people behind Truman's decision were an organization called Majestic 12 (MJ-12) Special Studies Group, set up on September 24, 1947, to handle the extraterrestrial issue.[34] It comprised twelve highly influential leaders drawn from America's scientific, intelligence, and military sectors, as revealed in a leaked Majestic document called the "Eisenhower Briefing Document."[35] In his 2005 book, *Top Secret/Majic: Operation Majestic-12 and the United States Government's UFO Cover-up*, veteran UFO researcher Stanton Friedman conducted an exhaustive investigation into the leaked document and concluded it was authentic. The MJ-12 Group was embedded within the National Security Council and was delegated great power – effectively making President Truman a puppet when it came to vital national security issues involving the UFO phenomenon.

Eisenhower, however, was very different from Truman in terms of his influence over the national security system. As a famous five-star general that successfully ran the European war against Nazi Germany, Eisenhower enjoyed the overwhelming loyalty of the US military and the general public, many of whom had served under him. The Ivy Mike test firmly suggested the MJ-12 Group wanted to lock Eisenhower and future US Presidents firmly on the path of developing thermonuclear weapons even though extraterrestrial visitors were explicitly warning against doing so. It was widely known at the time that Eisenhower was skeptical about the need for and use of nuclear weapons. MJ-12 wanted to prevent the incoming President Eisenhower from being unduly influenced by the extraterrestrial visitors to challenge the decision to move forward with the development of the hydrogen bomb.

It is helpful to appreciate how hydrogen 'fusion' bombs were a quantum leap in destructiveness when compared to 'fission' bombs used in the atomic bomb attacks against Japan. Ivy Mike's yield ranged between ten to eleven megatons (million tons of TNT). It was followed in March 1954 by the even more powerful Castle Bravo Hydrogen Bomb test, which had a yield of fifteen megatons. This was 1000 times the destructive power of the atomic bomb dropped on Hiroshima, which was 15 kilotons (1000 tons of TNT). As big as the US hydrogen bomb tests were concerned, these were dwarfed by the Soviet Union's Tsar bomb, which had a destructive yield of 60 megatons and sparked concerns that it could put the Earth's atmosphere on fire. Similar concerns had been expressed in the Ashtar Command warnings relayed by Van Tassel in 1952. Figure 5 gives a scaled comparison of the destructive yields of the US and Soviet hydrogen bomb tests with the atomic bombs dropped on Hiroshima and Nagasaki.

Figure 5. Size comparison of nuclear detonations

As best evidenced in the October 28, 1949, General Advisory Committee report described in the previous chapter, there were prominent American scientists opposed to the hydrogen bomb development program because of the quantum leap in the destructive power of nuclear weapons. [36] Dr. Robert Oppenheimer had emerged as the top scientist opposing hydrogen bomb development due to his pivotal role in developing the atomic bomb and chairmanship of the Advisory Committee. He was targeted by Senator Joseph McCarthy as a communist sympathizer and consequently investigated by the FBI. FBI Director J. Edgar Hoover delivered a damming report to President Eisenhower, which led to the revocation of Oppenheimer's 'Q' security clearance on December 3, 1953, only five days before President Eisenhower was scheduled to give a major address before the United Nations on nuclear weapons disarmament. The timing of these events indicated that there was a powerful factional struggle within the US national security establishment over hydrogen bomb development and nuclear disarmament.

At an infamous 1954 security hearing concerning the revocation of his security clearance, Oppenheimer reaffirmed his position, and that of the General Advisory Committee, of rejecting any development of hydrogen bombs on moral and technical grounds.[37] What is remarkable here is the similarities between Oppenheimer and the Committee's position to what George Van Tassel and Daniel Fry had respectively relayed from the Ashtar Command and the Galactic Federation about the dangers of such weapons. This does suggest that prominent American scientists were, at the very least, 'unknowingly' being influenced by positive extraterrestrial groups to oppose hydrogen bomb development. Another parallel was that we know from FOIA records that the FBI targeted Van Tassel and extraterrestrial contactees in general as communist sympathizers on spurious grounds.

We do know that Oppenheimer and Einstein were firmly opposed to the development of the hydrogen bomb and formally linked similar concerns to extraterrestrial visitors in their 1947 draft policy paper for President Truman, as discussed earlier. [38] This raises the distinct possibility that one or both of them were 'knowingly' communicating or working with the Galactic Federation. This raises an even more intriguing possibility. The targeting of Oppenheimer by Senator McCarthy and Hoover's damning FBI report were part of a behind-the-scenes power struggle between two factions of the US national security establishment. One faction appeared to be working with the Galactic Federation, while the other (McCarthy/Hoover allied) faction was apparently working with the Orion Grays and Draconian (Ciakahrr) Empire. If accurate, this meant that Senator McCarthy's targeting of Oppenheimer as a 'communist sympathizer' was a cover for him really being targeted for being a 'Galactic Federation' sympathizer!

Eisenhower and Atoms for Peace

President Eisenhower showed in the first year of his administration that he was also skeptical about the development of hydrogen bombs. On December 8, 1953, he gave a famous

31

speech at the United Nations General Assembly called "Atoms for Peace."[39] In it, Eisenhower talked about the need for the civilian sector to take control of nuclear weapons and that he was prepared to negotiate with other countries to set up a civilian authority to take away control and the development of nuclear weapons from the military, which planned to use them for destructive purposes. Eisenhower's Atoms for Peace speech was a very important sign that he was personally opposed to going down the path of developing ever more powerful generations of nuclear weapons as the mainstay of future national defense:

> The United States, heeding the suggestion of the General Assembly of the United Nations, is instantly prepared to meet privately with such other countries as may be "principally involved," to seek "an acceptable solution" to the atomic armaments race which overshadows not only the peace, but the very life, of the world."[40]

The reference to the threat that atomic weapons posed to all life on Earth was again similar to the language used by the Ashtar Command and the Galactic Federation representatives. If this wasn't bad enough, Eisenhower's next statement would have sent chills through the spines of the military industrial complex, which was eager to continue development and mass production of thermonuclear weapons:

> We shall carry into these private or diplomatic talks a new conception. The United States would seek more than the mere reduction or elimination of atomic materials for military purposes. It is not enough to take this weapon out of the hands of the soldiers. It must be put into the hands of those who will know how to strip its military casing and adapt it to the arts of peace.[41]

Here we clearly have Eisenhower saying in December 1953, before the United Nations General Assembly, that atomic weapons are very dangerous, and needed to be taken out of the hands of the military and put into the civilian sector where nuclear technology would be exclusively developed for peaceful purposes.

Eisenhower's Atoms for Peace speech gives us a clear answer to the question of "why was the Ivy Mike test detonated three days before the 1952 election of President Eisenhower?" The military industrial complex could count on Truman, who had authorized the use of two atomic bombs on Japan, but knew that Eisenhower was reluctant to go down the path of nuclear weapons development. The Military Industrial Complex clearly wanted the decision to develop thermonuclear weapons to be a *fait accompli* from which Eisenhower would not be able to extricate himself.

Nevertheless, a year after his election, Eisenhower proposed a civilian agency that would take control of American and Soviet national nuclear stockpiles and convert these for peaceful purposes. In his Atoms for Peace speech, he outlined what he had in mind:

> The more important responsibility of this Atomic Energy Agency would be to devise methods whereby this fissionable material would be allocated to serve the peaceful pursuits of mankind ... The United States would be more than willing--it would be proud to take up with others "principally involved: the development of plans whereby such peaceful use of atomic energy would be expedited.[42]

Even though Eisenhower was referring to placing material critical for nuclear fission bombs in the hands of the proposed civilian Atomic Energy authority, this would have also included the more powerful fusion bombs. This is because a nuclear fission reaction is needed to generate sufficient heat to start the nuclear fusion process that would detonate a thermonuclear weapon.

Consequently, Eisenhower's Atoms for Peace Initiative was not only proposing that fission atomic bombs be placed under this under the power of this civilian regulatory agency. More critically, his proposal would also prevent fusion hydrogen bombs from being developed because fission bombs would now be under the control of the civilian sector, not the military sector.

So what happened to Eisenhower's Atoms for Peace proposal? Unfortunately, the USSR didn't respond. Stalin's death on March 5, 1953, meant that the USSR at the time of Eisenhower's radical proposal eight months later before the United Nations caught the new Soviet Union leaders off guard. The Soviets were not in a position to respond because it now had a collective leadership, and no one wanted to appear weak or naïve by agreeing to hand over the Soviet nuclear stockpile to an international civilian body. Consequently, the Soviet Union ignored Eisenhower's Atoms for Peace proposal. The lack of response by Soviet leaders placed enormous pressure on Eisenhower to continue nuclear weapons development and move forward with the next hydrogen bomb test scheduled for March 10, 1954.

Nine days before the scheduled Castle Bravo test, which remains to this day the largest thermonuclear bomb ever tested by the US, the Galactic Federation intervened. What is not widely known is that in the late evening and early morning of February 19/20, 1954, President Eisenhower met with representatives of the Galactic Federation who formally requested that he end the development of thermonuclear weapons. From recently released information—about to be presented herein—we learn that Eisenhower was very agreeable to stopping thermonuclear weapons development since he wanted to work with the Galactic Federation. However, he was overruled by his national security advisers and leaders of the military industrial complex. 'Overruled' may be too kind of a word because it appears that Eisenhower did agree to work with the Galactic Federation, but instead, the Majestic 12 Group, which had been running extraterrestrial projects since 1947, had already agreed to work with a different group of extraterrestrials.

In my 2013 book, *Galactic Diplomacy: Getting to Yes with ET*, I discuss two sets of meetings that President Eisenhower had in 1954 and 1955. I presented multiple insider sources and circumstantial evidence to build a case that Eisenhower had two sets of meetings with rival extraterrestrial groups. The first of the groups (the Ashtar Command and/or the Galactic Federation) wanted him to end the thermonuclear weapons program, but the other group of extraterrestrials was comfortable with the US continuing its thermonuclear weapons development. This latter group of Tall "Nebu" Grays (allied with the Antarctic Germans and Draconian Reptilian Empire) was willing to share advanced technologies in exchange for several concessions.[43] It appears that this agreement was reached with the Majestic 12 Group behind Eisenhower's back.

Val Thor, Galactic Federation, and President Eisenhower

One of the human-looking extraterrestrials associated with the Galactic Federation got to spend a lot of time with President Eisenhower. His name was Valiant (Val) Thor, and he was secretly a guest of the Eisenhower administration from 1958 to 1961 at the Pentagon.[44] Val Thor was unsuccessful in getting Eisenhower and world leaders to work with the Galactic Federation simply because Eisenhower did not have the power to enforce or push any agreements reached with the Galactic Federation through the US military industrial complex. In fact, the military industrial complex was vehemently opposed to any agreement predicated on ending thermonuclear weapons development since the construction of hydrogen bombs represented a source of vast income and profits for many decades to come.

Even though Eisenhower worked very closely with Val Thor, he did not make any progress in getting the truth about extraterrestrial visitation out to the general public. There was a civilian, however, who was able to meet with Val Thor and let the world know about him visiting and meeting not just Eisenhower, but other world leaders as well. The Val Thor meetings were designed to promote international cooperation on key national and global security questions. However, the meetings were never revealed to the general public. The Reverend Frank Stranges was the first individual to reveal that such meetings were indeed taking place after he was allowed to meet with Valiant Thor at the Pentagon for the first time.

Frank Stranges was a Reverend and President of the International Evangelical Crusades and the International Theological Seminary of California. He also had a law enforcement background. Stranges' background made him a credible witness to an incredible event. He says that sometime in 1958, he was taken to the Pentagon to meet with Valiant Thor. He wrote a book about his experience titled *Stranger at the Pentagon,* which was first published in 1967.[45] In a subsequent interview, Stranges spoke about his encounter with Val Thor and how breakthrough health technologies could not be released due to their impact on the national economy:

> He told me his name was Valiant Thor. He grabbed my hand, his hand, skin soft as a lady's or a baby's skin, but it the grip of a man. And we spent 30 minutes, mostly me asking questions and he giving answers and he claimed that he was from the inside of the planet that our Bible calls the Morning and the Evening Star, the planet Venus.... Mr. Thor was at the Pentagon for three years, mind you, and he was going and coming at will. He was brought to the President of the United States Dwight Eisenhower and Richard Nixon, offered to give them information on how the American people could successfully live without sickness, without poverty, without disease, and without death.
>
> They told him, we're sorry that we cannot accept the information that you're freely giving us because it

will ruin the economy of this nation. Well sir, Commander Thor left on the morning of March 16th, 1960, on the outskirts of Alexandria, Virginia where his spaceship came down. He went into the spaceship and disappeared from sight.[46]

Up until recently, all that was known about Val Thor came from Stranges' book, newsletters, and interviews since he claimed to have continued meetings with Val Thor near Lake Mead, Nevada. That situation changed dramatically when new information concerning Val Thor appeared in Elena Danaan's book, *We Will Never Let You Down*.[47] In it, she talked about physically meeting with Val Thor on multiple occasions beginning in December 2020. Val Thor shared vital new information about Eisenhower and his problems with the MJ-12 Group. Val Thor told Danaan that he had convinced Eisenhower to work with the Galactic Federation of Worlds, but the MJ-12 group instead made agreements with the Orion Greys (aka 'Nebu') and Draconian/German alliance out of Antarctica behind his back. The MJ-12 agreements obliged Eisenhower to uphold their terms even though Eisenhower was working with and may have even reached an agreement with the Galactic Federation.

In the meantime, the Majestic 12 Group was operating behind Eisenhower's back, arranging meetings, conducting negotiations, and eventually even signing and implementing agreements with the Orion Grays and Antarctic German/Draconia Empire without Eisenhower's approval. This takes us to the conclusion that Eisenhower was betrayed. This is how Danaan describes the betrayal in *We Will Never Let You Down*:

> President Dwight Eisenhower decided, for the greater good of Humanity and his love for children, to make an agreement with the benevolent emissaries of the Galactic Federation, but the Majestic Twelve committed behind his back, instead, with the Grays…. The Military Industrial

Complex signed with the devil, with the blood of Humanity.[48]

Eisenhower apparently was betrayed since he wanted to work with the positive extraterrestrials (Galactic Federation), who insisted that thermonuclear weapons development had to be abandoned before they would begin to share advanced technologies. The Majestic 12 Group, instead, reached an agreement(s) behind his back with negative extraterrestrial factions that had no such pre-condition for reaching an agreement and beginning technological exchanges. This took the US and humanity down a very difficult path.

There is significant circumstantial evidence and witness testimony that the MJ-12 Group and the Military Industrial Complex had betrayed Eisenhower. The first case involved the reverse engineering projects that were underway at the S-4 facility located at Area 51 in the Nevada desert. The CIA, along with Lockheed Martin's Skunkworks, had carefully chosen the remote Area 51 region as the location for future classified research and development programs. It has been publicly confirmed that Kelly Johnson, the first head of Skunkworks, had flown with CIA officials to choose Area 51 as the site for building high altitude spy planes such as the U-2 and the SR-71 Blackbird.[49] However, Skunkwork's construction of "Top Secret" spy planes was actually a cover for an even more highly classified reverse engineering program involving captured flying saucer craft stored previously at secure military facilities such as Wright Patterson Air Force Base in Dayton, Ohio.[50]

The MJ-12 Group was formally in charge of all extraterrestrial-related projects, including reverse engineering efforts at S-4/Area 51. This quickly created a problem as Eisenhower was cut out of the loop. As Commander in Chief, he had a constitutional right to be briefed about all projects conducted at US military facilities. This constitutional right was not so clear when it came to joint corporate intelligence projects, which involved the proprietary interests of a private company. Of course, MJ-12 knew about this ambiguity and took full advantage of it. MJ-12 subsequently told the CIA not to share what was happening at S-4 with Eisenhower.

According to a former CIA agent and US Army cryptologist, who had been recruited after completing training with the US Army Signal Training Center, the situation over S-4 and Area 51 infuriated Eisenhower, who felt the chain of command had been willfully broken by MJ-12. Later, at age 77, with acute kidney problems and only months to live, the dying CIA agent consented to give video testimony for six former members of the US Congress attending the Citizens Hearing on Disclosure in May 2013. The agent explained that he and his CIA superior had been summoned to the Oval Office by Eisenhower to pass on a message to the MJ-12 Group. The agent revealed Eisenhower's fury when he explained how MJ-12 had told his administration that it had no jurisdiction over what was happening at S-4 and Area 51:

> We called the people in from MJ-12, from Area 51 and S-4, but they told us that the government had no jurisdiction over what they were doing.... I [Eisenhower] want you and your boss to fly out there. I want you to give them a personal message.... I want you to tell them, whoever is in charge, I want you to tell them that they have this coming week to get into Washington and to report to me. And if they don't, I'm going to get the First Army from Colorado. We are going to go over and take the base over. I don't care what kind of classified material you got. We are going to rip this thing apart.[51]

Eisenhower's threat to use the US Army to take over Area 51 and S-4 forced the MJ-12 Group to relent and give a limited briefing to Eisenhower and Vice President Nixon about extraterrestrial-related projects. Nevertheless, Eisenhower was very unhappy with being kept out of the loop. He knew that Area 51/S-4 would be a big problem for future Presidents wanting to learn about what was happening in extraterrestrial-related projects.

The above scenario was confirmed by a former US Army Judge Advocate General's Corps (JAG) officer, Stephen Lovekin, who had served in the White House Army Signals Corps during the Eisenhower administration prior to his JAG career.[52] Lovekin said that President Eisenhower personally told him that it was how the UFO issue was being handled by senior officials that led to him feeling betrayed:

> We would sit around with him when we were at Camp David, and he knew who each and every one of us [was] by name. That was the great thing about being under him. I was just a sergeant at the time. I was still privy to some stuff that some people wouldn't be privy to.... When he said the main thing we have to fear is the military industrial complex, he wasn't kidding, and he had the subject matter we are talking about [UFOs] in mind. He was quite explicit about that.[53]

Lovekin's testimony is an eyewitness account that Eisenhower believed that the danger posed by the military-industrial complex was directly related to the management of the UFO phenomenon. In another interview, Lovekin described Eisenhower's growing frustration with the way the UFO issue was being managed:

> This frustration, from what I can remember, went on for months. He realized that he was losing control of the UFO subject. He realized that the phenomenon or whatever it was that we were faced with was not going to be in the best hands. As far as I can remember, that was the expression that was used, "It is not going to be in the best hands." That was a real concern. And so it has turned out to be.[54]

Eisenhower's comment that management of the UFO subject "is not going to be in the best hands" is very revealing. It is worth recalling that his former job in running the European theater of World War II made him an astute judge of character and competence of the senior military personnel around him. Eisenhower's private admission to Lovekin shows that he had astutely gauged the personalities and expertise of the individuals managing extraterrestrial affairs, and concluded they were deficient in critical ways. Losing control of the UFO/extraterrestrial issue to rogue officials not willing to share information would certainly have left Eisenhower feeling deeply betrayed.

The betrayal over the management of extraterrestrial affairs was what Eisenhower was really conveying in his famous farewell address from January 1961, according to Lovekin, where he starkly warned the US public about the dangers posed by the military industrial complex:

> In the councils of government, we must guard against the acquisition of unwarranted influence, whether sought or unsought, by the military industrial complex. The potential for the disastrous rise of misplaced power exists and will persist. We must never let the weight of this combination endanger our liberties or democratic processes. We should take nothing for granted. Only an alert and knowledgeable citizenry can compel the proper meshing of the huge industrial and military machinery of defense with our peaceful methods and goals, so that security and liberty may prosper together.[55]

Consequently, it is very clear that Eisenhower's reference to the military industrial complex was an allusion to the MJ-12 group running highly classified extraterrestrial related projects out of Area 51/S-4 in conjunction with major aerospace corporations such as Lockheed's Skunkworks. The arrangement provided the pretext to deny Eisenhower access to classified projects, which were claimed to involve proprietary information of a private corporation and therefore out of Federal government jurisdiction. Eisenhower rightly felt betrayed, and he conveyed publicly and privately to trusted aides 'why' he was so angry with those running UFO/extraterrestrial projects—the Majestic 12 Group.

Eisenhower's farewell speech is conclusive evidence that he had been deceived by a powerful group associated with the Military Industrial Complex, which we know from Lovekin's testimony to be rogue officials managing the UFO issue—the MJ-12 Group. Also, we now know that Eisenhower's frustration went further than him not being informed about extraterrestrial-related projects at S-4. According to Elena Danaan, the deception involved MJ-12 reaching agreements with the Gray, Reptilian, and Antarctic German alliance, and ignoring what Eisenhower wanted or had agreed to do in his communications with the Galactic Federation.[56] This raises the question of whether there is any evidence that an agreement with the Galactic Federation had been reached by Eisenhower but was effectively overshadowed by agreements reached by MJ-12 with other extraterrestrial groups.

Leaked 1989 DIA Document Refers to a Possible Agreement with the Galactic Federation

A new leaked Majestic-12 document was released on June 14, 2017, describing various extraterrestrial-related encounters with humanity. This document includes claims that Nikola Tesla's pioneering radio broadcasts into outer space in the late 1800s alerted distant extraterrestrials to humanity's existence, which led to them traveling to our planet. President Eisenhower would establish full diplomatic relations with these visiting extraterrestrials in 1954. The human-like appearance and behavior of these extraterrestrials suggest that they belonged to the Galactic Federation.

The 47-page document was reviewed by several document authentication researchers and UFO experts, including the now-deceased Stanton Friedman, who found no evidence of forgery, according to Heather Wade, former host of the radio show *Midnight in the Desert.* This was the message posted on the show's website:

> Wade received documents last night [June 13] from a trusted source. She immediately had Stanton Friedman take a look at these documents who said, "I have never seen anything like this, this is new MJ12 information." Stanton Friedman is going to continue examining these documents for authenticity, but at this time we can find no evidence of forgery.[57]

Similarly, Dr. Robert Wood, another leading Majestic documents researcher, also shared his preliminary assessment in an email that the "stamps, markings, style, content, names" look genuine. Dr. Wood followed this up with an article published in the December 2018 edition of the Mutual UFO Network Journal in which he gave the first detailed analysis of the leaked 47-page document.[58] He wrote that there were several factors pointing to its authenticity and why it is an error to simply dismiss it, as many UFO researchers have done to date.[59] His detailed analysis of the typing, spelling mistakes, signatures, patents referenced, individuals mentioned, etc., in the document, led to his conclusion that it was a briefing dictated by a member of the Majestic 12 group to two typists. They typed up the 47 pages, a copy of which was preserved on microfilm by the DIA as Dr. Wood explained in his MUFON paper:

> If one contemplates why there were so many errors made in a document officially recorded on a microfilm, and you pronounce the word or phrase on the left and look at the correct one on the right, usually they sound essentially the same. This would be consistent with the document having been created as a result of taking dictation and having

two different typists implement the words on paper…

This would be consistent with MJ-12 (stated in this case to be individual MJ-1) having dictated a one-time entry-level summary for the new person, since one apparently was not available from prior written records at the time of the alleged briefing.[60]

An anonymous whistleblower source sent the document to Wade, who revealed its existence during her June 14, 2017, show, along with details about the document's background. Wade asserts that the whistleblower is known to her and is a reliable source, but to date, she has not released the person's identity. Additional information was provided to veteran UFO reporter Linda Moulton Howe that there are indeed two sources, both of whom are retired military personnel.[61] What follows is a description of the key points made in the document and their significance concerning the Galactic Federation reaching an agreement with President Eisenhower.

According to a cover page, the document is a "preliminary briefing" created by the Defense Intelligence Agency's Office of Counter Intelligence on January 8, 1989. The full title of the briefing package is "Assessment of the Situation/Statement of Position on Unidentified Flying Objects," and it is addressed to the Office of the President. The briefing officer is described as "MJ-1" who, based on historical precedent, has been the sitting CIA Director. The CIA Director at the time of the 1989 briefing was William Webster, who served as Director from May 26, 1987, to August 31, 1991. Previously, he was FBI Director from February 23, 1978, before heading the CIA under President Reagan. Webster is the only person ever to have held both the FBI and the CIA's directorships.[62]

Figure 6. Cover page of DIA document

Figure 7. MJ-1 is the briefing officer

The briefing document refers to four groups of extraterrestrial visitors which are listed in order of importance to our planet, and asserts whether they are friendly or not:

> There are four basic types of EBEs so far confirmed. And they are listed here in descending order of their influences on our planet.
>
> A.   Earth-like humanoids. There are several variations more-or-less like ourselves. The majority of these are friendly and are the bulk of our EBE contacts. Most have a high degree of psychic ability and all use science and engineering of an advanced nature.
>
> B.   Small humanoids or "Grays." The Grays, so–called for the hue of their skin possessed by most of this type, are a sort of drone. They are not unlike the worker ants or bees.... They are mostly under the psychic control of the Earth-like humanoids who raise them like pets (or a kind of slave). Assuming the Greys are under benign control, they are harmless.
>
> C.   Non-humanoid EBEs. These are in several classes and come from worlds where dominant morphology took a different evolutionary course. Many of these are dangerous not for organized hostile intentions, but because such creatures do not hold human life as sacred.... Thus far, contact has been minimal with only a handful of unfortunate encounters.
>
> D.   Transmorphic Entities. Of all the forms of EBE studied so far by Operation Majestic, these are the most difficult to understand or even to give a

> description of. Essentially, such entities are not "beings" or "creatures"... exist in some either dimension or plane which is to say not in our space or time. They do not use devices or travel in space.... In essence these entities are composed of pure mind energies. ... They are said (by other EBEs) to be capable of taking on any physical form that they "channel" their energy ... as matter. [63]

As the above description suggests, most extraterrestrial interactions are depicted as friendly, particularly those involving human-looking entities. Presumably, these belong to the Galactic Federation, which has engaged in several non-hostile interactions with humanity. This is consistent with what Fry wrote about the Galactic Federation monitoring the Earth over the course of many centuries.

The briefing document refers to the famed 1947 Roswell UFO Crash, and the national security mechanism that had been developed to investigate it and maintain a secrecy system. While the Roswell Crash is well known, the next case described in the document is not. There was a "controlled landing" of a flying saucer on March 25, 1948, in Aztec, New Mexico, which the briefing document describes:

> The controlled landing occurred in a small desert canyon on the private grazing land of a local farmer and rancher... about 12.2 miles northeast of Aztec, New Mexico. The ship was determined to be 99.983 feet in diameter. Inside the upper cabin .. the team found the bodies of two (2) small humanoids about four feet in height strapped into seats like those in a jet cockpit... The extraterrestrials were dead. [64]

The briefing document reported that the extraterrestrials had died because of an atmospheric leak caused by impact with a nearby cliff face. The report then described the discovery of cryogenic tubes with human-looking bodies in the lower level, four of which were successfully resuscitated:

> A closer look at the sealed tubes, which looked like the doors of clothes dryers at a laundromat revealed that they were a complex form of refrigeration system. Two were empty and twelve contained the bodies of what looked like human adults and small children as well as infants, all frozen as if preserved for specimens…. Eventually the medical team was able to resuscitate one adult Earth-like humanoid male and three (3) Earth-like humanoid infants, all about six (6) months of age: two male and one female. The rest of the infants and one more short, gray-skinned, large-headed EBE, perished. [65]

The adult survivor, according to the briefing document, looked human but was clearly an extraterrestrial who, though human-looking, had physiological differences, which included having two livers. The document describes how diplomatic negotiations began with the surviving adult extraterrestrial:

> After a hasty tele-conference with President Truman, it was explained to the visitor that if his intentions proved to be non-hostile and he cooperated in an information exchange, he would be granted diplomatic status and soon be repatriated to his own kind when the arrangement could be made. To this he readily agreed, provided he was not asked to give away any scientific secrets that could alter the course of our natural cultural development. [66]

What comes next details the year-long diplomatic exchanges between the extraterrestrial visitor and the Truman administration before he was returned to his people:

Altogether, the Aztec EBE lived under our protective custody on the Los Alamos complex for nearly a full year, from late April 1948 – until March of 1949. After that, he was sequestered at a private safehouse set-up by Army Intelligence ... during which time he met with the President and other top government and military administrators, prior to his being returned to his people in August of 1949. He gave the scientists and military debriefers a great deal of mostly non-technical information about his civilization and its motives for being on our Earth; a total of six hundred and eighty-three (683) pages of transcripts were made of recorded conversations. [67]

The document makes clear that President Truman met with the extraterrestrial diplomat—presumably a member of the Galactic Federation—along with top government and military administrators. According to Paul Blake Smith, author of *President Eisenhower's Close Encounters,* it is highly likely that Eisenhower was among the group of officials that met with the surviving adult extraterrestrial.[68] More importantly, Smith makes a strong case that Eisenhower was prepared for the return of the extraterrestrial and/or his colleagues soon to negotiate a formal diplomatic agreement.

In 1954, the briefing document referred to President Eisenhower traveling to Kirtland Air Force Base where he established full diplomatic relations with the human-looking extraterrestrials who had indeed returned:

The preceding diplomatic treaty was drafted by the director of the Majestic-12 operation and a joint committee of extra-terrestrial visitors and representatives of the U.S. Diplomatic Corps, as a statement of intent. It was ratified and signed at Kirtland Air Force Base ... on July the eighteenth,

1954 by President Dwight D. Eisenhower and an individual on behalf of the EBEs.[69]

It is critical to note here is that this draft treaty was a 'statement of intent.' Apparently, Eisenhower had only achieved the first step in a complex negotiation process with the Galactic Federation, which laid the foundation for future diplomatic negotiations that could culminate in a comprehensive treaty.

The diplomatic process appears to be very similar to how a very large international organization such as the European Union accepts new member countries.[70] First, a statement of intent establishes the procedures for future meetings, negotiations, and preliminary agreements that culminate in formal admittance that can take many years. As to how many civilizations belong to the Galactic Federation of Worlds, Elena Danaan estimates that it comprises "the union of hundreds of thousands of civilizations from this Galaxy … [that] protect the rights of all life.[71] For the Galactic Federation, signing a statement of intent with a developing planet such as Earth seems to be a predictable and reasonable first step. Eisenhower was basically telling the Galactic Federation, "I want to work with you guys, and we can cooperate on common areas of interest such as the danger of thermonuclear weapons." However, behind his back, the Majestic 12 group organized meetings and agreements with other groups of extraterrestrials—Orion Grays and Draconian Empire—that were not concerned by the US mass-producing tens of thousands of thermonuclear weapons that could lead to Earth's destruction. The betrayal effectively scuttled any plans Eisenhower had for a comprehensive agreement with the Galactic Federation.

Nevertheless, not all was lost as a major military service—the US Navy—began to secretly work with the Galactic Federation despite the agreements MJ-12 had reached with the Orion Grays and the Draconian Empire. In my 2017 book, the *US Navy's Secret Space Program and Nordic Extraterrestrial Alliance*, I presented evidence that the US Navy began formally working with a friendly group of human-looking 'Nordic' extraterrestrials in the early

1950s. According to multiple sources, the US Navy designed and built fleets of antigravity spacecraft for future space battle groups on the principle of a modern aircraft carrier battle group. One of these sources was William Tompkins, who worked for several decades as an aerospace designer and engineer for major corporations. Tompkins claims the US Navy secretly worked with the Nordics embedded in companies such as Douglas Aircraft, North American, TRW, etc., to design space battle groups that were secretly built in remote regions of Utah by major aerospace corporations. The Navy space battle groups became operational in the early 1980s.

In a private interview, Tompkins shared with me yet more startling information about the extent of the US Navy and 'Nordic' extraterrestrial alliance when it came to building the next generation of space battle groups:

> Tompkins told me about the Navy's current plan to replace its eight existing battle groups, which have become antiquated in comparison with other space programs, with twelve new battle groups... currently under development, and scheduled to become fully operational in the 2030s... Tompkins asserted that the next generation space carrier battlegroups are being built at an off-planet location, in an adjacent star system with the help of friendly human-looking Nordic extraterrestrials [Galactic Federation?], rather than the previous construction site in Utah.[72]

Tompkins never explicitly used the term "Galactic Federation of Worlds" to describe the extraterrestrial organization to which the Nordics belonged. However, the Nordics' behavior, appearance, and values in Tompkins' book series, *Selected by Extraterrestrials*, clearly points to an organization like the Galactic Federation. In an interview, the chief editor of Tompkins' book series, Dr. Robert Wood, asserts that the Nordics described in Tompkins' books belong to the Galactic Federation as described by Elena Danaan: "My opinion would be that the Nordics of Bill's... there are the same Nordics as the ones that are working with Elena Danaan now. The very same ones."[73] In her book, *We Will Never Let You Down*, Elena Danaan confirmed that the US Navy had indeed been working with the Galactic Federation, and this had been facilitated by Val Thor who spent three years embedded in the Pentagon:

> The Galactic Federation of Worlds secretly allied first with a structure called the "Navy." One of my numerous tasks was to start this project and prepare the groundwork for sending technicians and scientists from the Federation to Terra.[74]

Elena Danaan on the Galactic Federation of Worlds

Elena Danaan emerged into the public arena with her popular 2020 book, *A Gift From the Stars*. In it, she recounts her personal contact experiences, the most dramatic of which involved an abduction at age nine by five Gray aliens in the late 1970s. In the midst of medical procedures involving implants, she was rescued by two human-looking extraterrestrials using laser weapons to kill her Gray abductors. Danaan explains how her rescuers took her to their ship and repurposed one of the physical implants so they could subsequently remain in telepathic communications for her protection. She learned that her rescuers belonged to a Galactic Federation of Worlds that is helping Earth's 'Great Awakening'. Danaan's principal rescuer was a tall blond male from the planet Erra in the Taygeta star system in the Pleiades constellation named Thor Han Eredyon.

In her book and subsequent interviews, Danaan explains how the Galactic Federation became involved in Earth affairs after it was advised by another extraterrestrial organization, the Zenatean Alliance (aka Andromeda Council - to be discussed in

Chapter 6), that a future galactic tyranny could be traced back to Earth in the present era:

> They [Zenatean Alliance] have foreseen the future of Terra and, knowing this is a tipping point in its history after 5700 years of Reptilian occupation, they try to influence [Terrans] on the constructive and not the destructive path. They work at avoiding the Terrans to fall into a galactic tyranny, which may be stirred up right now, at this precise tipping point in time, from the alliance of Terran dark corporations and the Ciakahrr [Draconian], Orion, and Altairan collectives. They are, in fact, not only saving the Terrans but eradicating at the moment [of] its birth a galactic threat in the emergence of a new enemy.[75]

This matches the testimony of Alex Collier, who in the mid-1990s relayed his Andromedan contacts' discovery that the sudden appearance of a galactic tyranny about 350 years in the future could be traced back to the Earth, Moon, and Mars.[76] What Danaan and Collier's experiences tell us is that Earth has become the epicenter of a temporal war involving different extraterrestrial organizations. Danaan has ever since been relaying a lot of information about the multiple interventions by the Galactic Federation on Earth and in our solar system to prevent this galactic tyranny from occuring. In Part Two, I will discuss Danaan's startling updates.

Farsight Institute and the Galactic Federation

Independent support for the existence of a Galactic Federation currently intervening in human affairs as publicly expressed by Professor Haim Eshed comes from the Farsight Institute. After Professor Eshed's views about the Galactic

Federation created an international media frenzy, Dr. Courtney Brown organized a team of five remote viewers to gather intelligence on the Galactic Federation in multiple sessions conducted and publicly released in February 2021. He explained his rationale for the remote viewing session as follows:

> In quite a number of projects here at Farsight, the words "Galactic Federation of Worlds" have been used to reference a group of planetary civilizations that seem to be supportive of humanity and opposed to the influence of other groups and species that appear hostile to humanity. Well, now it is time to find out more about what those words mean.
>
> Exactly what is the Galactic Federation of Worlds? Or perhaps, who are they? Are they one species, or a group of species and civilizations, sort of like a United Nations of the galaxy? Do they have meetings? Do they work together on projects, such as a project that may involve Earth and us humans? Are they a diverse group with diverse interests, or are they all of one mind?
>
> And importantly, if they really do desire to help humanity in its hour of need within the context of a galaxy that contains a significant number of threatening or hostile forces, can the Galactic Federation of Worlds really do something helpful? What are its resources? Moreover, does it really need Earth humans to step up to the plate in order to help us out, or is it strong enough to help us out regardless of what we humans do?[77]

The results of the remote viewing sessions yielded many valuable insights into the existence of a Galactic Federation of

Worlds and other questions raised by Dr. Brown. This was particularly the case with understanding the Federation's command structure, its internal policy debates over the extent to which it should intervene in human affairs, how its intervention was part of a "temporal war" over the Earth's future, and what private individuals can do to support the Federation's efforts to assist our planet's evolution in a positive direction.

As with previous remote viewing sessions conducted by the Farsight Institute, the sessions were held under blind protocol conditions, and the participants were only told to focus on two targets presented to them in sequential order. No details of each target were given in order not to frontload the remote viewers' own personal views and biases into their observations. The two targets for the remote reviewing sessions were:

> Target 1: The headquarter of the Galactic Federation of Worlds / The most relevant meeting of the GFW dealing with the subject of Earth and humanity.

> Target 2: The command ship for the GFW responsible for Earth now and its commander.[78]

The remote viewers' reports on the two targets were remarkably consistent in their overall observations even though details varied from case to case. As far as both targets were concerned, there were several notable observations, among which were:

- The Galactic Federation of Worlds (GFW) is a large and diverse body holding many viewpoints about how to deal with humanity.
- There were members of the GFW who were opposed to further intervening in human affairs.
- The enemy of the GFW, powerful rival extraterrestrial coalitions, had a tight grip over humanity and would not be easy to displace.

- There were significant armed conflicts between the GFW and its rivals over the Earth, and this had placed great stress on the Federation's military commander.
- If the GFW stopped its operations, there would be significant planet-wide destruction and Earth would descend into a post-apocalyptic nightmare.
- The GFW leadership is aware that rival extraterrestrial alliances were more powerful in overall military terms, but the latter would abandon Earth operations if the GFW was committed.

The opposing interplanetary forces that the remote viewers are referring to are the Draconian Reptilian (aka Ciakharr) Empire and the Orion Alliance (aka Collective), which have been discussed in previous remote viewing sessions focusing on Nazis and Reptilians in Antarctica,[79] and US Presidential meetings with extraterrestrials.[80]

In his evaluation of the data given by the multiple remote viewers, Dr. Brown offered up the following conclusions and insights over these competing extraterrestrial alliances vying over control of humanity:

> Regarding the Galactic Federation of Worlds, let's pull things together. I will get straight to the point. We humans on Earth need to realize and soon that we are in a very precarious situation. The Galactic Federation of Worlds clearly is trying to help us, but the resources are limited. They are up against forces that seem huge even to them. They do seem to have the ability to help us, but it really looks like they will need our help in order to do it.
>
> There were two reasons. First, the membership of the Galactic Federation of Worlds seems to be divided. Most of the membership clearly desires to help, but there are huge doubts within the

organization regarding their actual ability to do this, especially on the level of military capabilities. Earth is a relatively backwater planet on a peripheral part of the Galaxy, so that is a factor in our favor. If opposing galactic forces were to make a major effort to stop the Galactic Federation of Worlds from assisting humanity, well, it seems clear that those opposing forces could push the Galactic Federation of Worlds aside; but, on the other hand, are we worth such a major effort?

It appears that part of the thinking process of the Galactic Federation of Worlds is the calculation that the opposing forces would not be interested in a major confrontation regarding Earth at this time. If it is going to cost the opposing forces a lot, then they are likely to pass on the big confrontation idea.[81]

The opposing galactic forces—the Draconian Empire and the Orion Alliance—have a powerful hold over Earth humanity through their respective minions and controlled assets, which allow these alien alliances to manipulate humanity's destiny. William Bramley succinctly describes this process in his book, *The Gods of Eden* (1993), which traces out centuries of contrived extraterrestrial conflicts through controlled political elites designed to manipulate Earth humanity's evolution.[82]

Dr. Brown next draws attention to the long-term involvement of the Galactic Federation of Worlds in human affairs and what this entails:

Clearly, many in the Galactic Federation of Worlds consider [Earth] humanity to be a successful end result of a project that they started long ago from an evolutionary point of view. Probably one that resulted from a lot of genetic and cultural manipulation, and adaptation over a great many years. We are their children, they care for us, and they want to protect us, but what would any parent do if the child does not want to be helped at some point? All parents need to let go to allow their children to determine their own forward path, but if children openly recognize the challenges that they face and if these same children then turned to their parents for needed assistance which parents would not want to help their own children?

So, this is the key. The greatest inhibiting factor that the Galactic Federation of Worlds faces right now is internal disagreement. If they were strongly united and wanted to help humanity in its hour of need against a very threatening and hostile set of aggressors, then they could do something with meaningful success.[83]

The idea that one or more extraterrestrial civilizations are responsible for seeding or creating humanity on Earth dates back to Erich von Daniken's groundbreaking 1968 book, *Chariots of the Gods*. He was followed by others, including Zecharia Sitchin, author of *The 12th Planet* (1976), who devoted considerable attention to extraterrestrials genetically creating our human ancestors, according to ancient records from Sumer and elsewhere.

According to Dr. Brown's analysis drawn from his remote viewing team, the Galactic Federation of Worlds has been involved in Earth's history for a very long time and was part of the genetic seeding of humanity. The Galactic Federation and the Ashtar Command that have been discussed so far are not the only positively oriented or benevolent extraterrestrial organizations that have been intervening in human affairs or have been involved in long-term genetic engineering experiments. Another important organization is the Confederation of Planets, which also plays a critical role in current human affairs.

CHAPTER 3

Confederation of Planets aka Galactic Confederation

The space people tell us that before we are ready to be received back into the universal confederation of planets, certain social and economic reforms on our planet are necessary.

—New York Dispatch, 1959.

A more spiritually oriented galactic association has intervened in human affairs in a very different way to the organizations described so far. Terms such as 'Confederation of Planets,' 'Galactic Confederation,' 'Confederation of Light,' etc., have been used to describe this organization. In contrast to the 'Galactic Federation' and the 'Ashtar Command,' which are more military-oriented and interventionist in dealing with the problem of negative extraterrestrial influences, the Confederation of Planets takes a more long-term spiritual approach emphasizing nonviolence, cosmic consciousness, education, and love. In short, the "Confederation" is a loosely bound non-interventionist, almost pacifist, galactic alliance in contrast to the 'Federation,' which has a more tightly integrated structure that includes a unified military that facilitates direct intervention in galactic conflicts. A good way to illustrate the difference is to contrast the interventionist policies of the USA—a tightly integrated federation of self-governing states with a unified national military—with the European Union, a confederation of nations-states without a unified military, which consequently takes a more non-interventionist pacifist approach to international conflict.

Gabriel Green, Robert Renaud & the Confederation of Planets

The first public reference to a Confederation of Planets was made on July 13, 1959, when an extraterrestrial contactee by the name of Gabriel Green, was cited by a number of US newspapers at a Los Angeles convention that Green had organized. In *The York Dispatch* in York, Pennsylvania, reported Green saying: "The space people tell us that before we are ready to be received back into the universal confederation of planets, certain social and economic reforms on our planet are necessary."[84] Green was speaking at the inaugural convention of the Amalgamated Flying Saucer Clubs of America, which he created in 1957. He explained the problems confronting Earth and the goals of his organization as follows:

- To help create greater understanding and cooperation between the people of earth and the people of space;
- To help initiate, through political and economic action, the procedures for providing abundance for all;
- To help establish 'the universal brotherhood of all mankind' and 'the kingdom of heaven on earth.'[85]

Green said that he had been contacted by members of the Confederation who came from the planet Korendor in a star system called Korena.[86] He said that members of the Confederation were walking among humans and helping raise consciousness to bring about the "kingdom of heaven on earth. He wrote a book about his contact experiences called *Let's Face Facts about Flying Saucers,* in which he described what he had learned. Green was not the only person at the time who claimed to have had contact with extraterrestrials from a planet called Korendor.

Flying Saucer Club Blasts Earthlings For Doubts

LOS ANGELES, July 13, UPI— The Almagamated Flying Saucer Clubs of America wound up its first annual convention with a blast at persons who doubt that "space people" and earthlings have met.

"Every new idea is met with ridicule," said Gabriel Green, 34, of Los Angeles, an ex-photographer who is director of the organization. "Television once was considered impossible."

Green maintains he has seen more than 75 space-ships in isolated areas near Los Angeles although, he said, he never personally met space people until the convention opened.

Shortly after the convention opened, he said, spacelings who looked almost exactly like earthlings were attending the meeting.

Green, who says he receives his information about outer space from other earthings who have met inter-planetary travelers, shrugged off a shaply-worded telegram he received from the National Investigations Committee on Aerial Phenomena.

'Carnival' Blasted

The telegram from Major Donald E. Keyhoe, U. S. Marine Corps (Ret.), director of N. I. C. A. P., said in part:

"Your carnival approach to the subject of unidentified flying objects is . . . off-setting serious work by N. I. C. A. P. and other . . . fact-finding U. F. O. groups."

The T. T. list of numerous lectures at the flying saucer convention included such topics as "Landing at Butte," "Universal Vibration," "Aura Rhanes of Venus Speaks" and "Spiritual Significance of Space Ships."

A number of the speakers here have told of their frequent rides into space and back aboard spaceships.

Meanwhile, Green, in his publication "Thy Kingdom Come," outlined the purpose of the flying saucer organization:

—"To help create greater understanding and co-operation between the people of earth and the people of space."

—"To help initiate, through political and economic action, the procedures for providing abundance for all."

—"To help establish 'the universal brotherhood of all mankind' and 'the kingdom of heaven on earth.'"

John Believer Talks

In his publication, Green said he learned of "a wonderful future for our planet" after "several interviews" with a man whom he called John Believer.

He said the man he called Believer "wore a beard and had long, wavy hair to his shoulders. He looked to be about 30 to 33 years of age."

According to Green, space people can help earthlings solve their problems because space people are more advanced.

"This is proven by the fact that they have achieved inter-planetary travel," he said.

One of the main ways to equal the level of the space people, he said, is to form what he termed "God's political party."

He suggested naming this organization the Economic Security Party "since nearly all of our problems are in some way directly connected with economics or the lack of security in the lives of our people."

He added:

"The space people tell us that before we are ready to be received back into the universal confederation of planets, certain social and economic reforms on our planet are necessary."

**The York Dispatch
York Pennslvannia
13 July 1959. p.7.**

*(Note: Confederation of Planets
mentioned at end)*

Figure 8. First public reference to Confederation of Planets

Robert Renaud was an 18-year-old amateur ham radio operator when in 1961, he began having radio communications with a group of extraterrestrials also claiming to be from the planet Korendor, which belonged to a powerful galactic organization that was intervening on Earth. Renaud was told that there were two positive extraterrestrial organizations intervening on Earth to bring about a desirable future for humanity, and both had infiltrated Earth society with human-looking operatives embedded within major corporations, government institutions, and the general public. The first of these benevolent organizations is described as the United Worlds Alliance—aka the "Galactic Federation of Worlds"—which allowed the use of military force to bring about positive outcomes for worlds such as Earth being threatened by negative extraterrestrial groups. The second positive organization is called the Confederation of Planets (aka Galactic Confederation), which takes a nonviolent path to resolve galactic conflicts.

These two 'positive' galactic organizations collaborate when it comes to helping Earth free itself of the influence of two 'negative' extraterrestrial alliances called the 'Omegans' and the 'Syndicate,' which are using the Earth in a proxy war against the Galactic Federation and the Confederation. The descriptions Renaud gives of the respective behaviors of the hostile organizations make them functionally equivalent to what we know of the Draconian Empire (Omegans) and the Orion Collective (Syndicate). Renaud explains that in addition to extracting Earth resources for their needs, the negative groups want to recruit Earth's military forces as mercenaries to fight in their galactic conflicts.

> The Omegans [Draconians] are creating a dispassionate, unfeeling military force to wage interstellar war and conquer worlds. Desensitizing mankind to the horrors of war is part of the process. The terrorists of 9/11 had the sort of cold, unfeeling, almost robotic dedication to death and destruction that the Omegans want to instill in us as a species.

> They might have done it in the name of their religion, but the goal is for mankind to become uncaring machines of violence and conquest devoid of any rationale other than the insatiable thirst for power.[87]

Significantly, William Tompkins said something very similar about the creation of a human proxy force that could "wage interstellar war and conquer worlds." He said this was precisely what the Draconian (aka Ciakharr) Empire was doing through its German proxies in Antarctica:

> Holy cats, the thing went way beyond that [world conquest]. Again, what we just said about this was the tip of the iceberg of what they were doing. Already Reptilians were doing it to other stars' planets all over this area of the Galaxy.... It was a massive program. The [Nazi/Reptilian] mission was to take over the planet, kill off all of the ones that were a problem, and the rest of them make slaves out of them. Everybody on your planet, then [the] second phase was to leave the planet with large squadrons of UFOs, after you've got them all built, and do the same thing to other stars' planets.[88]

According to Renaud, the Confederation's commitment to nonviolent solutions meant that even when it recognized the advantage of using military force in solving a galactic conflict, it would at best only intervene indirectly in supporting any Galactic Federation military operation. In response to a question from Gabriel Green, this is how the Korendians explained the Confederation's nonviolent policy, which involved surrender rather than a direct military response except in dire cases of planetary genocide:

> To be sure, the provocation that would force them
> to action would be considerably more severe than
> might be the case to instigate Alliance [Federation]
> response, and given a choice, they would usually
> consider surrender if it would spare violence. They
> would never consider a retaliatory strike such as we
> made on the Omegans' [Draconian] Sirius
> headquarters planet, and would in most cases not
> fight back unless a Confederation world was in
> imminent danger of total destruction. We have
> never seen their weaponry in use, but we know that
> it exists.[89]

The Confederation of Planet's nonviolent approach led to some resentment from members of the Alliance/Federation, as can be seen in the following statement:

> The Confederation remains firmly committed to
> exploring every possible avenue to a non-violent
> solution, and still firmly opposes any interference or
> military action in another world's affairs. However,
> out of necessity and dire reality they're also
> becoming a bit more pragmatic, and looking toward
> appropriate means of (to euphemize a bit) covering
> their tushes. If it means acceding in principle to an
> Alliance program of direct -- and if need be, violent
> -- action, then they will forego their high-minded
> principles and (at least indirectly) support such a
> policy.[90]

What is particularly striking about Renaud's information is the reference to a highly advanced intergalactic civilization/ organization monitoring the battle between positive and negative extraterrestrial groups over the Earth's future:

It has been revealed to me that the entire confrontation involving the Alliance, the Confederation, The Omegans and the "Syndicate" is being watched impassively by a highly-advanced intergalactic race some 80 million years older than any other civilization that the Alliance has ever encountered.

Dubbed "The Moderators" (they have offered no formal diplomatic contact or full identification), they have been in control of the local cluster of galaxies for at least 75 million years. Until the onset of this business, they've been content to stand aside and simply observe the activities of the various races and organizations in the galaxies.

They have occasionally left tantalizing traces of their presence, but only recently did they reveal themselves simultaneously to all parties, and establish the ground rules outlined in my last letter. They are serving as judges of the ongoing conflict, and will award governing of this galaxy to whichever side proves victorious. [91]

This reference to highly evolved extraterrestrial race or organization acting as judges of conflicts between less evolved extraterrestrial civilizations and awarding governance of galaxies and solar systems to victors in an ongoing galactic war is highly significant. In Chapter 7, I will present information that this is precisely what has very recently happened in our solar system.

In another communication, Renaud explains that highly evolved extraterrestrial species which are not part of the Galactic Federation or the Confederation of Planets are involved in genetic seeding projects:

By Alliance estimates of worlds with intelligent life, 37% are at or beyond the level of Earth and about 3% are vastly beyond the Alliance. The majority of the 3% do not wish to be aligned with the Alliance or Confederation. They are loosely aligned with an organization that predates the Alliance by millions of years. They have in the past engaged in seeding other worlds.[92]

In Chapter 5, I describe an Intergalactic Confederation comprising twenty-four highly evolved extraterrestrial civilizations involved in intergalactic seeding of human life and monitoring their progress, which closely matches what Renaud described.

It is worth emphasizing that Gabriel Green worked directly with Robert Renaud in learning about the complex situation on Earth involving the different extraterrestrial organizations intervening on Earth. Green was the first to publish Renaud's information in his magazines from 1963 to 1969, and the sequence of articles are available online.[93] In addition, many of Green's questions were answered by the Korendians and compiled into a collection called "The TerraKor Files."[94]

In 1989, Green asked a series of questions related to contemporary politics and the prospects of future cataclysmic events. The answers show that in the more than twenty years since communications had begun, the Confederation of Planet's non-interventionist policy had not fundamentally changed:

Question #2 -- the Confederation is itself powerless to carry out an effective intervention in your affairs, just because of their steadfast and seemingly unchangeable adherence to their non-interference directives. We do not expect that this position will be materially altered in the immediate future. Therefore, if the Confederation intends to intercede on your behalf, it will be after, not before a cataclysmic occurrence on Earth. By definition, this would no longer constitute interference with a viable culture, and such an intercession is encompassed within the wording of their directives.[95]

Robert Renaud continues to post updates on his Terrakor files website, which contains a wealth of data on his contacts and communications with the Korendians since 1961.

South American Contactees & the Confederation of Planets

A decade after Green and Renaud began discussing a Confederation of Planets (Galactic Confederation) involved in human affairs, contactees from South America also began discussing a Confederation dedicated to encouraging spiritual evolution and moral development. The first and most prominent of these contactees has been Sixto Paz Wells, who was approached in 1974 by members of what he described as the "Galactic Confederation of Stars" or the "Confederation of the Galaxy." He described this Galactic Confederation of Stars as like-minded extraterrestrial civilizations that cooperate with one another in protecting their worlds and introducing advanced spiritual knowledge to other planets. The 'Confederation' is headed by a Council of 24 Elders, which Paz Wells describes as follows:

> The Council [of 24 Elders] is formed by the highest spirits of beings who have reached a high degree of enlightenment and wisdom. These 24 Masters from different worlds and higher planes of development have been designated by the mentors or regions the highest authority of the council of the central Galaxy of Andromeda, the council of nine from Andromeda in charge of guiding different civilizations.[96]

The reference to a Council of Nine that works alongside or under a Council of 24 Elders, both of which act as higher supervisory bodies or oversight groups for an association of extraterrestrial worlds— the Galactic Confederation—is highly significant. In later chapters, I will discuss a Council of Nine that the famed biophysicist Andrija 'Henry' Puharich first encountered in 1952, how it relates to the organization mentioned by Paz Wells, and a possible connection to a leadership council from the Andromeda Constellation.

Paz Wells described the Galactic Confederation as having a major base on Jupiter's moon Ganymede. The role of Ganymede as a Galactic Confederation base in our solar system is also critical to understand. Chapter 12 will discuss three contactees who claim to have traveled to Ganymede where they encountered extraterrestrial civilizations.

In his book, *The Invitation*, Paz Wells describes a meeting he had with members of the Council of 24 Elders:

> You, along with hundreds of other missionaries of the light, are being freed from organizations and structures that hinder the teachings of love and understanding. A new humanity is being forged today with the purity of your ideals. On this day you have come upon the support of the **profound love of the cosmic consciousness**. Do not permit anyone to restrict the spontaneity of your service be truthful and always work in the new humanity. [97]

This encounter gives us a clear idea of how the Galactic Confederation emphasizes nurturing "cosmic consciousness" in the citizens of civilizations in the early stages of technological development. Paz Wells explains how the Confederation regards the spiritual condition of the multiplicity of extraterrestrial civilizations operating in our galaxy and beyond:

> Not all alien races have reached a highly evolved spiritual state. There are those whose desire for

conquest is stronger than their interest in evolving as beings. The spaceships of the Confederation have always been able to protect the evolved and evolving worlds with the help of spiritual forces **whose power of love surpasses all else**.[98]

The power of a transformative love ethic appears to be the core driving principle underpinning the activities of the Galactic Confederation. The idea of "spiritual forces whose power of love surpasses all else" in protecting worlds and resolving galactic conflicts appears to be a practical application of the love ethic as taught by historical figures such as Jesus Christ. It is worth pointing out that Mahatma Gandhi and Martin Luther King developed a practical application of a love ethic in the early to mid-twentieth century to resolve intractable social and political conflicts. Gandhi and King believe nonviolence, personal suffering, and forgiveness were the keys to transforming intractable conflicts and bringing about long-lasting solutions.[99] The Galactic Confederation extends the same practical application of the love ethic into the galactic arena.

While the Galactic Federation of Worlds and Galactic Confederation appear to be separate organizations with different behaviors and beliefs, they recognize the same galactic oversight bodies—the Council of Nine and the Council of 24 Elders, which I discuss in the next chapter. The Federation uses a carrot and stick approach to galactic conflicts—rewarding a civilization if it behaves in accord with universal law but using military force if violations occur. In contrast, the Confederation is more tolerant of extraterrestrial civilizations that violate universal law and tries to help all parties in a conflict by transforming a situation through nonviolence, self-suffering, forgiveness, and love.

Sixto Paz Wells created an organization called "Mission Rama" that rapidly grew throughout South America in the 1970s and 1980s after a prominent Spanish journalist, JJ Benitez, favorably covered his contact experiences in several major newspapers of the time.[100] After a reorganization caused by Wells' departure, it was renamed "Mission Rahma," and it continues to operate today, offering training seminars and spiritual retreats for those interested in extraterrestrial contact. This is how Mission Rahma views itself:

> Mission Rahma is a contact bridge between extraterrestrial civilizations and human beings. This connecting experience is attempting a rescue in which man saves himself by using the only force that can generate a transformation in his inner self and in all of the Universe: Love. For this reason, we say that Rahma is to love. The word Rahma means "Sun on the Earth" (Ra=Sun, Ma=Earth, and h=the connection created by humanity). This means to be a beacon of light and to shine for the planet. Rahma is a contact group, but above all, it's a mission in favor of our planet and of ourselves.[101]

On the Mission Rahma website, it describes the Confederation of Planets as follows: "It is a voluntary grouping of Galactic Planets in the Milky Way. It is an association of all those planets that have reached a high degree of evolution."[102]

Another prominent South American contactee is a professional architect, Luis Fernando Mostajo Maertens, who has also written and spoken about the role of the Confederation of Planets in humanity's evolution:

> It is a mission of contact because the evolved worlds that are in this galaxy, who form the *Confederation of Planets*, have seen, at this time, not only the changes of this Earth, but also of the whole galaxy. They claim that this planet as we know it is not finished evolving. It is still transforming itself. Within this transformation, it is up to us to take a part, a role, in this planet regarding these changes that are happening. They claim, firstly, that the whole

70

universe is pure energy, and, secondly, that this energy is dynamically acting upon all stars in the galaxy, which are continually transferring information. The universe, as we see it at night, is constituting itself into the universal consciousness.[103]

Like Sixto Paz Wells and others associated with Mission Rahma, Luis Fernando emphasizes the importance of cosmic consciousness and how the Confederation of Planets nurtures this to the greatest extent possible for developing worlds such as ours.

Another vital element in Luis Fernando and other South American contactees' writings is the emphasis on "Masters of Wisdom," "Ascended Masters," or "Elders" who can help develop cosmic consciousness. These 'Masters' are well described in literature released by the Theosophical Society in the early 1900s. A good example is the book series authored by Baird Spalding, *Life and Teachings of the Masters of the Far East* (1924), which elaborates upon the activities and philosophies of these Masters who emphasize cosmic consciousness and universal love.[104] In a 2008 conference presentation describing his meeting with one of these "Elders" based under Lake Titicaca, Luis Fernando said:

> I was able to know and integrate myself with these elders who are very, very old. They are the guardians of human history. Today they have opened the doors so that this wisdom and knowledge can reach humanity ... That's what I experienced during my travels to the internal retreat of Lake Titicaca. These are the islands of the small lake. This is one of the passages to the internal retreat. This is the actual Paititi, the lost city, The Eternal City, which is beneath the lake ...[105]

Consequently, Luis Fernando conducts regular consciousness-raising workshops and initiations at his retreat next to Lake Titicaca, Bolivia.

Another South American contactee, Enrique Castillo Rincon, gives a vivid account of one of these meetings with a Master of Wisdom facilitated by a Pleiadian extraterrestrial. At the time of his physical contacts that began in 1973, Rincon worked as a professional civil engineer and traveled widely in South America to work on large-scale construction projects. His professional background meant that he had a lot to lose if he went public and his testimony was ridiculed or debunked by critics. Nevertheless, Rincon believed that the experiences were so important that he decided to risk his career by revealing to the world what had happened. In 1995, the Spanish edition of Rincon's book, *UFOs: A Great New Dawn for Humanity* was published after a nearly two-decade delay.

Rincon explains that in one of his contact experiences, he and other human contactees (24 in total) were taken to a remote location in the Andes where they were given ambassadorial training to prepare humanity for the truth about extraterrestrial life. A key component of the ambassadorial training was the development of higher ethics and consciousness as taught by the extraterrestrial visitors. Rincon's information reveals that the Confederation of Planets trained a select group of individuals for open contact, helping them to become emissaries ready for the day when the truth would be exposed to the world.

In addition to being trained to report on technical and historical details about extraterrestrial life and technology, Rincon and his fellow emissaries were guided to develop an appreciation for developing cosmic consciousness. The extraterrestrials with whom Rincon collaborated arranged for him and other contactees to meet with a "Master of Wisdom." The incident, vividly described by Rincon, shows that the Confederation of Planets is training their contactees in higher consciousness by having them meet with highly evolved beings that radiate love and wisdom. Rincon was an engineer by training, so he had no idea of the literature at the time of Ascended Masters, Masters of Wisdom, etc., making the incident he described even more remarkable.

According to the situation described by Rincon, he and the other emissaries-in-training met one of these Masters of Wisdom in the Andean mountains. It is worth pointing out the irony that the Pleiadians had to introduce an earthling to a human master of wisdom, who presumably Rincon would not have even believed existed. However, because Rincon was so awed by the technological superiority of the Pleiadians, he naturally assumed that whatever they had to share would be monumental information for the rest of humanity. The Pleiadians, however, wanted to open Rincon and the other emissaries' minds by making it clear that the off-planet visitors did not regard themselves to be at the apex of evolution. They introduced Rincon to someone much further along the evolutionary ladder – a human Master of Wisdom based in the Andes.

Rincon explains what happened when he and the others were taken to a cave located high in the Andean mountains:

> The instructor [an extraterrestrial] approached the entrance to a tunnel carved in the living rock and clasped his hands twice. He retired to one side, and the most incredible Being made his appearance. We were astonished beyond description. That being looked exactly like Jesus, the Master. I thought immediately that the Pleiadians had brought us here with the purpose of meeting Jesus Christ, who was here again, fulfilling the prophecies..."[106]

When the Master of Wisdom addressed Rincon and the others, one of the first things he did was to dispel their belief that he was Jesus Christ:

> I am not who you believe I am. My name is a thousand names, give me any, and That I Am. I am ancient before you, not in age, but in knowledge...

73

My name is Age, for I am the Ages and the Time. I
am Wisdom, and my name is Wisdom. I hold thirty
five percent of universal wisdom.[107]

The individual Rincon described just stood there in front of the
cave, radiating an enormous energy field of love and wisdom that
made Rincon believe he could only be an advanced being like the
Jesus described in Christian literature. However, this Master of
Wisdom simply said no, "I'm not who you believe I am." His claim
of holding "thirty five percent of universal wisdom" reveals the
highly evolved status of this particular Master but also implies that
there are others in the universe holding far more. This takes me to
another source on the Confederation of Planets and the emphasis
it places on cultivating cosmic consciousness.

Law of One & the Confederation of Planets

Among the most authoritative sources helping us
understand a Galactic Confederation (aka the Confederation of
Planets) is the Law of One material presented in a series of five
books. They are transcripts of channeling sessions that took place
from 1981 to 1984 and involved physics professor, Don Elkins,
trance channeler, Carla Rueckert, and Jim McCarthy, who set up
the sessions. Elkins would ask a series of probing questions and
receive answers channeled through Rueckert from an
extraterrestrial collective calling itself the Ra Social Memory
complex. Ra was a very highly evolved 6th density collective
consciousness.

Ra described a positive group of extraterrestrials as the
Confederation of Planets, which included members from over 50
highly evolved civilizations:

Ra: I am one of the members of the Confederation
of Planets in the Service of the Infinite Creator.
There are approximately fifty-three civilizations,

comprising approximately five hundred planetary consciousness complexes in this Confederation. This Confederation contains those from your own planet who have attained dimensions beyond your third. It contains planetary entities within your solar system, and it contains planetary entities from other galaxies. It is a true Confederation in that its members are not alike, but allied in service according to the Law of One.[108]

Significantly, the Ra material refers to members from Earth occupying higher densities/dimensions than our own 3rd density existence. Presumably, they are referring to inner Earth civilizations and the survivors of ancient Earth cataclysms who were able to develop spacefaring capabilities prior to planetary catastrophes from different historical epochs.

When Elkins asked a question about the formation of the Confederation, he received a very telling response:

Questioner: Thank you very much. Can you tell me how the Confederation of Planets was formed and why?

Ra: I am Ra. The desire to serve begins, in the dimension of love or understanding, to be an overwhelming goal of the social memory complex. Thus, those percentiles of planetary entities, plus approximately four percent more of whose identity we cannot speak, found themselves long, long ago in your time seeking the same thing: service to others. The relationship between these entities as they entered an understanding of other beings, other planetary entities, and other concepts of service was to share and continue together these commonly held goals of service. Thus, each voluntarily placed the social memory complex data in what you may consider a central thought complex available to all. This then created a structure whereby each entity could work in its own service while calling upon any other understandings needed to enhance the service. This is the cause of the formation and the manner of the working of the Confederation.[109]

Once again, the emphasis is on developing the love ethic, but this is applied to planetary collectives and not just individuals. This is how the love ethic became the guiding principle for multiple planetary civilizations forming a Confederation. Thus, the members of the Confederation practice a love and service-to-others ethic in their dealings with one another and with other civilizations such as here on Earth. This desire to be of service forms the core philosophical distinction in the Law of One material of how different planetary civilizations interact with one another. Those worlds practicing "service-to-others" help the advancement of civilizations on different worlds by spreading "love and light," while those practicing "service-to-self" seek to exploit more primitive worlds such as Earth for their own benefit.

The "service-to-self" extraterrestrial group that the *Law of One* material focuses on is the Orion Crusaders (aka Orion Collective).

Questioner: I don't know if this is a short question or not, so we can save it till next time, but my only question is why the crusaders from Orion do this. What is their ultimate objective?...

Ra: I am Ra. This is not too long to answer. To serve the self is to serve all. The service of the self, when seen in this perspective, requires an ever-expanding use of the energies of others for manipulation to the benefit of the self with distortion towards power.[110]

The *Law of One* material gives us a better understanding of how a more spiritual or ethically oriented extraterrestrial organization (the Confederation of Planets) interact with their rivals (Orion Crusaders) in galactic conflicts.

In conclusion, there are multiple independent sources describing a Confederation of Planets that practices a love ethic, emphasizes the development of cosmic consciousness, works closely with "Masters of Wisdom," and adopts nonviolent approaches to galactic conflicts. This distinguishes the Confederation from the more military-oriented Galactic Federation and Ashtar Command in their respective interactions with negative or service-to-self extraterrestrial organizations such as the Orion Collective and the Draconian Empire. This creates a complex dynamic between these different extraterrestrial organizations. A dynamic conflict that is overseen by an even more highly evolved extraterrestrial organization than those discussed so far—the Council of Nine.

CHAPTER 4

The Council of Nine

[Gene] To whom am I talking? Do you have a name?
[Tom] I am Tom. I am the spokesman for the Council of Nine. In Truth I am Tehuti. Yes. I am also Hamarkos, I am also Herenkar, I am known as Thomas, and I am known as Atum.

—Gene Rodenberry questioning Tom/Council of Nine, 1974.

The first reports of a "Council of Nine" can be traced to the paranormal research of an American biophysicist, Andrija 'Henry' Puharich, who received an M.D. from Northwestern University in 1947. In 1948, Puharich set up a private research laboratory called the Round Table Foundation in Glen Cove, Maine where he began working with different psychics. What distinguished Puharich's paranormal research over the subsequent decades was that he secured funding from wealthy supporters to build Faraday cages, i.e., metallic grids blocking outside electromagnetic interference, where prospective psychics could be tested. There was great interest from US and French military officials when Puharich discovered that a Faraday cage significantly increased a psychic's performance.

In 1952, Puharich presented his research in a paper titled "An Evaluation of the Possible Uses of Extrasensory Perception in Psychological Warfare" at a classified Pentagon meeting.[111] Puharich's paranormal research was an early example of the military intelligence community seeking to learn whether psychic phenomena could be weaponized and/or used for intelligence gathering purposes. In December 1952, Puharich invited to his laboratory an Indian mystic, Dr. D.G. Vinod, who claimed to be channeling extraterrestrial entities. Puharich's biographer, H.G.M. Hermans, described what subsequently happened:

> When he [Vinod] entered the great hall, a curious thing happened. Without saying a word or even taking off his overcoat, he walked straight to the library as if he had been there before. He sat down on a sofa and immediately went into a trance.
> Then, at exactly 9 p.m., a deep sonorous voice came out of his mouth, totally unlike his own high-pitched, soft voice, saying in perfect English without an accent:

> "M calling: We are Nine Principles and Forces, personalities if you will, working in complete mutual implication. We are forces, and the nature of our work is to accentuate the positive, the evolutional, and the teleological aspects of existence. By teleology I do not mean the teleology of human derivation in a multidimensional concept of existence. Teleology will be understood in terms of a different ontology. To be simple, we accentuate certain directions as will fulfill the destiny of creation. We propose to work with you in some essential respects with the relation of contradiction and contrariety. We shall negate and revise part of your work, by which I mean the work as presented by you. The point is that I want to begin altogether at a different dimension, though it is true that your work has itself led up to this.

> I deeply appreciate your delicateness to the great cause of peace, which is fulfillment of finitesimal

existence. Peace is not warlessness. Peace is the integral fruitage of personality. We have designed to utilize you and thus to fulfill you. Peace is a process and will be revealed only progressively. You have it in plenty; I mean the patience that is so deeply needed in this magnificent adventure. But today, at the moment of our advent, the most eventful and spectacular phase of your work begins.[112]

Thus began a new phase in Puharich's life and research. Puharich and a small group gathered at the Round Table sessions to hear Dr. Vinod's channeling of the "Nine Principles and Forces" (the Council of Nine), who claimed to be the ancient gods in Egyptian mythology—the Ennead (from the Greek 'ennea,' nine).[113] The Egyptian Ennead was the earliest creation myth and described the nine gods who had come out of the one, which had earlier emerged out of the void.[114] The following is a quote attributed to one of these early Round Table communications with the Nine:

> I am the beginning. I am the end. I am the emissary. But the original time I was on the Planet Earth was 34,000 of your years ago. I am the balance. And when I say "I" – I mean because I am an emissary for The Nine. It is not I, but it is the group ... We are nine principles of the Universe, yet together we are one.[115]

At the end of January 1953, Dr. Vinod returned to India, and Puharich began what would turn into a 20-year quest with different psychics to reestablish communications with the Council of Nine, confirm their existence, and release their teachings to the world.

Puharich's new quest, however, was rudely interrupted by the US Army, which decided to ignore a previous medical discharge issued in 1947 and recall him into military service in February 1953 as a Captain in the Medical Corps at the Army Chemical Center, Maryland. Thus began a controversial phase in his life when he was linked to Army research into chemical, radiological, and bacteriological warfare being conducted at the nearby Fort Detrick facility in Maryland. Puharich's groundbreaking psychic research had been classified, and he was denied a security clearance to continue his Round Table research unless he joined the Army. This turn of events led to him feeling "muzzled." [116] He complained about the situation in a letter:

> If the intent of the Army people was not to use my experience, but to slow down my work in Maine, they certainly had done a good job. Although I realize that I could not have obtained a security clearance unless I was in the Army under 24-hour surveillance, it was a high price to pay. [117]

Puharich's recruitment so soon after meeting Vinod and establishing a clear line of communications with the Council of Nine and the classification of his psychic research was not accidental. It is worth reflecting here that just as the Council of Nine had mysteriously appeared in his life with a powerful conduit into higher teachings and reliable information from a positive extraterrestrial source, the "other side"(negative extraterrestrials) wanted to shut this possible collaboration down as quickly as possible. Recruiting him into the US Army appeared to be an effective way of achieving this goal—muzzling Puharich, as he had said.

After completing his Army service in 1955, Puharich's had to resurrect his Round Table organization, which had folded during his absence. He continued to find different psychics to work with, but in all cases a reliable connection with the Nine could not be reestablished. The psychics he worked with would suffer from many emotional and psychological problems raising again the possibility that some external force was sabotaging Puharich's efforts. In 1971, Puharich met the young Israeli psychic, Uri Geller, who began receiving messages from an entity calling itself 'Spectra' (allegedly a conscious supercomputer on a spacecraft) that agreed with Puharich's suggestion that it was linked with the "Nine Principles." Geller channeled messages from Spectra/Nine that "alerted Puharich to his life's mission, which was to use Geller's talents to alert the world to an imminent mass landing of spaceships that would bring representatives of The Nine."[118]

Puharich brought Geller to the US to have him tested in August 1972 by paranormal researchers at the Stanford Research Institute (SRI), who published a detailed report supporting Geller's psychic abilities. The SRI report led to much controversy, with *Time Magazine* publishing a hit piece using comments by two Pentagon scientists rebutting the SRI report and calling Geller a fraud. Nevertheless, the controversy turned Geller and Puharich into national celebrities and led to them speaking before large university audiences around the country. Prominent scientists such as Dr. Tom Beardon commented on the controversy and the threat that psychic research posed to the dogmas of materialistic western science and the power of the 'shadow government' to manipulate public opinion:

> Geller's (and rapidly others') performances under laboratory conditions posed a monstrous new threat to the notion that a human is just a robot and the brain is just a meat computer. The hue and cry – and the commotion - stirred up by the "Geller phenomenon" and its rapid spread of interest in paranormal phenomena was indescribable. Puharich strode through this suddenly emerging counterculture on the world scene, electrifying the younger generation on several continents. From some quarters, the malice and venom directed against Andrija mounted to near frenzy.
>
> Secretly, behind the scenes, the shadow government – that serves not the electorate but the wealthy persons who run the world – was worried. The shadow control of the populace depends upon

convincing them of materialism, and setting group against group to keep everyone isolated and hence powerless. The evocation of Man's spiritual and moral nature is their greatest enemy, for it continually leads to unification of large groups of people, who thus attain political and economic power by harmony rather than dissonance. And now here was an upstart Shaman, in their view, who posed an unacceptable threat to the status quo because his work was electrifying and unifying across the artificial boundaries that had been established between groups.[119]

Puharich subsequently wrote a book about Geller simply titled *Uri,* which became an international bestseller in March 1974. Puharich's research and his book *Uri* launched Geller's career and made him into an international psychic superstar. Geller, however, became frustrated with Puharich's relentless efforts to convince the scientific community about the reality of psychic phenomena through rigorous experiments, which Geller had found tedious and exhausting.

By July 1974, Geller decided to stop working with Puharich and the Council of Nine, which led to Puharich lamenting: "The list of people who have been exposed to the aeons [Council of Nine] is now quite long, and everyone has failed in taking on commitment and responsibility. I must go on!"[120] Serendipity quickly stepped in, however, and Puharich accidentally found another channel for the Council of Nine who would have the necessary commitment and emotional stability.

The psychic healer and channeler, Phyllis Schlemmer, began channeling the Nine when helping Puharich deal with another psychic healer, 'Bobby', who was experiencing emotional problems. In one of these first channeling sessions, 'Tom' (T), the spokesperson for the Council of Nine, commented on Andrija Puharich's (AP) 22 year-long effort to re-establish communications after encountering Dr. Vinod in 1952:

84

T: You have worked with us for many, many years without proof, and for that we are forever grateful.

AP: I seem to be in a strange position in that I do not have dreams, do not have visions. I don't have special insights.

T: You have knowledge inside.

AP: I seem to go on faith.

T: Knowledge is faith. Just know that from now on we will be with you. You are being guided, and you are following in the right direction.[121]

Figure 9. Andrija Puharich with Uri Geller (on right)

After another of Schlemmer's channeling sessions held on July 20, 1974, a British aristocrat and millionaire, Sir John Whitmore, decided to commit himself to help the Nine by sponsoring future research efforts. The reasons why Whitmore decided to support the Nine with his significant resources are described by Puharich's former wife and biographer, H.G.M. Hermans:

> On the morning of July 20, 1974, after another channeling session, John Whitmore made the decision to commit himself to the 'Management," as the Nine called themselves. The main thing that had convinced him that the communications were not the ordinary psychical phenomenon, but came from an external source, was the extent and variety of the information they disclosed. The Management had evidently been observers of the Earth for thousands of years. Their communications contained a wealth of detail about the origins and progress of civilization, the origins of languages and mythologies, and the roles of historical figures. Also, there was an entire cosmology, comprising information about five different extraterrestrial civilizations, their inner-relations, their technology, and about how the earth related to this cosmic scheme. The Management knew about contemporary political situations and events on Earth, and sometimes gave some intriguing information about what went on behind the scenes.[122]

Consequently, a more than 20-year association between Schlemmer, Puharich, and Whitmore began on the Council of Nine and the voluminous information that was being shared since 1974.

While the sessions began with Puharich as the central pillar around which the collaboration revolved, this changed over the years, especially after his Ossining Lab 9 Laboratory was burned down by two arsonists on August 7, 1978. It was only by luck that none of the individuals living at Ossining, which included family members, had been harmed. Puharich firmly believed the arsonists had been sent by the CIA that wanted to shut down his latest biophysics research. At the time, he was researching the effect of Extremely Low Frequencies (ELF—3 to 30 Hz) that were secretly being transmitted through the Earth by giant radio transmitters by the defense and intelligence communities of the Soviet Union and the US. Each side was testing ELF technology against their respective populations and territories. This abuse of technology that was pioneered by Nikola Tesla back in 1899 with his giant Magnifying Transmitter at Colorado Springs—which used the Earth's natural resonance to transmit ELF waves—was the subject of a book Puharich tried unsuccessfully to have published due to pressure on prospective publishers by CIA operatives.[123] Puharich fled to Mexico, frightened of being assassinated before finishing his book. This undeclared war using "Tesla Technology" only ended with a secret ceasefire reached between Ronald Reagan and Mikhail Gorbachev during their Geneva (1985) and Reykavik (1986) summits on nuclear weapons disarmament.[124] In the meantime, Schlemmer and Whitmore continued the channeling sessions with the Council of Nine without Puharich during his long absence and difficulties.

Puharich & the CIA

It is worth pausing here to discuss a damning critique of Puharich as a CIA asset, according to the influential book, *The Stargate Conspiracy* by Clive Prince and Lynne Picknett, since such a claim has clear implications for subsequent information about the Council of Nine.[125] What follows is their view on Puharich and the CIA, which many others have extensively cited as valid:

> Recent research has revealed Puharich to have a distinctly sinister side. As an Army doctor in the 1950s, he was deeply involved with the CIA's notorious MKULTRA mind control project... He – together with the infamous Dr. Sidney Gottlieb – experimented with a variety of techniques to

change or induce actual thought processes... even to creating the impression of voices in the head. These techniques included the use of drugs, hypnosis and beaming radio signals directly into the subject's brain. And, significantly, he was engaged in this work at exactly the same time that The Nine made their first appearance at the Round Table Foundation. The Foundation itself is now known to have been largely funded by the Pentagon as a front for its medical and parapsychological research. Puharich was still working for the CIA in the early 1970s, when he brought Uri Geller out of Israel.[126]

It is certain that the CIA took a keen interest in Puharich's paranormal studies, dating back to his 1952 paper delivered at the Pentagon and the classification of his research. Prince and Picknett further claimed that Puharich was part of the infamous MK Ultra mind control program, with the implication that the Council of Nine channelings were a byproduct of a CIA/Pentagon psychological operation.[127] These claims need to be closely examined, and objective analysis shows they are demonstrably wrong.

It is essential to point out that the experiences with Dr. Vinod that started Puharich's lifelong interest in the Council of Nine were unplanned, spontaneous, and pointed to genuine communication with highly evolved ("higher density") extraterrestrial beings, rather than a product of psychological warfare. Puharich's subsequent recruitment into the US Army in February 1953, only a month after Vinod returned to India, pointed to an attempt to either co-opt Puharich's pioneering research in psychic communications with extraterrestrials or to stop him. It is not hard to fathom why the Pentagon would want to shut down Puharich's independent communications with extraterrestrials using scientific protocols such as a Faraday cage, and recruit him into a classified psychic program so they could effectively control and muzzle him. The initial years of the Eisenhower administration (from 1953 to 1961) were critical for setting up a framework of secret agreements with different extraterrestrial groups. The last thing the Majestic 12 Group wanted was for independent scientists such as Puharich to gain any support or prominence in their investigations and communications with different extraterrestrial groups outside of MJ-12's approved list.

During his second stint in the US Army as a Captain from February 1953 to 1955, Puharich wrote several research papers which confirmed official Pentagon interest in paranormal events and psychic abilities.[128] On March 16, 1953, only weeks after his Army service began, he delivered a paper on "Researches in Decreasing or Increasing Telepathy" at the Aviation School of Medicine, US Air Force, Randolph Field, Texas. Later that year, on December 4, he presented a paper on "A Physical Technique for Amplifying Telepathy" at the Armour Research Foundation, Illinois Institute of Technology. On April 20, 1954, Puharich gave a paper on "Biochemical Foundations for Extrasensory Perception" at the Army Chemical Center, Edgewood, Maryland. As to what Puharich was working on during the rest of his time with the US Army, we get an idea from a paper published in the winter 1957 edition of *Tomorrow*, "Can Telepathy Penetrate the Iron Curtain?"[129] Consequently, during his Army service, Puharich continued to develop and use telepathy and other paranormal abilities for various military applications, including intelligence gathering and espionage.

In reviewing Puharich's extensive list of publications, there is no evidence that he "experimented with a variety of techniques to change or induce actual thought processes," as claimed by Picknett and Prince. Nor did Puharich ever show any interest in or conduct research into trauma-based mind control techniques used in the infamous CIA MK-Ultra experiments associated with Dr. Sidney Gottlieb.[130] Such work would require a specific skill set concerning pain and different tolerance thresholds that could be used to unlock inherent human abilities. Puharich, while certainly interested in psychic abilities and enhancing these through means such as Faraday cages and psychedelic mushrooms, never showed any interest in experimental research designed to unlock such abilities through involuntary methods or subjects.[131] Consequently, Puharich's research into telepathy and paranormal abilities for the US Army and as an independent researcher needs to be considered separate from what the CIA was doing in its MK-Ultra program. Therefore, Picknett and Prince were wrong to implicate Puharich in such research simply based on his coerced recruitment into the Army and the similarities in his paranormal research with what the CIA was doing.

In conclusion, while it is true that the Army forced Puharich to work in a variety of medical research projects to study and enhance human paranormal abilities from 1953 to 1955, there's no evidence that he used involuntary methods or subjects. While it is possible that during his Army service, he was ordered to work in MK-Ultra experiments conducted by the CIA in some official capacity, there is no evidence that this actually happened. In Puharich's defense, however, it is important to point out that he was forced to join the Army against his will, his psychic research becoming classified, and he was genuinely chafed at being muzzled by the Army during the birthing phase of his paranormal research. After being released from Army service in 1955, his Round Table laboratory had to be rebuilt from scratch and new funding sources found, which effectively set Puharich back years in his paranormal research. Picknett and Prince's claims that the Round Table was a front for Pentagon research into paranormal abilities overlooks the inconvenient fact that Puharich's involuntary recruitment into the Army, during a critical phase beginning in 1953, led to the Round Table's collapse.

It is true that CIA and Pentagon officials were very interested in psychic, paranormal, and extraterrestrial affairs and tried to recruit Puharich over the subsequent decades. This was to be expected since his financial affairs as an independent researcher were always precarious, and he was constantly seeking funds for new research projects. Whatever the relationship between Puharich and the CIA since 1952, it is clear that they parted ways acrimoniously in 1978 after his Ossining laboratory was burned down. He had to move to Mexico to escape the CIA that wanted to stop his exposure of the Pentagon and CIA misuse of Tesla technologies in a covert war with the USSR. In 1982, Puharich's former wife cited a highly significant comment from Puharich's private journal about his difficulties with the CIA, along with her own comment about what he subsequently did:

> I seem to be over a terrible four-year period. The CIA now recognizes what I did was right, and have asked me to work for them. I declined the offer. (He told them that he didn't want to work for liars, thieves and murderers.)[132]

Picknett and Prince's book, *The Stargate Conspiracy*, takes a debunking approach to claims of highly evolved extraterrestrial intelligence communicating through human psychics. When combined with false assumptions and factually wrong conclusions, such debunking, as demonstrated in their biased analysis of Puharich's paranormal research, does much damage to the quest to find an objective balance in understanding what is genuinely happening. While there is indeed an official campaign of psychological warfare to confuse and distract the public concerning paranormal abilities and the extraterrestrial topic through contrived experiences using MK-Ultra mind control victims, this is done to discredit genuine claims of extraterrestrial contact. In other words, one shouldn't throw out the baby with the bathwater when it comes to psychological operations and their deleterious effects today when it comes to psychic abilities and extraterrestrial contact. Official government agencies would routinely feign disinterest in the contacts and communications of private individuals with extraterrestrial intelligence, but in reality, seriously investigate and study the results.[133] This is not that surprising when one considers the limitations of electronic and other traditional intelligence gathering techniques when it comes to extraterrestrial visitors, and therefore the need for alternative intelligence methods for discerning what the visitors are doing.

Today, there is much skepticism towards the Council of Nine as a direct result of Picknett and Prince's flawed work in the *Stargate Conspiracy.* That is an unfortunate fact, and hopefully, my preceding comments will help the reader come to a better understanding of the Council of Nine and the significance of their information for humanity today.

Phyliss Schlemmer & the Council of Nine

There are three noteworthy developments concerning Schlemmer's channeling of the Nine. First, the initial sessions were conducted out of a Faraday cage that shielded her from disruptive electromagnetic frequencies, along with negative astral and extraterrestrial influences. These disruptive influences quickly emerged as a problem as the sessions progressed, and the Faraday cage effectively blocked these negative influences while allowing communications with the Nine to proceed unaffected. Stuart Holroyd, a British journalist who visited Lab 9, Ossining, in 1975, described the Faraday cage where the Council of Nine channeling sessions with Schlemmer were conducted:

> Their Faraday cage is a rectangular metal box of dimensions 8 x 8 x 12 feet, which is lined with copper and placed on insulating supports and constitutes a complete electrical vacuum. When the door is shut no electro-magnetic waves can penetrate the cage, and the electrical environment within the cage can be controlled for experimental purposes. Inside the cage there were three chairs and a table on which stood some expensive-looking recording equipment and a small portable TV set. John demonstrated the electro-magnetic shielding property of the cage by switching on the TV set and slowly shutting the door of the cage. The picture remained on the screen up to the point when there was just about a quarter

inch crack for the signal to get through. Then John sharply pulled the door shut, the screen became blank.[134]

The Faraday cage demonstrated that human communications with lower astral and negative extraterrestrials involve an electromagnetic element, while communications with higher density beings operate entirely outside the electromagnetic spectrum. The fact that a Faraday cage had been made available in the most synchronistic of circumstances, as the need emerged, showed that hidden forces wanted the communications with the Nine to proceed at Puharich's new private research laboratory (Lab Nine) at his Ossining, New York estate.

The second development is that Gene Roddenberry, creator of the Star Trek series, sat in on the early channeling sessions from 1974 to 1975, asked many probing questions, and was so impressed by the Council of Nine's answers that he wrote a semi-biographical film script called "The Nine ." As I've discussed in the *US Navy's Secret Space Program & Nordic Extraterrestrial Alliance* (2017), Roddenberry had a relationship with US Navy intelligence through Leslie Stevens IV, creator of the Outer Limits TV series and son of Vice Admiral Leslie Stevens. I made the case that the original Star Trek series was 'soft disclosure' of a future Navy secret space program and an alliance with positive human-looking extraterrestrials. I will later discuss the relationship between the Council of Nine, Roddenberry, and the subsequent *Star Trek Series, Deep Space Nine.*

A third development is that prominent officials, industrialists, celebrities, and paranormal researchers attended the Lab Nine channeling sessions. Among them was the researcher, Dr. JJ. Hurtak, who was made Puharich's second in command by the Nine.[135] This was no doubt due to his own paranormal experiences described in his 1973 book, the *Keys of Enoch*. In it, Hurtak described being taken off-planet and being told about the critical role the Council of Nine played in governing our local galactic supercluster:

> I was taken from this region of the stars into the Mid-Way station of Arcturus, the major programming center of the galactic council serving the Father on this side of our Galaxy, which is under the direction of the Council of Nine - the governing body of our local universe. There I was shown the network and the courts used by the spiritual brotherhoods who adjudicate decisions pertaining to the planets involved in our region of space.[136]

The communications that Schlemmer, Puharich, Whitmore, and Roddenberry had with the Nine and the resulting activities are described in two books. The first, *Briefing for the Landing on Planet Earth,* was written by Stuart Holroyd, initially released in 1979 and re-published in 1995 under the new title, *The Nine: Briefing from Deep Space.* The second book, *The Only Planet of Choice,* was written by Schlemmer and published in 1993. It's worth pointing out that this is the same year that the Star Trek series, *Deep Space Nine*, was launched with mysterious entities called 'the Prophets' that were based on the Council of Nine, as I will later show.

In Schlemmer's, *The Only Planet of Choice*, much is written about the identity of the Council of Nine:

> [T]he principle of the Nine is infinite intelligence, and what we try to bring to this planet is this type of intelligence. We are of nine principles of the Universe, yet together we are one. We are separate and one at the same time. Each represents a portion of energy, knowledge, wisdom, love, kindness, technology, and in continuity it goes on until each portion of a spiral is composed of all that is important to bring complete understanding to each atom, until it becomes one with us. There are in actuality multiplications and more, but in principle there are nine.

> We are what is described in the Hebraic tradition as the Elohim. We wish you to know we are not God. We are collective and become one. We wish you to know that we are you as you are we. [137]

The reference to "nine principles of the Universe" corresponds to Dr. Vinod's first channeling sessions where the Nine are equated with the creator gods of Egyptian mythology—the Ennead. The reference to the 'Elohim' is also highly significant given the term is used extensively throughout the Holy Bible to denote the creators of humanity. Chapter 1 of the Book of Genesis describes the role of the Elohim in the creation story.:

> [1] In the beginning **Elohim** created heaven and earth....

> [3] Then **Elohim** said, "Let there be light!" So there was light. [4] **Elohim** saw the light was good. So **Elohim** separated the light from the darkness. [5] **Elohim** named the light *day*, and the darkness he named *night*. There was evening, then morning—the first day...

> [20] Then **Elohim** said, "Let the water swarm with swimming creatures, and let birds fly through the sky over the earth." [21] So **Elohim** created the large sea creatures, every type of creature that swims around in the water and every type of flying bird. **Elohim** saw that they were good. [22] **Elohim** blessed them and said, "Be fertile, increase in number, fill the sea, and let there be many birds on the earth." [23] There was evening, then morning—a fifth day.

> [24] Then **Elohim** said, "Let the earth produce every type of living creature: every type of domestic animal, crawling animal, and wild animal." And so it

> was. [25] **Elohim** made every type of wild animal, every type of domestic animal, and every type of creature that crawls on the ground. **Elohim** saw that they were good.
>
> [26] Then **Elohim** said, "Let us make humans in our image, in our likeness. Let them rule the fish in the sea, the birds in the sky, the domestic animals all over the earth, and all the animals that crawl on the earth."[138]

Most biblical scholars use sophistry to interpret the Elohim in the creation story as a single all-powerful deity (aka God), but it is widely accepted that the term 'Elohim' means a plurality of gods.

The Council of Nine goes on to describe itself in relation to the many other universal forces in existence, especially those that are involved in directing human affairs from behind the scenes. The Nine present a unique way of understanding the relationship between positive and negative forces using the principle of balance:

> We are in the center. And we do not wish to sound as if we are perfect or as if we are egotistical, but on either side of us there is the positive and there is the negative. And when I say this I mean there is the positive that is not balanced, and there is the negative that is not balanced. We are in the center, and we are balanced. We are trying to bring those other forces into balance. We have never been out of balance. It is other things in the Universe that are not in balance. We exist at the pivotal point of the Universe. There is a balance. Within each of you there is all of the positive and all of the negative of the universe.[139]

The idea that positive and negative forces can be in balance or out of balance is critical for understanding extraterrestrial intervention on Earth. What the Council of Nine is revealing here is that positive groups can be out of balance. This might occur, for example, if benevolent extraterrestrial forces fail to act against negative groups due to an overly strict interpretation of a non-intervention principle. On the other hand, negative forces might be in balance if they take aggressive action against corrupt planetary civilizations whose time for removal has come, thereby performing a similar destructive/cleansing function as attributed to the Hindu God Shiva.

Council of Nine, *the Law of One* Material & the 24 Elders

There were references to the Council of Nine in the *Law of One* material that was channeled by Carla Rueckert in response to questions from the retired physics professor, Don Elkins, from 1981 to 1984. Given the reputation of the *Law of One* material today as among the most reliable channeled information ever released, it is noteworthy that it confirmed important elements of Council of Nine material and the integrity of Puharich in facilitating the public emergence of such communications. In fact, Rueckert and Elkins had attended Council of Nine channeling sessions at Puharich's Ossining estate in 1977 and 1978, and this undoubtedly inspired them about the potential of channeled information for understanding extraterrestrial life and contact.[140] They also accompanied Puharich to Mexico to study the psychic healer Pachita.

In the Ra Material, one of the sessions features a dialogue between Elkins and 'Ra' (a sixth density Social Memory Complex) about the Council of Nine:

> **Questioner:** I have a question here, I believe, about that **Council** from Jim. Who are the members, and how does the **Council** function?

Ra: I am Ra. The members of the **Council** are representatives from the Confederation and from those vibratory levels of your inner planes bearing responsibility for your third density. The names are not important because there are no names. Your mind/body/spirit complexes request names and so, in many cases, the vibratory sound complexes which are consonant with the vibratory distortions of each entity are used. However, the name concept is not part of the **Council**. If names are requested, we will attempt them. However, not all have chosen names.

In number, the **Council** that sits in constant session, though varying in its members by means of balancing, which takes place, what you would call irregularly, is nine. That is the Session **Council**. To back up this **Council**, there are twenty-four entities which offer their services as requested. These entities faithfully watch and have been called the Guardians.[141]

The above passage suggests that the 24 entities, the Guardians, act as a backup to the Council of Nine, helping it achieve its primary tasks. The passage goes on to explain these primary tasks:

The **Council** operates by means of, what you would call, telepathic contact with the oneness or unity of the nine, the distortions blending harmoniously so that the Law of One prevails with ease. When a need for thought is present, the **Council** retains the distortion-complex of this need, balancing it as described, and then recommends what it considers as appropriate action. This includes: One, the duty of admitting social memory complexes to the Confederation; Two, offering aid to those who are unsure how to aid the social memory complex requesting aid in a way consonant with both the call, the Law, and the number of those calling (that is to say, sometimes the resistance of the call); Three, internal questions in the **Council** are determined.

These are the prominent duties of the **Council**. They are, if in any doubt, able to contact the twenty-four who then offer consensus/judgment/thinking to the **Council**. The **Council** then may reconsider any question.[142]

The last paragraph implies that the Council of Nine is subordinate to the 24 'Guardians' who lend assistance in dealing with complex galactic issues. As to the identity of this group of 24 'Guardians' assisting the Council of Nine, the Book of Revelations offers an important clue:

Surrounding the throne were twenty-four other thrones, and seated on them were twenty-four elders. They were dressed in white and had crowns of gold on their heads….

Whenever the living creatures give glory, honor and thanks to him who sits on the throne and who lives for ever and ever, the twenty-four elders fall down before him who sits on the throne and worship him who lives for ever and ever.[143]

Interestingly, JJ Hurtak also discussed the 24 Elders (aka Guardians) in *The Keys of Enoch*:

Twenty Four Elders. Lords who sit in the presence of YHWH exchanging their commissions and glory with periodically with other Masters. They control twenty-four Thrones and Dominions which administer the Law of Central Control through

Councils of Light to all universes which recognize YHWH. [144]

This is a very telling statement since it shows that the Council of Nine is among the administrative "Councils of Light" bodies found throughout our universe. The Ra Material, along with Hurtak's *The Keys of Enoch*, affirms that there is a spiritual hierarchy governing our universe, and the Council of Nine is an integral part of it but does not sit at the apex.

Another helpful passage from the Law of One Material confirms that Andrija 'Henry' Puharich and Uri Geller's communications with the Council of Nine were genuine:

> Questioner: Is the Council of Nine the same nine that was mentioned in this book? (Questioner gestures to Uri [authored by Puharich].)

> Ra: I am Ra. The Council of Nine has been retained in semi-undistorted form by two main sources, that known in your naming, as Mark and that known in your naming as Henry [Puharich]. In one case, the channel became the scribe. In the other, the channel was not the scribe. However, without the aid of the scribe, the energy would not have come to the channel.

> Questioner: The names that you spoke of. Were they Mark Probert and Henry Puharich?
> Ra: I am Ra. This is correct.[145]

The above passage from the Law of One should settle any lingering doubts about the integrity of Puharich that was raised by Picknett and Prince in their book, *The Stargate Conspiracy*. The Council of Nine was not a product of a psychological operation, as Picknett and Prince asserted, but was a genuine advanced extraterrestrial intelligence making contact with humanity, according to the Law of One material.

Figure 10. William Blake. The Four and Twenty Elders Casting their Crowns before the Divine Throne, c. 1803–5

When Uri Geller briefly channeled Spectra/Nine for Puharich, a major theme was future mass landings of extraterrestrial civilizations that would precede a return of the Nine. The same theme of mass extraterrestrial landings and a return of the Council of Nine were also very prominent in

Schlemmer's channelings of the Nine. What is particularly noteworthy here is the role of a prominent television series creator in learning about such a future—Gene Rodenberry.

Gene Roddenberry, Council of Nine & Mass Landings/Return of the Nine

The creator of the Star Trek television and movie franchise, Gene Roddenberry, was deeply impacted by the Council of Nine channeling sessions which he personally attended from 1974 to 1975. Schlemmer's book, *The Only Planet of Choice* (1993), gives a hint of the impact in the acknowledgments to her book where she wrote in appreciation:

> The late Gene Roddenberry, creator of *Star Trek* for his courage, curiosity and desire to communicate with the Nine, and the semi-autobiographical film script he created for us called, 'The Nine.' [146]

The semi-autobiographical film script Roddenberry wrote was never released. Two years after his 1991 death, however, a new Star Trek series was launched, *Deep Space Nine*. It aired for seven seasons (1993-1999), achieving much success as a novel contribution to the Star Trek franchise. Two of Roddenberry's associates, Rick Bergman and Michael Piller, were considered the series creators. However, we know from Schlemmer's book that Roddenberry wrote a film script based on what the Council of Nine shared about their identity and activities. It is certain that Piller had access to Roddenberry's unpublished film script, given their close relationship. Therefore, it is highly likely that Piller, who wrote the pilot episode for *Deep Space Nine*, 'Emissary,' incorporated elements from Roddenberry's 'The Nine.'

Rather than a group of disembodied higher intelligence calling itself the Council of Nine, the Nine would appear in the new Star Trek series as disembodied beings living outside of the normal space-time continuum inside a wormhole. In short, the prophets depicted in the Deep Space Nine series are clearly adaptations of the Council of Nine encountered by Roddenberry during the Schlemmer channelings he attended.

The questions Roddenberry asked the Nine are particularly revealing as they indicate the extent to which he was probing them for answers as to why extraterrestrials did not just reveal themselves and end all public debate over their existence:

> Gene: There's a question that I cannot avoid asking; why do you not give strong and definite signs of your existence or proximity, on top of approaching humanity by indirect means such as these channelings or other ways? Obviously, you have your reasons, but this question does matter to me.

> Tom: it is of great importance for you to understand that the governments of your world of Earth have refused to believe, or to convey to the people, our existence. If there were an attempt by the [extraterrestrial] civilizations to land upon Planet Earth in a mass situation, which in truth will come to pass in the course of time, the people upon Planet Earth would panic, for they have not the understanding, the knowledge, that we would mean no harm to them.[147]

The predicted future mass landings led to Roddenberry creating the pilot episode for a future television series, *Earth: The Final Conflict,* that would air in 1998, seven years after his death. Roddenberry was credited as the series creator, but the series was not formally linked to the Star Trek franchise and therefore was not very successful.

This concludes my historical discussion about the Council of Nine. There is more to the story, as will become apparent in Chapter 12, where I examine Elena Danaan's claims of recently having met with them and an intergalactic body—the 24 Extraterrestrial Civilizations—that work directly under the Nine. The 24 extraterrestrial civilizations that figured prominently in Schlemmer's *The Only Planet of Choice* now need to be examined.

CHAPTER 5

Intergalactic Confederation
aka 24 ET Civilizations

The preparation of the Twenty-Four civilizations in gathering forces is to make people upon planet earth aware and alert to bring the prevention of greater difficulties. Apocalyptic prophecies are not necessary to be fulfilled, if those that exist upon planet earth have awareness and understanding.

—Council of Nine, *The Only Planet of Choice*, p. 69.

Multiple sources have referred to an association of extraterrestrial civilizations that originally seeded humanity and have ever since been running long-term genetic experiments. This extraterrestrial association is described as human-looking and committed to ensuring the success of human evolution. This 'positive' group is opposed by other extraterrestrials viewed as negative, opportunists, or disrupting human evolution. The similarities of this scenario to the story of the Garden of Eden are not accidental. Both 'Jehovah' and the 'Serpent,' depicted in biblical texts, represent opposing extraterrestrial groups and their respective efforts to either help or sabotage the human experiment.

The first public reference to this positive association of extraterrestrials overseeing human evolution comes from the Council of Nine channeled communications dating from 1974 to 1993. The Council of Nine revealed the existence of an association they describe as the "Twenty-Four physical civilizations" that abide by Cosmic law and with whom they were working:

> In relationship to us there are Twenty-Four physical civilizations in another dimensional realm. Each is a total collective consciousness that oversees and from these civilizations, physical beings have incarnated upon your planet earth, and at times have intervened, when necessary. These physical civilizations, the Twenty-Four, each in its own dimension, are total and complete units of one collective consciousness that have agreed to be in that collective consciousness. They have evolved to that point form of action to oversee, to pass through information of great importance and help other physical civilizations in their evolutionary process.[148]

The Council of Nine is here emphasizing that while they are incorporeal and reside in a dimensionless non-temporal void, this is not the case with the Twenty-Four civilizations. The latter physically interact with humanity, and even incarnate on Earth from time to time as great prophets, teachers, inventors, artists, etc. This is how the Council of Nine described the process by which four out of the Twenty-Four Civilizations interact with humanity:

> There is in each civilization a different manifestation of love. Altea will proceed with technology, to bring forth knowledge of non-destructive technologies, which work in unison with the nature of Planet Earth – to help with production without destruction.
>
> Aragon will come with knowledge and wisdom, and the ability to release disruption and pain within a physical body, for it is Aragon's concern to relieve humans of bondage, arising from the influence of physical pain – such relief can free the mind...

Ashan will awaken the creativity in humans upon Planet Earth, and through great music and great art will educate in the ways of the Universe.

With great love Hoova of the Nazarene comes to bring love to the Planet Earth. They will set down a system to begin, to teach humans what they must do for themselves to help Planet Earth and the souls that are trapped.... Most important: they will instill in humans that life does not cease upon the death of the physical body, so you cannot escape the consequences of what you have done.[149]

The Council of Nine gave examples of how the Twenty-Four civilizations relate to ancient human civilizations – Atlantis and the Israelite Hebrew nation being the two most prominent cases:

An example would be the civilization of Altea; as we are in another realm of existence, we depend upon Altea for communicating with you. They guard the body of our being while you are in communication with us, and they provide the technology for us to communicate. Altea was also the head of what you know as the physical civilization that manifested upon planet earth as Atlantis.

There are other civilizations - and there are amongst you incumbent souls from those civilizations who have come to help Planet Earth. One of these civilizations, Hoova, was the civilization that originally seated Planet Earth, as did some of the others, but Hoova re-seeded Planet Earth on three occasions. Hoova is the civilization from which the Hebrews derive: hence the importance of the Hebrews. Hoova is the civilization that brought forth the Nazarene.[150]

The reference to the Nazarene (aka Jesus Christ) is highly significant as it directly links the Hoova civilization to the birth and life of Jesus. It raises the intriguing possibility that the Star of Bethlehem was a Hoova spacecraft playing an unknown role in Jesus' birth. His unusual abilities as a child and desire to seek esoteric knowledge led to him spending extended periods with the Essene Community hidden in the Qumran region, as explained in Dolores Cannon's groundbreaking book, *Jesus and the Essenes*.[151] Her book investigated the past life memories of a client who was one of Jesus' Essene community teachers. What truly separated Jesus from others at the time was his absolute focus on the 'love ethic' in all his teachings and activities, as Cannon pointed out. The 'love ethic' was a revolutionary teaching at the time, even for the reclusive Essene community, and raises the possibility that he was connected in a powerful way with the Hoova extraterrestrials attempting to influence human evolution with a revolutionary love ethic.

When asked whether this association of positive extraterrestrials could be called a "Council of Twenty-Four and the 'Elders' and so on?" the Council of Nine replied: "it would be the Congress."[152] A Congress is defined as "a formal assembly of representatives, as of various nations, to discuss problems."[153] The Nine's reference to 'the Congress' suggests that the Twenty-Four Civilizations is a formal organization that deliberates on galactic-wide problems associated with the evolution of human-populated worlds, rather than an ad hoc or informal body that is relatively short-lived.

The Council of Nine described how the Twenty-Four civilizations would have other extraterrestrial races working under them, thereby forming a hierarchal system with the Nine at the apex:

> The members of the Council of Nine are not, and have not been, in physical form. There are the Twenty-Four civilizations that are in physical form, and then there are what we could call helper-

civilizations that are in more physicalness than the Twenty-Four. Example: Altea is a civilization of the Twenty-Four. That civilization has one thought, one being. In other words, it is a collective consciousness of a very high caliber and is of millions of souls that support, create and survive with each other. They know all in their location and in their knowledge. They in turn have underneath them other civilizations that you would term workers or helpers of ... we do not wish to use the term 'sub-civilization' but there are those that filter down.[154]

The diversity of these different extraterrestrial races and their intervention on Earth has led to multiple long-term genetic experiments, and the rise and fall of many civilizations on Earth. The extraterrestrial races involved in these numerous genetic experiments and human societies coordinate with one another in a formal Congress and work under the authority of the Council of Nine. This association doesn't preclude competing agendas and activities by the Twenty-Four civilizations, but it does minimize conflict between them and their respective helper civilizations.

Gene Roddenberry & the 24 Civilizations

In 1975, when Gene Roddenberry attended the Council of Nine channeling sessions with Phyllis Schlemmer, Andrija Puharich, and John Whitmore that were held inside a Faraday cage at Ossining, New York, he was particularly intrigued by the Council's statements that the Congress of Twenty-Four Extraterrestrial civilizations would facilitate a large-scale mass landing in the near future. Roddenberry asked the Council of Nine for more details:

Gene: You mentioned that at some stage there might be a large-scale landing of the civilizations. I think the next questions involve who and where, how and why; the first such question most people would ask is how? In other words, what method of transportation would be used in such a landing; are we referring to physical vehicles?

Tom: Yes. That would be in the nature of what you would call a physical vehicle. If you have the desire to go and touch it, as you have with an automobile, you would be able to touch it.

Gene: Can you tell me anything about the relative size and shape and so on? Would they hold a large number of people, or ...

Tom: These would be vehicles of different sizes and different designs. There would be some with the appearance of a glass top, but it is not in truth a top, it will just have its appearance. There will also be those that will remain in your atmosphere that are very large, that will then send out smaller ones... you have, upon your oceans, carriers that send out ships that fly, is that not so?

Gene: That is correct.

Tom: It would be similar, but instead of being upon your oceans, it would be in your sky.[155]

It is helpful to keep in mind that extraterrestrials have long been observed to use motherships in orbit around Earth from which smaller craft would operate. This is what was revealed in 1952 by George Van Tassel in his communications with the Ashtar Command. Fortunately, the contactee George Adamski took a famous sequence of photographs of six scout craft emerging out of a larger cigar-shaped vessel high in our atmosphere.

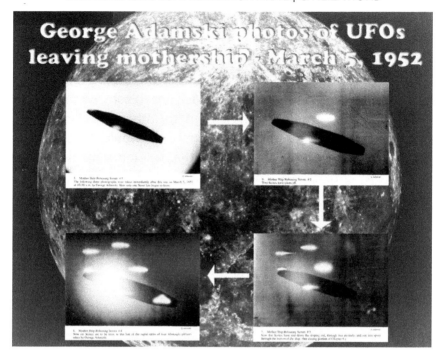

Figure 11. Sequence of photos taken by George Adamski in 1952

Roddenberry next asked whether the Twenty-Four civilizations showing up uninvited would lead to conflict with Earth governments. The Council of Nine's answer revealed much about which civilizations' would be involved and their motivations:

> Gene: Landings would undoubtedly be judged by humans and governments in a variety of ways, which includes the almost certainty that some would view your landings as a threat. Do you have a method of defending yourself from attack?

> Tom: We wish you to know that we are talking about the civilizations, not us, the Council of Nine. We do not need to manifest in the physical. There would be a method to stop people from attempting to destroy those of the civilizations. It will be done with love

and gentleness. Those of the civilizations that are in service to us will not attempt to destroy, nor harm in any manner, any physical being on Earth. We will have a way of preventing them from attempting to destroy us. But we would wish not to come without giving some prior knowledge, for otherwise people would begin to believe that we would seek to control them. We have not the desire nor the need to control, we come only to benefit.[156]

In a later session, the Council of Nine [Tom] explained how "lesser" extraterrestrial groups would respond to the Twenty-Four civilizations conducting mass landings on Earth in response to questions by Sir John Whitmore:

Tom: Those lesser civilizations who have been viewing Planet Earth, who have made contact with governments, and who are in portion in beings upon Planet Earth and in this realm as well, would have warlike conflict with the Twenty-Four civilizations or those who work with them: therefore that would mean a destructive device in the atmosphere of Planet Earth. Humankind in its great fear would not have acknowledged or understood that there were those of goodness also.

John: Because they would only see two groups … destroying each other.

Tom: That is correct, and that would then create a nightmarish pollution destructiveness of portions of Planet Earth. We must find another way of removing these others at this time.[157]

Here the Council of Nine was showing their full awareness that these "lesser extraterrestrial groups"—Draconian (Ciakahrr)

Empire and the Orion (Gray) Collective—which had contacted and reached agreements with various Earth governments, would orchestrate a terrible planet-wide catastrophe using destructive weapons if the Twenty-Four civilizations openly arrived to help humanity's evolution. Aside from the few government leaders who were aware of what was really happening, the rest of humanity would not be able to distinguish between the positive and negative extraterrestrial visitors and would conclude we were under a planet-wide alien attack.

The Council of Nine succinctly described the situation created by the 'lesser civilizations' working with human elites to control the rest of humanity, and effectively preventing the Twenty-Four civilizations and their helpers from openly landing or revealing themselves:

> Remember this: there are also certain civilizations, not of the Twenty-Four or their helper civilizations, that have a great desire to control Earth, to keep souls in bondage. And these civilizations have landed at times on Planet Earth and have caused difficulty, which they forced on Earth people. It is important that there is no panic amongst those that exists on the Planet Earth that the knowledge be brought to them in gentleness, that those are the Twenty-Four civilizations mean no harm to them. This is of great importance for if there was panic, humans may then attempt to end their own life, and also the lives of their families and neighbors, which would not serve any purpose. [158]

As mentioned earlier, when it came to distinguishing between positive and negative extraterrestrial groups, the Council of Nine took a unique approach. It distinguished between balanced and unbalanced positive and negative extraterrestrial races and organizations. The Council of Nine regarded itself as the point of balance between these different tendencies in the multitude of extraterrestrial civilizations in the universe, a select group of which are currently visiting or interacting with humanity.[159] The Nine gave an example of "unbalanced positive" individuals and how they could create problems: "Remember: those that are so positive in their approach that they have no sense, create just as many problems as those that live on greed, anger, frustrations, and fears."[160]

The Nine's example here implies that those that take a negative approach to their interactions with others but do so using 'sense' (a basic understanding of cosmic law) are an example of 'balanced negativity.' This term could apply to predatory extraterrestrial races such as the Draconian Empire, who take steps to ensure their conquests of other worlds are done in alignment with basic universal law. This is achieved if they only infiltrate, attack, or take over civilizations out of balance in some fundamental way (e.g., Earth) and leave alone balanced societies (e.g., the 24 Civilizations). In nature, this is mirrored in the way predatory animals typically hunt isolated, wounded, sick, or old animals and leave healthy mature animals alone.

The Council of Nine is not alone in positing negative forces, and actions can be 'balanced' in ways that bring them in accord with universal law. The *Law of One* Material also takes the approach that negative polarity "service to self" individuals and groups have an evolutionary path that can lead to ascension (harvest) to higher densities.

> **Questioner:** What must be the entity's percentage, shall we say, if he is to be harvested for the negative?
>
> **Ra:** I am Ra. The entity who wishes to pursue the path of **service** to **self** must attain a grade of five, that is five percent **service** to others, ninety-five percent **service** to **self**. It must approach totality. The negative path is quite difficult to attain

harvestability upon and requires great dedication.[161]

At this point, it is worth exploring whether there have been other credible sources supporting the existence of a supra-galactic congress—the Twenty-Four Extraterrestrial Civilizations—overseeing galactic genetic experiments that have been visiting Earth since antiquity.

French Contactee & the Intergalactic Confederation

Robert L. is an extraterrestrial contactee from France who says that in 1969 he spent nearly a year in a secret base in the Himalayas where he participated in a genetic experiment to seed human life on a planet in another galaxy. After completing his year-long stay at the base, Robert was returned to France and was told to remain silent, which he did for nearly 40 years until 2005 when he first went public. He contacted a well-known French UFO researcher, Georges Metz, who was so impressed that he included Robert's case in a 2011 book *Ovnis en France: Les enquêtes de Georges Metz* (*UFOs in France: The Investigations of Georges Metz*).[162] The book was published but not translated into English, making most in the English-speaking world unaware of Robert's remarkable story and its significance.

What makes Robert's story especially relevant today is that he described the extraterrestrials as belonging to an "intergalactic confederation" managing life on planets such as Earth, and this confederation worked under the supervision of a mysterious group of nine very highly advanced extraterrestrials. This is a translation of the relevant passage in Metz's book:

> The visitors gave me information and advice. The Guide said to me: "Your parents are good people - You have characteristics that interest us. We are all scholars. Star explorers from another galaxy. We are

20,000 years ahead of your civilization that we have been watching for a long time. We are responsible for keeping life safe on inhabited planets like the Earth. We are part of a kind of intergalactic confederation overseen by nine unknown superiors who manage the galaxies. We visit the planets in development like yours. We know your whole story and all the languages spoken on Earth.[163]

This closely matches the two extraterrestrial groups described in Schlemmer's *The Only Planet of Choice*—the Council of Nine and the Congress of Twenty Four Extraterrestrial Civilizations. It is important to point out that Robert was never told how many extraterrestrial civilizations made up the "Intergalactic Confederation," but the similarities with Schlemmer's material suggest that it was the same twenty-four civilizations that the Council of Nine repeatedly referred to. What is noteworthy here is that when Elena Danaan claims she was taken to visit an "Intergalactic Confederation" in November 2021 (to be discussed in Chapter 12) she was told it comprises 24 civilizations. This confirms that the Intergalactic Confederation and the (Congress of) Twenty-Four Extraterrestrial Civilizations are the same organization.

Robert at first believed the extraterrestrials were angels. They told him they were simply humans, like him, but only more evolved with life spans of up to 500 years. They told him they were scientists that came from another galaxy. Robert mainly interacted with three extraterrestrials he respectively called "the Guide" (a male); "the Biologist" (a beautiful female approximately two meters tall); and "the Ethnologist" respectively. In September 1968, the extraterrestrials asked if Robert was willing to be part of a genetic experiment where he would help seed human life on a planet in another galaxy. Robert was told he would spend a year at a remote base in the Himalayas where he would contribute his biological material, which was very suitable for the galactic seeding project. Robert agreed to participate, and in early January 1969, he was taken by spacecraft to the base.

In Metz's book, Robert described its location as somewhere near Ladakh, a strategic mountainous region that straddles the borders of China and India. Metz cited several articles from 2004 referring to UFO activity at an alleged extraterrestrial base in the region, which helped corroborate Robert's story.[164] Robert asserted the base was located entirely underground, with only an elevator connecting it to the surface. He said that the elevator exit to the surface was well disguised, making it very difficult for the base to be found. Georges Metz created an illustration of the base that was located one kilometer (~3000 feet) below the surface of a remote mountainous area.

Robert said the base's interior was very futuristic, and its walls did not appear to be those of a cavern. The base was filled with advanced extraterrestrial technologies such as holographic television monitors, which could monitor distant areas such as his home and village. He realized that the balls of light he and his family had first encountered in June 1967 were monitoring devices whose outputs could be viewed on these holographic monitors. Robert was allowed to roam freely inside the base, which had three levels. He regularly met human-looking extraterrestrials that treated him courteously in corridors and reception areas. He was only restricted from three rooms that contained powerful electromagnetic energies that could harm him.

In Metz's book, Robert described what the extraterrestrials told him about government leaders hiding the truth and how many UFO sightings involve the off-world visitors revealing themselves, so the public awakens to the truth:

> Your governments are afraid of us. Why? Are they uncomfortable not being alone in the Universe? They know very well that we don't want to harm any inhabitants; they are partially aware of the capacity of our technology. Why don't they want to tell the citizens? They ridicule the reports of those who have

seen us and have spoken up. So the Intergalactic Confederation decided to show our capacity to the greatest number of people possible. The world over needs to know that we exist and that Manifest Intelligence is everywhere in the Universe.[165]

The extraterrestrials that Robert met and spent a year with at the Himalayan base are described as very tall, with long arms, and having a white complexion. The description matches one of the "seeder races" that Elena Danaan says she met near Jupiter's moon, Ganymede, which will be discussed in Chapter 12. These extraterrestrials are, however, only one from among the 24 seeder races involved in running genetic experiments on Earth.

Extraterrestrials Running 22 Genetic Experiments

While we know that the Intergalactic Confederation (aka Twenty-Four Extraterrestrial Civilizations) have been seeding human life throughout many galaxies—Earth being only one example of this—the Council of Nine never specified how many genetic experiments were taking place on Earth. Popular researchers such as Zechariah Sitchin described the creation of humanity by one race of extraterrestrials described as the Anunnaki.[166] His information matched biblical references to the Elohim as the creators of humanity. Yet we know that more than one extraterrestrial civilization is lending its genetic diversity to humanity in planetary seeding experiments, according to what the Council of Nine has revealed. They described the interventions of the Altea, Hoova, Ashan, and Aragon civilizations in human affairs, which involved seeding their genetics into societies stretching far back into remote antiquity.

According to information supplied by the extraterrestrial contactee, Alex Collier, and secret space program insider Corey Goode, 22 distinct genetic experiments are currently being conducted on Earth. This approximates what we know from the

Council of Nine's information about the Twenty-Four Civilizations/Intergalactic Confederation intervening in human affairs. In short, the Intergalactic Confederation is running 22 genetic experiments, as described by Collier and Goode.

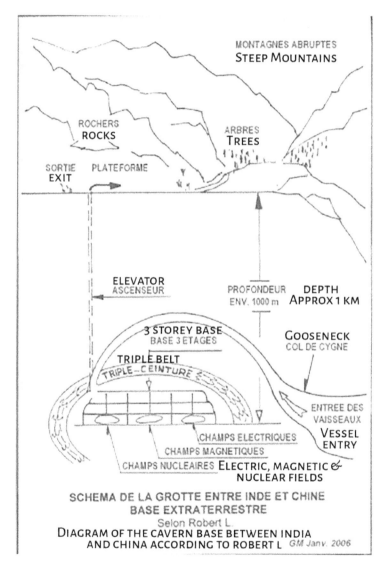

Figure 12. ET Base in the Himalayas. Illustration by Georges Metz. 2008. English translation added to original French

Collier, who claims to have been contacted by extraterrestrials from Andromeda, was the first to describe these 22 genetic experiments soon after his public emergence in 1991. In one of his early lectures, compiled in the book *Defending Sacred Ground*, Collier pointed out that "we have the genetic coding of 22 different races in our bodies."[167] Collier explained that this theory of extraterrestrial genetic intervention (aka Intelligent Design) is more accurate than Darwinian notions of natural selection:

> Now, ladies and gentlemen, you are all truly awesome beings. We have inside our DNA the genetics and racial genetic memories of 22 different races. You know, science teaches us that the body is a 'pool of chemicals' evolved from monkeys. It just didn't happen that way. The physical forms that we are 'in' were genetically altered, and then they were 'tinkered' with by many of the different races that have come here. [168]

In a 2002 lecture, Collier illustrated what he was told by referring to the different human racial characteristics—body types—dispersed over Earth's geographical regions:

> [W]hat we are going to be talking about is the 22 [extraterrestrial] races... In a nutshell, we are a composite of a lot of different races, 22 to be exact. It is a physiological fact that there are 22 different body types on the planet. And that is the result of the extraterrestrial races.[169]

According to Collier, the fact that we are a composite of 22 different extraterrestrial genetics makes us unique and capable of extraordinary abilities. He claims that these innate genetic abilities make us royalty in the eyes of the more advanced civilizations:

> [W]e, as a product of extraterrestrial genetic manipulation, are possessors of a vast gene pool consisting of many different racial memory banks, also consisting of at least 22 different races. Because of our genetic heritage, and because we are spirit, the benevolent extraterrestrial races actually view us as being royalty.[170]

While Collier's information about us being genetic royalty may appear hard to believe, we need to go back to the case of Robert L who was told by one of the extraterrestrial seeder races belonging to the Intergalactic Confederation that his genetics was to be used to seed human life in another galaxy. This seeding would only be possible if human genetics was considered exceptional by highly evolved extraterrestrials involved in intergalactic seeding experiments. This exceptionality supports Collier's claim that the Andromedans and other highly evolved extraterrestrial races consider us a kind of genetic royalty.

Another source that has spoken about 22 extraterrestrial genetic experiments being conducted on Earth is secret space program insider Corey Goode. In a July 14, 2015, interview aired on Gaia TV, Goode spoke about the 22 genetic experiments:

> There was a group of 40 human-looking ETs that were pretty much always present, and up to 60 at other times that were present. There were 22 genetic programs that were going on…. Of the 22 different programs, they've been going on for different lengths of time. But the genetic manipulation of what we are has been going back at least 250,000 years.[171]

Goode [CG] described the extraterrestrial races involved in running the 22 genetic experiments as a "Super Federation" in response to questions from David Wilcock [DW]:

> CG: ... What I've described as this Federation Super Council, (Okay) this is a Super Federation made up of other federations, councils, and other different organizations and groups.
>
> DW: So hence the word 'Super.'
>
> CG: 'Confederations' I've heard used .... And it's kind of like a giant UN of all of these different federations, confederations, councils, that come to meet, and there are 40 main groups with 20 other groups that are there a fair amount of the time but not all the time.[172]

Goode's information is similar to what Robert L. had earlier described regarding the Galactic Confederation running human genetic seeding programs in this and other galaxies. Goode's information also matches what the Council of Nine had to say earlier about primary extraterrestrial civilizations working with helper races in running the genetic experiments on Earth stretching far back into antiquity. While Goode posits 40 main extraterrestrial groups with 20 support groups running the genetic experiments on Earth, the Council of Nine refers to 24 main groups with an unknown number of helpers.

Goode said the extraterrestrial races involved in running the 22 genetic experiments were improving our genetics to enhance our spiritual development and abilities:

> CG: I actually heard that it was a part of the Grand Experiment from these 22 different genetic experiments from these 40 groups. This experiment was not only genetic in nature, but it was also spiritual in nature and that they were trying to enhance us in a spiritual way and that the pineal gland and something also to do with our light body were something that they were manipulating to try

to help us become more spiritual and more developed in that way. They are obviously at odds with this Draco Alliance group.

DW: So that would imply that the Super Federation is not all negative.

CG: No. Like I said, it's all point of view. They have their agendas and why they're manipulating us the way they're doing.[173]

This also approximates what Alex Collier had to say about some of the higher extraterrestrial groups viewing humanity as genetic royalty—our genetics gives us the capability of doing things through consciousness that other races can only achieve through technological means. Given these similarities, it would not be unreasonable to conclude that Goode's "Super (Con)Federation" is directly connected to the 24 Civilizations described by the Council of Nine, or the 'Intergalactic Confederation" described by Robert L and Elena Danaan. It may be that the Super Federation described by Goode is the local branch of the Intergalactic Confederation.

What Goode had to say about where the Super Federation (aka Intergalactic Confederation) is based is worth reviewing. He said in an interview:

Now, these groups are more of the human-looking, human type, and their bases seem to be mainly on the back of the Moon and on moons of some of the gas giants, especially Saturn, so much so that there are areas around certain moons of Jupiter and Saturn that our vessels were completely forbidden from going anywhere near. And this is in our own solar system. These areas were off limits. [174]

The reference to the Moons of Jupiter is especially important given recent information that the Intergalactic Confederation has only recently arrived in our solar system in a very large fleet, which will be discussed in chapter 12.

CHAPTER 6

Andromeda Council

The Andromedan Council consists of 133 representatives of planetary systems and races, much like a United Nations of our galaxy. Their intent is to help develop consciousness ... The Council has operated for thousands of years under strict codes and guidelines of conduct... We are not to look at the Andromedans as saviors. In fact, they say we really gain nothing by having someone come down here and literally save us, because they take us off the hook, and we don't gain the experience of evolution ourselves.

—Alex Collier, "ET Overview," 1994.

The Andromeda constellation is 44 light years away from Earth and contains sixteen main stars with at least 24 exoplanets that have been confirmed so far by different scientific methods.[175] In addition, there is also the famous Andromeda or M31 galaxy, which is a staggering 2.5 million light years away in the same line of sight as the constellation—the galaxy appears as a point of light in the Andromeda Constellation. While it is not surprising that there have been contactees who claim to have met or communicated with extraterrestrials from the Andromeda constellation possessing advanced spacecraft, it is their references to the important role of an Andromeda Council in galactic affairs and in our solar system that is critical to understand.

Billy Meier and the Andromeda High Council

The first reference to an Andromeda Council emerged in the "Contact Notes" of Eduard Billy Meier. In 1975 Meier went public with his claims, photos, and videos of contact with human-looking extraterrestrials from the planet Erra in the Taygeta star system of the Pleiades constellation. Meier wrote down what he was told by a beautiful female extraterrestrial called "Semjase," and these were compiled chronologically to be eventually released as the Contact Notes. Meier's claims and evidence were studied by multiple UFO researchers, including the legendary Lt. Col. Wendelle Stevens (USAF retired). In addition to his book about Meier, *UFO Contact from the Pleiades: A Preliminary Investigation Report* (1982), detailing his research conclusions,[176] Stevens also edited a four-volume series of books called *Message from the Pleiades: The Contact Notes of Eduard Billy Meier* (1988-1995).[177] Stevens and other researchers found Meier's information to be genuine. The information in the Contact Notes gave many insights into the history of the galaxy and the emigration of human colonies from one star system to another seeking refuge from different enemies and planetary disasters.

In Meier's account of what he was told about the history of one of these galactic migrations, he described how the Plejarans (aka Pleiadians) encountered a highly evolved race of extraterrestrials in the Andromeda constellation that would subsequently become advisors to the Plejarans and their new colonies. Meier's contact note from January 6, 1977, described what happened:

> In the run of the next 8,000 years, the Pleja nations developed themselves up to a very high spiritual level, in result of which, they made alliances with every possible similar and other strange nations of nearby and far-away systems, and unanimously lived for evolution. In this way then together

126

developed another great alliance, in the cause of which they performed new expeditions, and found in 1951, years ago in Earth chronology, a semi-spiritual world in the Andromeda Star System, which was inhabited by semi-spiritual creatures, an already extremely high developed form of life, which still existed semi-materially, but as well semi-spiritually, too. By agreement among these forms of life, they all decided that in the future, these beings in Andromeda should guide and govern, by their gigantic knowledge and wisdom, the fates of their nations and their great alliance, which plan was welcomed joyfully by all nations. In consequence, it was decided by agreement of the spiritual leaders, who were human creatures and spiritual teachers, that all fates should be in the future be guided by the, now best friends, semi-spiritual creatures. The manner of guidance should be that one of a council from the side of the higher spiritual level, in consequence of which this control and guidance was called the "High Council", and is maintained this way until today, and will never change. Since then, all nations of all races allied to us remain under the guidance of the "High Council," which never orders any commands, but only offers a "high advice," the observance of which is at the disposal of each single form of life, and which normally is observed, too, without exception.[178]

The "High Council" comprising "semi-spiritual" beings from the Andromeda constellation is what we today call the Andromeda Council. Particularly relevant is the Plejarans/Pleiadians assertion that the High/Andromeda Council had "gigantic knowledge and wisdom" which led to them being accepted as guides. Very significant is the observation that the Andromeda Council does not issue orders or commands to extraterrestrial races that accept the

127

Council's guidance but offers "high advice." Meier was not the only individual claiming contact with a highly advanced race of beings from Andromeda that Wendelle Stevens would come across in his pioneering UFO research.

Professor Hernadez and the Andromedans

Stevens found another contact case that involved a tenured professor in the medical school at the University of Mexico. The professor was a senior member of Mexico's Instituto Nacional de Energia Nuclear (National Institute for Nuclear Energy) and used the pseudonym of 'Prof Hernandez' to release his amazing story. Prof. Hernandez worked with a Mexican journalist, Zitha Rodriguez, who investigated his case and eventually published the notes of his contact meetings.[179] He discussed how a beautiful extraterrestrial female, Elyense, from the constellation Andromeda had befriended him and revealed her origin. Zitha Rodriquez explained how Prof. Hernandez first approached her while she was researching another story about earthquakes at the Instituto Nacional de Energia Nuclear.

> In 1978-1979, I directed the magazine *OVNI* [UFO]....
> Well, ... I was writing a book on earthquakes. A
> friend suggested I talk to a certain person in the
> Instituto Nacional de Energia Nuclear, one Professor
> Carlos Graef, who was an experienced
> seismologist... One day, desperate to make contact
> ... I went in to look for someone, and when I came
> out I passed Professor Hernandez. The professor
> immediately showed interest in what I was doing
> and how was my work. He had important
> responsibility at the institute and was a high
> executive at the university ... I went into his office
> the first time without knowing exactly what was
> going to happen.... He invited me to sit down and

began to question me... He asked me if I knew any people who had seen UFOs and I told him yes... He got up, walked around his desk, struck the desk with his fist and made an unusual confession. I have traveled in a ship and have a friendship with a woman who said she came from ... Andromeda. I at first did not believe it, said the professor, not all of it.[180]

Prof. Hernandez described in detail the free energy principles, advanced technology, and galactic history he learned about from his Andromedan contact. Elyense told him that humanity was descended from extraterrestrial civilizations that had established themselves on Earth. Yet more corroboration that members of the 24 Civilizations/Intergalactic Confederation had regularly seeded Earth with their genetics. After destructive conflicts involving advanced technology, the DNA of the survivors began to degenerate. Elyense told Prof. Hernandez that the Andromedans and other extraterrestrial civilizations were giving assistance to restore humanity's inherent abilities and former stature. Elyense also revealed that some extraterrestrial groups were trying to sabotage these efforts and were dedicated to exploiting humanity:

> You had asked me if there were beings more aggressive than the Earth humans inhabiting this universe. I mentioned that there were and spoke about those who have been coming on various occasions to your world... they scorn mercy to your empiricism and the rickety form of science that you possess. They have been coming to your world with complete freedom and have captured living beings, children, ancients, men, women, animals, fish and they rob you of oxygen, hydrogen and even absorb electric fluid of the supplies flowing to your great cities. Humans who unfortunately disappear and do

not return anymore have been kidnapped by them.[181]

Once again, this corroborates information presented earlier about negative extraterrestrial groups (the Draconian Empire or the Orion Collective) abusing humans and interfering in Earth's evolution.

Prof. Hernandez described how the Andromedans had made an effort to prepare humanity to deal with the threats confronting it by giving needed information to scientists. Elyense told him that the Andromedans had contacted senior officials in the political and scientific establishments but had been spurned: "we have had contacts with ambassadors, with tenured professors and with other people of your civilization. They simply do not believe us."[182] The Andromedans claimed that they could not directly intervene to prevent future threats. The Andromedans were primarily scientists and ambassadors and did not have a military force. This matches what Meier was told about the Andromeda Council insofar as it provided scientific advice and guidance rather than a powerful military force to help other civilizations.

Prof. Hernandez explained how his mental and psychic abilities increased dramatically because of his interactions with the Andromedan female:

> My mind had expanded and my power of concentration had become sharpened. I could perceive any sound in great detail and surprisingly, could repeat such any time I desired and analyze it completely, including its musical derivations, if it had any... [W]hen I see a man, whatever his ancestry might be, I perceive various characteristics, his extraordinary ones – levels of vibrational frequency, his origins, his blood chemistry compositions ...[183]

Unfortunately, Prof. Hernandez invoked the wrath of his wife, who was convinced that he was having an affair with a student and succeeded in having him committed to a mental asylum for one month in 1989. Upon his release, Prof. Hernandez disappeared and has not been found since, despite the best efforts of his family and investigators. Subsequent investigations by Zitha Rodriquez were unable to extract his papers and records from Mexican security officials or his distraught family. The Hernandez case was also investigated by Wendelle Stevens, who was able to corroborate Zitha Rodriquez's research and the identity of Prof. Hernandez. The Hernandez case showed how dangerous it was for prominent scientists to come forward with accounts of contact with advanced extraterrestrials willing to share life-changing information and technologies that could revolutionize our planet. Subsequently, the Andromedans found another individual, a non-scientist, through whom they could disseminate their information.

Alex Collier & the Andromeda Council

From the testimony of another contactee, Alex Collier, who publicly came forward in 1991, we learn most about the Andromedans being part of a "High Council" or "Andromeda Council" that guides other extraterrestrial races, such as Meier's Plejarans. Collier was a professional accountant and had worked for the Internal Revenue Service for several years. After contact experiences that revealed his life mission, he began giving lectures, interviews and publishing a regular newsletter called "Letters from Andromeda."[184] Some of these lectures and interviews were compiled in the book *Defending Sacred Ground,* released in 1997.[185] I have met, interviewed, and worked with Alex Collier on numerous occasions, and my conclusion is that he is very sincere and credible.

Collier says the Andromedans are direct descendants of the Lyrans who experienced some difficulty when first leaving the Lyran system due to predatory extraterrestrial races. The Lyrans eventually settled in the Andromeda constellation in the star system 'Zenetae.' Collier describes the nature of the Andromedans as follows:

131

> Everything that they create technologically is used for the advancement of their race. It is for educational purposes only. But, it can be used in defense. No, they do not have a military, per se. They are scientists. What they do is send their children to school anywhere from 150 to 200 years, in our linear time. They teach their students all of the arts and sciences. They are literally masters at everything. Then, at that point, they have the choice in what it is they want to do, and they can change their minds anytime and do something else. So, they are given all the tools. Everything is for education. Nothing is for distraction. They would never conceive of creating television as a distraction. Never. Everything is to help them evolve, and their science and their technology can be used for defensive purposes -- mostly the holographic stuff.[186]

This is very similar to what Prof. Hernandez was told by his Andromedan contact, Elyense, about the scientific and ambassadorial services they offered, rather than military assistance since they did not possess an organized military.

The most significant contribution of the Andromedans to galactic life is that they were instrumental in creating the Andromeda Council, which is a grouping of approximately 140 star systems that deliberate upon stellar affairs and provide guidance to less evolved civilizations such as the Plejarans, as first explained by Meier. In a 1997 interview, Collier described the Council's warning to other extraterrestrial races regarding a future galactic threat that involved the Earth:

> Now, in our galaxy there are many councils. I don't know everything about all those councils, but I do know about the Andromedan Council, which is a group of beings from 139 different star systems that

come together and discuss what is going on in the galaxy. It is not a political body. What they have been recently discussing is the tyranny in our future, 357 years from now, because that affects everybody. Apparently, what they have done, through time travel, is that they have been able to figure out where the significant shift in energy occurred that causes the tyranny 357 years in our future. They have traced it back to our solar system, and they have been able to further track it down to Earth, Earth's moon and Mars. Those three places.[187]

It is important to note the similarity of the threat Earth was facing with what Elyense told Professor Hernandez. Furthermore, in chapter 2, I discussed the Galactic Federation and how it was approached by the Andromeda Council about the future problem involving the Earth. It makes sense that the Andromeda Council, which comprises scientists and diplomats, and does not possess an organized military, would approach an organization such as the Galactic Federation, which does. Collier next gave details about the Andromeda Council's deliberations about what to do about Earth being a future threat to the entire galaxy:

The very first meeting the Andromedan Council had was to decide whether or not to directly intervene with what was going on here. According to Moraney, there were only 78 systems that met this first time. Of those 78, just short of half decided that they wanted nothing to do with us at all, regardless of the problems. I think it is really important that you know why they wanted nothing to do with us. We are talking about star systems that are hundreds of millions of light years away from us. Even some who have never met us. They just knew the vibration of the planet reflected those on it. The reasons why they wanted nothing to do with us is that, from their perspective, Earth humans don't respect themselves, each other or the planet. What possibly can be the value of Earth humans? Fortunately, the majority of the council gave the opinion that because Earth has been manipulated for over 5,700 years, that we deserved an opportunity to prove ourselves - to at least have a shot at proving the other part of the council wrong.[188]

It is interesting to note that Collier says that the first meetings of the Andromeda Council involved discussion of the future threat the Earth, Moon, and Mars formed to the rest of the galaxy. This matches what Meier revealed about the Andromeda (High) Council forming in 1951.

More Contactee Accounts of the Andromedans

Another contactee with the Andromedans is an individual who uses the pseudonym 'Tolec,' whom I have personally met and interviewed. He appears to be having genuine contact and communications with extraterrestrials. Tolec emerged into the public arena in early 2011, claiming to have been taken onto an Andromedan mothership and recruited to be a representative to Earth for the Andromedan Council. He claims:

The Andromeda Council is an intergalactic and interstellar governance and development body of aligned benevolent star systems and planets of sentient intelligent life... for worlds in both the Milky Way and Andromeda galaxies. The Andromeda galaxy is also known as M31 to the people of Earth. The chaired members of the

Andromeda Council comprise a total of twelve (12) different, distinct member worlds & races.[189]

Tolec says that he is in regular communication with the Andromedan Council, and coordinating with them on how to best transform the Earth into a Galactic society. His website has much material about recent Andromedan activities and echoes the earlier testimony of Alex Collier who Tolec supports as a genuine contactee.[190] Tolec offers no physical evidence to support his claims and believes that his material stands by itself.

More recently, Elena Danaan has released more information about the Andromeda Council that she was given by her Galactic Federation sources. In her book, *A Gift from the Stars*, she writes about the ancient galactic movement of civilizations that led to the colonization of the Andromeda constellation:

> They are a Lyran colony who left Vega to settle in the Zenatean system, Andromeda constellation.... Their higher caste of sages can reach up to the 12th Density and their life-purpose is principally based around learning, as Zenae nourish a passion for science. They created the Andromeda Council, which in fact is the Zenatean Alliance, which regroups about 140 different species. The high council of this alliance is composed of uniquely spiritually highly advanced races. It is a non-political body. They are interacting a lot at the moment for Terra, alongside the Galactic Federation of Worlds but also by sending envoys (starseeds) to help in this switching point in the evolution of the Terran species.[191]

Interestingly, this matches what Meier had to share about ancient migrations of human colonies from the Lyra constellation to other star systems. Most important is Danaan's corroboration for what Alex Collier had revealed about a galactic tyranny in the future and how this related to the Earth.[192] According to Danaan, the Andromeda Council notified the Galactic Federation of Worlds about the future galactic threat, which was instrumental in the Federation deciding to upgrade its monitoring of our solar system, and to militarily intervene to remove the threat in what was essentially a temporal war. The Galactic Federation's military intervention has had an enormous impact on the physical presence of negative extraterrestrial races in our solar system (i.e., Draconian Empire and Orion Collective) and made it possible for humanity to finally cleanse itself of the infestation of dark energies that have plagued humankind for millennia.

My examination of the Andromeda Council brings Part 1 to an end. I will now examine how these different extraterrestrial organizations collaborate with Earth's governing elite and secret space programs to manage the momentous changes underway as humanity steps into its Star Trek future. The place to begin investigating this transition is our solar system's largest planet, Jupiter, which is a historical hub for extraterrestrials arriving in our solar system, and where meetings have recently taken place to decide humanity's destiny.

CHAPTER 7

Jupiter Agreements – The Solar System's Yalta

When we met at Yalta, in addition to laying out strategic and tactical plans for the complete and final military victory over Germany, there were other problems of vital political consequence…. Never before have the major allies been more closely united- not only in their war aims but also in their peace aims. And they are determined to continue to be united, to be united with each other – and with all peace-loving nations – so that the ideal of lasting peace will become a reality.

—President Franklin D. Roosevelt, Speech to US Congress, March 1, 1945

Three months before the collapse of Nazi Germany during World War II, the three major Allied powers—the US, the Soviet Union, and Great Britain—met at Yalta on the Crimean Peninsula. They discussed the post-war order of Europe that would emerge with the impending defeat of the Nazis. What is noteworthy about the Yalta agreement was that Nazi Germany had still not surrendered during the meetings and was fighting desperately to stem the tide of the advancing Allied armies upon Berlin. Therefore, it was very significant that a similar set of meetings were claimed to have taken place in a floating city/base controlled by the Ashtar Command in the upper atmosphere of

Jupiter to discuss the new order in our solar system that would emerge with the military collapse of the Dark Fleet and its Draconian, Orion, Deep State, and corporate allies. Elena Danaan was the first to publicly claim such meetings took place, according to information she received from her primary extraterrestrial contact, Thor Han Eredyon. What makes her claim well worth considering is compelling circumstantial evidence that the Jupiter meetings really did happen and important agreements were reached.

Danaan revealed that the Galactic Federation of Worlds had a series of meetings in early to mid-July 2021, with the representatives of an "Earth Alliance" comprising the leaders of national space programs to discuss the new order in our solar system. She contacted me on July 17, 2021, with the dramatic news of the meetings that had been completed in Jupiter's atmosphere at the Ashtar facility and of the different nations that were involved through their respective space programs. Danaan said the final meeting had concluded only a day earlier with an agreement being reached that would establish a multinational space alliance between the Earth's spacefaring nations under US leadership. US Space Command would take the lead in organizing Earth's planetary defenses.

This is what Danaan wrote in the first of two emails sent to me on July 17:

> Agreements have been passed on Jupiter yesterday between the different progressive galactic coalitions and Terran military forces, to share the use and the protection of this star system, regarding to economic and military domains, in preparation for the future. Territories of action have been set. Terran Humans are officially taking ownership of their system. The US was the lead representative in these series of meetings; they were chosen by the GFW because of their abilities, resources, and goals,

best able to guarantee a sustainable and glorious future for off-world humankind.

Long years of secret collaboration with the nations of Terra have come to completion, but we still need to bring closure to this war for the liberation of this system. Until then, we will need to work hard, and when this day comes, we will all be ready to step into a new era of fraternity and cooperation together.

To further clarify what had just happened, Danaan sent me a second email on the same day, with additional information about what she was told about the meetings from Thor Han Eredyon:

Thor Han wasn't part of these meetings; he was just part of the escort for the representatives of the GFW [Galactic Federation of Worlds], and he stayed in orbit of Jupiter. But he knows this:

There was a series of meetings, and this had been going on for a while. There were twelve meetings in total, first occurring among specific groups, separately, and then these last days, three big meetings: the first gathering everyone, the second a selected group, and the third the final agreements with the leading selected group. Each group was made of space force military officials and (progressive) corporations' CEOs.

So, a delegation of the GFW has been auditing separately different Earth representatives, military officials responsible for space forces, as well as heads of certain progressive corporations to determine safety zones and who would serve best the interests of the many.

It is very significant that Danaan used the term "safety zones" to describe the areas of multinational space cooperation and what served the interests of most nations. This term matches the language used in the Artemis Accords (which I will shortly discuss) something she was not familiar with prior to our communications.[193]

In an August 6, 2021, interview where we discussed the Jupiter meetings, Danaan sent me a diagram to illustrate the sequence of meetings that took place above Jupiter.[194] The diagram succinctly describes what happened, along with her comments for each stage of the meetings. Based on the sequence of meetings, it appears that the chief purpose was a selection process to determine which of Earth's spacefaring nations would be primarily responsible for coordinating all human space operations and liaising with the Galactic Federation of Worlds.

Here is how Danaan summarized the meetings based on Thor Han's initial messages and what she has subsequently learned:

> There was a series of meetings and this had been going on for a while. Each Terran group attending these meetings combined space force military officials and progressive corporation CEOs. There were twelve meetings at first, occurring as twelve separate groups. Each group was composed of officials from galactic institutions, auditing a specific Earth nation's representatives in the space military and corporate domains.

Put simply, the Galactic Federation was reviewing Earth's spacefaring nations in terms of their respective capabilities, histories, and leadership potential. Danaan went on to explain what happened after the initial set of 12 meetings.

> Then, three big meetings occurred: the first of the three meetings was a gathering of six selected

nations' programs. The second meeting gathered a selected group of four from this previous group of six to decide who would be best able to lead the group of six. The third and final agreement was between the galactic representatives and the winning nation selected from the previous group of four.

Figure 13. Elena Danaan Illustration of Jupiter Meetings in sequence

Danaan says that Thor Han was forbidden from identifying the different nations participating in the meetings. It can be speculated that the six nations that participated in the first of the three final meetings were those with the oldest and largest functioning national space programs. These are in order of their first satellite launches: Russia (1957), the United States (1958), France (1962), Britain (1962), China (1970), and Japan (1970).

It should be noted that the first five nations from this group of six are all permanent members of the United Nations Security Council. Each has a long history of being deeply involved in Security Council decisions concerning international affairs. It is, therefore, no great surprise that this same group of nations would perform a similar function for regulating human activities in our solar system.

It can be further speculated that the four countries that participated in the penultimate meeting out of which the Galactic Federation would choose the nation that would be given the responsibility of coordinating all Earth's nations in space affairs were the US, Russia, China, and France. From this group, the Galactic Federation chose the US as the nation with the most support from the total group of 14 nations and the CEOs of the space companies in attendance. In his initial message, Thor Han said, "there are actually fourteen countries involved in space programs, who were represented there." This meant the 12 meetings involved representatives from 14 countries with space programs with officials from the Galactic Federation, Andromeda Council, Ashtar Command, and other extraterrestrial organizations. To understand who these fourteen nations were and how they participated in the sequence of meetings that resulted in the US being selected as the lead nation, we need to review the Artemis Accords.

Artemis Accords and the Jupiter Meetings/Agreements

What corroborates claims about secret meetings held above Jupiter is the signing of the Artemis Accords, less than a year earlier, by countries with functioning space programs that desire to expand commercial, civil, and military cooperation into space. The Artemis Accords are bilateral accords negotiated between the US and seven spacefaring nations, signed on October 13, 2020: Australia, Canada, Italy, Japan, Luxembourg, United Arab Emirates, and the United Kingdom.[195] The Accord's primary goal was to establish a multinational space coalition that would support NASA's Artemis missions to the Moon, and would also support joint missions and asteroids, and eventually human missions to Mars.

The Artemis Accords provide the legal underpinning for human expansion and resource extraction throughout the solar system.[196] Since the launch of the Artemis Accords, Brazil, South Korea, New Zealand, Ukraine, Poland, Mexico, and Israel, have all subsequently joined. On November 10, 2021, President Emmanuel Macron affirmed the intent of France to also join the Artemis Accords.[197] Other major spacefaring nations, such as Germany and India, are expected to join the Artemis Accords.[198]

The Artemis Accords have established the founding principles of a multinational space alliance under US leadership. The Accords make possible the pursuit of joint economic and scientific activities in space along with a multinational military alliance that will protect these activities through "safety zones."[199] These are areas designed to prevent "harmful interference" in the space operations of signatory nations, as the Artemis Accords explains:

> [Section 11] 6. The Signatories intend to use their experience under the Accords to contribute to multilateral efforts to further develop international practices, criteria, and rules applicable to the

143

definition and determination of safety zones and harmful interference.[200]

Importantly, the Artemis Accords is here recommending a multilateral process where signatories develop rules and practices for creating safety zones, which would be enforced by a mix of diplomatic, economic, and military means. As mentioned earlier, the idea of 'safety zones' was an important topic of discussion for the Jupiter meetings. Furthermore, the continued expansion of the Artemis Accords since their October 2020 launch is circumstantial evidence supporting claims that the Galactic Federation and other progressive extraterrestrial alliances such as the Andromeda Council and Ashtar Command have recently reached agreements with Earth's major spacefaring nations above Jupiter.

It is also important to point out the surge of nations forming space commands after the passage of the Artemis Accords. These newly created Space Commands involve the military forces of the different signatory nations that are increasingly working together in space related issues. Britain (2021),[201] Germany (2021),[202] Italy (2021),[203] and Australia (2022)[204] have all recently created space commands. They all follow the US (1985/2019),[205] France (2010),[206] Russia (2011),[207] and China (2015),[208] which previously set up space commands for integrating their respective military activities in space. Most significantly, in October 2020, NATO set up a Space Center that will run all its space operations out of Ramstein Air Base in Germany.[209] All these recent military developments concerning outer space corroborate claims that agreements have been recently reached with Earth's major spacefaring nations.

As to the question of why choose only one nation as the chief spokesperson or liaison for Earth in discussions with the Galactic Federation of Worlds, Danaan's second email on July 17, 2021, gave the following answer:

> The GFW only wants to work with a unified global civilization, not with a clutter of different rival space forces playing power games. Thor Han said that

there are actually fourteen countries involved in space programs, who were represented there, but a top six have programs recognized by the GFW as most progressive and durable, and fit to join forces with them. The eight others were just in for commercial reasons benefiting the many.

Thor Han was also speaking about a "horizontal" coalition of these top six, coming up as a unified space department. Would we be witnessing, as you said it Michael, the birth of Starfleet?

It is understandable why the Galactic Federation of Worlds would be insisting on a "unified global civilization" that partners with it in space affairs, rather than the current situation of competing spacefaring nations with conflicting agendas. The formation of an alliance of spacefaring nations working within a unified command structure makes much more sense. Based on the current membership of the Artemis Accords, it can be speculated that four of the six countries identified as the "most progressive and durable" would be the US, France, Britain, and Japan. The US, France, and Britain had, on February 13, 2020, reached agreements on integrating their space assets and operations through the "Combined Space Operations Initiative."[210] A month later, Japan agreed to cooperate on military space operations and placed a full-time liaison officer at US Space Command Headquarters.[211] The other two nations would be China and Russia, upon which I will elaborate shortly.

In my book, *Space Force: Our Star Trek Future* (2021), I explain how the multinational space alliance being currently created under US leadership is the antecedent of a future Starfleet, not unlike that envisaged by Gene Rodenberry. In fact, I present evidence that Rodenberry's Starfleet was modeled on a future multinational space coalition that he was clandestinely briefed about in the 1960s! As I will show, the secret agreements reached on Jupiter have resulted in significant extraterrestrial assistance for the creation of a future Starfleet. The other eight nations participating in the Jupiter meetings would be primarily drawn from Artemis Accord members.

At the time of the Jupiter Agreements, there were twelve countries that had signed the Artemis Accords: Australia; Brazil; Canada; Italy; Japan; Luxembourg; New Zealand; United Arab Emirates; South Korea; Ukraine; United Kingdom; and the United States. There were also six countries with national space programs which had not signed the Artemis Accords: China; France; Germany; India; Israel; and Russia. Israel joined the Artemis Accords on January 27, 2022.[212] As mentioned earlier, President Emmanuel Macron publicly affirmed France would join, and Germany and India are expected to eventually follow. Only China and Russia are not expected to sign on to the Accords anytime soon.

If only 14 out of these 18 nations participated in the Jupiter meetings, then it can be speculated that some of the smaller nations in terms of either population or space resources, e.g., Luxembourg, New Zealand, United Arab Emirates, or Ukraine, delegated to strategic allies to represent their space interests. Consequently, the 14 countries which almost certainly attended the Jupiter meetings are the following (Artemis Accords signatories identified by the alphanumeric 'A'): Australia (A); Brazil (A), Canada (A), China; France; Germany; India; Israel (A); Italy (A); Japan (A); Russia; South Korea (A), United Kingdom (A), and the United States (A).

This leads to the critical question of what kind of leadership role China and Russia play in this emerging multinational space alliance that collaborates directly with the Galactic Federation and other extraterrestrial organizations? Danaan's July 17, 2021, message from Thor Han provides us an answer:

> Thor Han showed me also the only visual memory he had of these events: viewed from his ship, three ovoid crafts leaving the orbit of Jupiter after the second of this series of three ultimate meetings. Each craft had Earth military delegates onboard, by

country. He didn't tell me what the third was, but two of them were carrying Chinese and Russian officials, and he was told that both these crowds were very unhappy. He said that the USA won the responsibility to organize the new Earth's united space coalition.

Danaan drew a graphic of what Thor Han saw departing after the penultimate meeting. Three spacecraft were seen carrying the unsuccessful delegates of the nations not chosen to be the liaison or spokesperson for Earth in future coordination with the Galactic Federation. Danaan says that two of the craft carried the Russian and Chinese delegations that were unhappy with the outcome. According to Danaan and my speculation, the third craft carried the French delegation. The cigar-shaped craft presumably belonged to the US Navy's Solar Warden space program.

Figure 14. Elena Danaan drawing of three craft with delegations from penultimate Jupiter meeting

What corroborates Danaan's information here is that no other spacefaring nation has joined China and Russia in their proposed International Lunar Research Station initiative launched with their bilateral agreement of June 2021.[213] Only the US has succeeded in creating a multinational space coalition through the Artemis Accords, which Russia declined to join since it was "too US-centric,"[214] and China was excluded from joining due to its continued theft of intellectual property and industrial espionage.[215] Consequently, it does not come as a great surprise that Chinese and Russian delegations "were very unhappy" with the agreements reached above Jupiter that gave the critical liaison role to the USA. Now that we have a fair idea of which nations participated in the Jupiter meetings and their respective positions, it is worth exploring what corporations attended.

Progressive CEOs and the Jupiter Agreements

In his original July 17, 2021, message to Elena Danaan about who attended the Jupiter meetings, Thor Han referred to "progressive corporation CEOs." Thor Han was very likely referring to representatives from companies such as SpaceX, Blue Origin, Virgin Galactic, and Bigelow Aerospace, as opposed to CEOs from older larger aerospace corporations such as Boeing, Airbus, Lockheed Martin, Northrup Grumman, etc., which worked with the now-discredited Interplanetary Corporate Conglomerate, a major ally of the German Dark Fleet. Prominent CEOs such as Elon Musk, Jeff Bezos, and Richard Branson, therefore almost certainly attended the Jupiter meetings. Flights into space by both Bezos and Branson support this contention. Branson flew to the edge of space (defined by US authorities as 50 miles altitude) on July 11, 2021, in a Virgin Galactic craft.[216] He was followed by Bezos, who flew into space on July 20 in a crewed Blue Origin flight.[217] These two very public space flight events, it turns out, were covers for Branson and Bezos to attend the Jupiter meetings.

At this point, it is important to emphasize that in the shadowy world of Special Access Programs involving the military-industrial complex engaged in "above Top Secret" programs, cover stories are routinely developed. This practice enables secrecy to be maintained by plausible cover stories used by participants in military, intelligence, and corporate programs when describing their activities. What this means in practice is that a program involving classified or proprietary technologies (e.g., a commercial spaceflight) is routinely used to hide a more highly classified program from public scrutiny (e.g., a classified spaceflight to Jupiter). On Oct 10, 2014, Peter Maass and Laura Poitras writing for *The Intercept,* released powerpoint slides from leaked NSA documents concerning highly classified programs that are hidden from public scrutiny.[218] The documents, originally leaked by Edward Snowden, reveal that "Sentry Eagle" is used as an umbrella term for hiding the NSA's most sensitive programs that are classified "Exceptionally Controlled Information" (ECI). Several powerpoint slides show how ECI programs are hidden beneath less classified programs as a cover. The leaked documents prove that cover stories and programs are routinely used to hide the most classified military intelligence and corporate secrets from public scrutiny.

Musk also likely attended the Jupiter meetings using another mode of transportation and cover story. The cover story appeared on July 23, 2021, when SpaceX announced it had been awarded a contract to launch NASA's "Europa Clipper" mission to Jupiter's moon Europa in October 2024.[219] That means that when Branson and Bezos were involved with their trips to the edge of space, Musk was working with NASA officials on an announcement concerning a future mission to Jupiter—a plausible cover story for Musk secretly flying to Jupiter to attend the meetings. In NASA's announcement of the Europa Clipper mission, what is noteworthy here is its recent behavior of increasingly awarding contracts for space exploration to SpaceX or Blue Origin rather than older established aerospace corporations. NASA's award of contracts to these newer companies is critical circumstantial evidence that there has been a major change in how space is being managed by national governments and the aerospace corporations they are supporting.

In a 'physical contact' with Thor Han that occurred in mid-August 2021, Danaan provided fresh new details about the Jupiter Meetings, which confirmed my speculations about the CEOs in attendance. This is Elena Danaan's (E) recollection of what she was told by Thor Han (T):

E: About the CEOs, was Michael right?

T: Yes.

E: All of them?

T: And many more.

While Branson and Bezos very publicly televised their relatively few minutes floating inside capsules sent to Earth's upper atmosphere, Thor Hans' response suggests they kept secret that they were about to or had already spent many hours in the upper atmosphere of Jupiter negotiating the future of our solar system.

It is worth pointing out that this is not the first time that Jeff Bezos has been involved in top-level negotiations involving secret space programs. In early February 2018, the German-led Dark Fleet operating out of Antarctica conducted high-level meetings with the Trump administration, as first revealed by former Forbes Magazine author Benjamin Fulford.[220] What corroborated Fulford's claim was that Trump's Secretary of State, Rex Tillerson, did travel to Bariloche, Argentina where secret negotiations were allegedly held with the Dark Fleet to reveal its existence and release some of its advanced technologies. What added even more credence to Fulford's claims was that Bezos was also in Bariloche at the same time, where he almost certainly joined Tillerson in these secret negotiations, which I covered in a February 11, 2018, article.[221]

This takes me to the question of why corporate CEOs with questionable backgrounds were involved in the Jupiter meetings. Thor Han's response suggests a dire contingency is on the horizon that makes urgent the need for the Galactic Federation to work with them for planetary defense. This is the relevant portion of the dialogue between Elena Danaan [E] and Thor Han [T]:

> [E] Why them? People on Earth are going mad about it.

> [T] Because these are the ones who are ready now. There's no other choice. We don't have time, we can't afford to wait that new corporations form and equip themselves with brand new fleets, we take the ones who are available here and now. I know they are not pure-hearted but they are the only ones able to lead the Terran species into the future. As corporations, their agendas are financial. They go with the winners. Their old allies are losing, so these corporations have turned their back to them.

Thor Han's response that "we don't have time" is very troubling. It corroborates that the Galactic Federation sees some impending planetary emergency that makes the development of large space fleets imperative.

Danaan continued her dialogue with Thor Han about Musk, Bezos, and Branson as follows:

> [E] But do you trust them?

> [T] No, we don't. Remember, I told you that we were watching them proving their good intent. Now, you must not tell this publicly until I say it is the right time because civilians on Terra do not possess all the elements yet to grasp the whole perspective. There are many other reasons why we do not disclose

everything for the moment, as it does not involve only ourselves.

Thor Han is correct that most on Earth do not possess the necessary "big picture" perspective. Many will undoubtedly focus on the shortcomings of Musk, Bezos, and Branson at the Jupiter meetings as "progressive corporate CEOs" without understanding that they have built the necessary infrastructure to quickly expand their operations to construct large fleets of spacecraft for either military or civilian purposes.

When I first heard the information from Danaan, my initial thought was that the most likely candidate for such a dire planetary emergency was a micronova or 'solar flash' event happening in the near future—a possible event which I have discussed in a number of articles.[222] Ben Davidson, the founder of Space Weather News, has for several years now been urgently warning about the growing evidence that a micronova event will happen by the 2030 time period.[223] Similarly, a secret space program insider, Corey Goode, has since 2015 been warning that a "solar flash" event is predicted to happen in the near future.[224] Historical evidence shows that micronova events have happened before and wiped-out advanced civilizations on Earth and within our solar system. I surmised that large space fleets would be very helpful for a significant percentage of humanity evading any future planetary catastrophe caused by a micronova or geophysical pole shift. After all, Musk's SpaceX, Bezos' Blue Origin, and Branson's Virgin Galactic have spent a decade or so developing rocket-propelled spacecraft to get to their current positions. Now they can safely begin building fleets of spacecraft for moving a significant number of humans into space and out of harm's way.

It later became clear, however, that Thor Han was instead referring to the return of the negative extraterrestrial alliance that was being forced to leave our solar system, as I discuss at length in the next chapter. The view of the Galactic Federation was that this opposing alliance would return with reinforcements, thereby mirroring the fictional scenario depicted in the sequel to the famous *Independence Day* movie – *Resurrection*. According to the Galactic Federation, there is little likelihood that the Earth will be devastated by a cataclysmic solar flash event, as warned by Davidson and Goode. Thor Han's reference to there being "no other choice" and that there is insufficient time for "new corporations [to] form and equip themselves" suggests that the dire contingency is not that far in the future.

Danaan shared more of Thor Han's response about the corporate CEOs, which gives us some clues into what lies ahead:

> The Galactic Federation offered to these corporations a deal: that if they comply to the progressive rules of the new agreements, we will support and protect their commercial interests. Because it is in our spirit to entice unity and progress, not division. We believe that everyone in this universe deserves a second chance; this is a process part of the evolution; learning from our mistakes. And also, by including your opponents in your circle, they cease to be an enemy and they become an ally. This is how you make peace, and also why our Federation works hard at welcoming cultures that were once regressive. Unity is progress.[225]

Thor Han is here acknowledging that Musk, Bezos, Branson, and other CEOs at the Jupiter meetings had previously collaborated with the Deep State in various ways. However, with the impending defeat of the Deep State and their space allies—the Dark Fleet, Draco Empire, and Orion Alliance—Musk, Bezos, and Branson have realigned themselves. Thus they have been given a second chance though they are being closely watched by their new partners, the Galactic Federation, in terms of complying with the "progressive rules of the new agreements."

Galactic Organizations at the Jupiter Meetings

While the Ashtar Command hosted the Jupiter Meetings at its Jupiter facility, it does not appear that it played a prominent role at the meetings. Elena Danaan shared more details about the galactic organizations that met with the 14 Earth delegations in choosing the leadership team that the Galactic Federation would coordinate with in the future:

> So the delegations of the Galactic Federation of Worlds, Council of Five and Andromedan Council, audited separately different Earth officials responsible for space forces and progressive corporations, to determine safety zones and who would serve best the interests of the many. The Galactic Federation of Worlds only wants to work with a unified global civilization, not with a compound of different rival space forces playing power games.

> Thor Han said that there are actually fourteen countries involved in space programs, but a top six have programs that were recognized by the Galactic Federation of Worlds as most progressive and durable, and fit to join forces with them. The eight remaining others were in for commercial accords benefiting the many. Thor Han was also speaking about a "horizontal" coalition of these top six, coming up as a unified space department under the leadership of the US.[226]

What makes the scenario described by Danaan/Thor Han credible is that it is consistent with what is known about the Artemis Accords, which continue to grow in popularity among spacefaring nations. In contrast, Russia and China's rival international space coalition for a joint International Lunar Research Station initiative has gathered no support. Therefore, it is very understandable why the Galactic Federation and affiliated galactic organizations—Andromeda Council and Council of Five— would choose the US as the go-to nation for future collaboration between the Federation and the rest of humanity.[227]

US Groomed for Decades to Lead the Earth Alliance

In her communication with Thor Han [T] over the Jupiter Meetings in mid-August 2021, Danaan [E] received vital information about the role of the Galactic Federation in grooming the US to play the leadership role among the Earth's spacefaring nations:

> [E] This explains why, as I thought, in the recent agreements on Jupiter, countries such as Russia and China were voted to be under the management of the United States of America. But why the USA?
>
> [T] Because they are the best able to fit the task, and because we know what the future is made of. We have been secretly grooming the USA into secret programs since the 1950s, because we knew...
>
> [E] I closed my eyes as Thor Han sent me a telepathic image. It was three similar logos. From left to right, as an unfolding timeline: Star Trek's Starfleet, Artemis Accords, and Space Force. All three blended into one. Just after that, I saw eight ships of Solar Warden passing by the GFW station (where I was). What a good omen![228]

Danaan's response highlights the Artemis Accords' importance and US leadership for the immediate years ahead as humanity's presence in space expands greatly beyond its present levels. The Artemis Accords create a framework for the civilian, corporate and military sectors to work side-by-side in meeting the challenges of quickly expanding humanity's presence far into our solar system.

In addition, Danaan's information confirms the testimony of William Tompkins, who told of human-looking extraterrestrials (the Galactic Federation) helping the US Navy develop a secret space program (Solar Warden) since the 1950s.[229] I analyzed Tompkins' testimony at length in the *US Navy's Secret Space Program and Nordic Extraterrestrial Alliance* (2017). Tompkins further stated that the Navy's Solar Warden program has been building new fleets of space carriers that are scheduled to come online sometime in the early 2030s. All of this suggests that in the immediate years ahead, the Navy will begin revealing its Solar Warden assets through the newly re-constituted US Space Command, which is fast becoming the hub for a future multinational space alliance. This is evidenced in the expanding "Combined Space Operations Initiative" whereby the space commands of Australia, Canada, France, Germany, New Zealand, United Kingdom, and to a lesser extent Japan, are closely coordinating with the US Space Command and Space Force.[230] I discuss this exciting emergence of a future multinational military space alliance—a modern-day Starfleet—in my 2021 book *Space Force: Our Star Trek Future*.

The US Navy will certainly play a key role in preparing humanity for the challenges that lie ahead. Over the last few years, the Department of the Navy has been releasing some of the advanced space propulsion technologies used in Solar Warden through scientists such as Dr. Salvatore Pais.[231] Five US patents have been submitted by Dr. Pais, all on behalf of the Secretary of the Navy, which contain the necessary components for the civilian sector to build fleets of advanced antigravity space vehicles and powerful electromagnetic shielding technologies that can be used to protect humanity either in deep space or on Earth from electromagnetic storms and Coronal Mass Ejections.[232] Furthermore, all of these patents and more will be vital for building future fleets of spacecraft that can be used either for planetary defense purposes; or to ride out the devastating effects of a solar micronova or other catastrophic planetary events.

In what appears to be the most powerful corroboration to date that the Jupiter meetings and agreements did actually happen, the US Space Command's leader, General James Dickinson, made some very revealing comments at the US Space Foundation's 36th Space Symposium. During the conference week, beginning August 23, 2021, he said that over 100 agreements had been reached with different countries, agencies, and corporations for space-related activities. A reporter paraphrased General Dickinson's comments as follows:

> Spacecom has more than 100 data sharing agreements with allies, inter-governmental teammates and commercial partners, he said. These agreements exchange information, enhance space domain awareness, increase the safety of spaceflight operations, and lay the foundation for future collaboration in space operations.[233]

What is noteworthy about his remarks is that only a month earlier, it is alleged that General Dickinson had attended the series of meetings high in Jupiter's atmosphere where comprehensive agreements were reached between the Galactic Federation of Worlds and 14 spacefaring nations, including CEOs from major aerospace companies. It is highly likely that the Jupiter agreements are among the more than 100 agreements Space Command had signed with various entities.

In conclusion, there is significant circumstantial evidence that the Jupiter meetings did in fact occur in mid-July involving 14 nations and CEOs of relatively new aerospace companies, as claimed by Elena Danaan. First, the number of countries in attendance (14) is close to the number of known spacefaring nations (18). Second, the flights to the edge of space by Richard Branson and Jeff Bezos were very likely cover stories for them physically attending the Jupiter meetings. Third, Musk's announcement of SpaceX's selection to launch the 2024 Europa Clipper Mission shows that Jupiter was very much on his mind during the meetings. Fourth, the growing acceptance of the Artemis Accords by leading spacefaring nations (with the exceptions of China and Russia) makes it very plausible that the Galactic Federation chose the USA as the liaison for future communications and coordination in deep space. Finally, General James Dickinson's remarks that over 100 agreements had been reached between different entities and US Space Command, points to the Jupiter agreements being among the agreements.

What is clear from the Jupiter meetings is that elaborate preparation is underway for our solar system entering an era when the power of the Dark Fleet and their Ciakharr Empire and Orion Collective allies (aka the Dark Alliance) would be significantly reduced, if not eliminated altogether. Based on the information presented in this chapter, it appears that a Yalta-like set of meetings and agreements had indeed occurred in anticipation of the impending defeat of the Dark Fleet and its allies. This takes me to further supporting intel about the alleged Liberation of the Moon, Mars, and the rest of the Solar System from the Dark Alliance.

CHAPTER 8

Did Mars & Phobos Just Go Through
a Planetary Liberation War?

Mars was once Earth-like in climate, with an ocean and rivers, and for a long period became home to both plant and animal life, including a humanoid civilization. Then, for unfathomable reasons, a massive thermo-nuclear explosion ravaged the centers of the Martian civilization and destroyed the biosphere of the planet.

—Dr. John Brandenburg, American Institute of Aeronautics &Astronautics Conference, Sept 2016

Introduction to Recent Mars History

The history of Mars is shrouded in mystery. Richard Hoagland's groundbreaking 1992 book, *The Monuments of Mars*, opened the door to understanding some of its ancient past through scientific analysis of artificial structures found on orbital images from NASA's 1976 Viking mission.[234] The pyramids and other artificial structures found in the Viking images led to the CIA secretly commissioning remote viewers to learn about the ancient history of Mars, as confirmed through documents released under the Freedom of Information Act.[235] Decades later, Dr. John Brandenburg analyzed orbital data from subsequent missions in his 2015 book, *Death on Mars,* and found compelling evidence of radioactive isotopes in Mars' upper atmosphere that pointed to an ancient nuclear war.[236] But did this nuclear war occur in remote antiquity as Brandenburg had concluded, or did he stumble upon evidence of a much more recent atomic war on Mars? For an answer, I need to summarize the information I first presented in my 2018 book, *Antarctica's Hidden History*.[237]

The human colonization of Mars began in the 1950s when the Draconian and Orion Alliance helped the breakaway German colony, which had established bases in Antarctica, to also build bases on the Moon and Mars. Advanced Haunebu-class flying saucer craft and cigar-shaped Andromeda class ships made up the German's Dark Fleet (aka Nacht Waffen) that were utilized to create off-planet colonies. It needs to be emphasized that all of the German colonies continued the policy of slave labor that had been established in Nazi Germany during the war. Slave labor was a vital part of the Third Reich's post-war plans for Europe, as confirmed by Hitler's armaments minister, Albert Speer, in his 1991 book, *Infiltration*. Despite the defeat of Hitler's Third Reich, the secretive "Fourth Reich" birthed in Antarctica and South America continued the policy of slave labor, as Speer had warned in his book.

As a result of agreements reached between the Eisenhower administration and the German Antarctica Colony (aka the Fourth Reich), the Dark Fleet's bases on the Moon and Mars were significantly expanded.[238] Regarding Dr. Brandenburg's discovery of scientific evidence of a nuclear war found in Mars' upper atmosphere, secret space program insider Corey Goode claimed the US military provided the Dark Fleet with nuclear weapons that were then used against the indigenous Martian population.[239] This comprised local Reptilians, Insectoids, and other less evolved species that resisted the Dark Fleet's colonial expansion. Goode revealed that the Dark Fleet had used nuclear weapons on Mars for both excavation purposes and as a weapon against native Martians encountered under the planet's surface.

Goode described two species of intelligent native Martians, Reptilians, and Insectoids that the Germans encountered. He said that hundreds of thousands of Martians were killed in replays of Nagasaki and Hiroshima in the various nests discovered by the Germans. The nuclear weapons used were of an advanced generation that did not leave much radioactive residue, according to Goode. This may answer the question raised by Dr. Brandenburg's discovery of radioactive isotypes in Mars' upper atmosphere. The radioactive residue was not necessarily created in an ancient Martian nuclear holocaust but could well have been a legacy of more recent nuclear weapon strikes used by the German Dark Fleet against the indigenous Martians.

The infamous brain-drain of the 1960s and 1970s, launched under cover of the US Apollo Program, led to the exponential growth of the Dark Fleet's presence on Mars.[240] Millions of people—many of whom were highly skilled and taken from Earth under false pretenses—expanded the German colonies and created new ones in conjunction with major Earth corporations. These new corporate-run colonies have been called the "Interplanetary Corporate Conglomerate." It is run by a 'superboard' comprising retired or serving CEOs from major corporations, according to Goode.[241] With the help of the Draconian and Orion Alliance, the Mars colonies became so technologically advanced that they eventually were trading with a multitude of extraterrestrial civilizations. The Mars colonies were equipping mercenary forces recruited from all major countries on Earth to join the Dark Fleet for distinct periods of service on Mars, elsewhere in our solar system, and in interstellar locations. The infusion of personnel, equipment, and resources from all over Earth enabled the Dark Fleet to expand its operations significantly throughout the latter half of the 20th century and well into the 21st century.

The Dark Fleet now possessed powerful fleets of spacecraft with well-armed and genetically enhanced troops that could fight alongside Reptilian and Orion extraterrestrials in interstellar wars of conquest. This meant that the bulk of the Dark Fleet's operational forces, at any one time, would be located outside of our solar system. This brief background provides important context to understand better the complex exopolitical situation on Mars, which had dramatically affected the red planet's indigenous species with the infusion of human bases and their aggressive colonial expansion. As to what was happening inside these human bases and their interactions with the indigenous Martians, three secret space program insiders provide us with a clear overview— Randy Cramer, Corey Goode, and Tony Rodrigues.

Randy Cramer and Corey Goode on Mars

In April 2014, I interviewed Randy Cramer (aka "Captain Kaye"), who claims to have served in a "20 and back" secret space program, the first 17 years of which were spent on Mars as a space marine.[242] In 2019, Cramer was interviewed on Gaia TV, where he successfully passed a polygraph lie detection test concerning his groundbreaking testimony.[243] Cramer was the first person to come forward to claim he had served in a "20 and back" program since Michael Relf emerged back in 2000. Relf's experiences were published in a two volume book series by Stephanie Relf, titled *The Mars Records*.[244] Cramer said his main purpose as part of a contingent of space marines was to protect the five civilian bases within the "Mars Colony Corporation" from indigenous Martians and a non-indigenous extraterrestrial race. Cramer describes how he first traveled to a secret Moonbase (the Lunar Operations Command) to sign papers committing him to a 20-year tour of duty. He was then transported to a well-equipped military base on Mars, where his marine unit engaged in territorial battles with the native Reptilian and Insectoid Martians.

Another extraterrestrial species on Mars was described as non-indigenous Alpha Draconians. Cramer asserted these were master manipulators. He explained how his unit commanders came to understand the complex exopolitical situation on Mars, which involved both indigenous and non-indigenous Reptilian races facing off against each other, an Insectoid species, and human colonists—all involved in a series of armed conflicts over territory and resources:

For a number of years, we just assumed that a Reptile was a Reptile was a Reptile, and they were all part of the same group, even if they were different in size, shape, or color. They just must be different kinds of ranks, or distinctions, or individual races, that they are working with. We presumed for a long time that all the Reptiles were the same, and they weren't. There was an invasive Reptoid species, they were Draconians, Alpha Draconians. For a long time, we thought the two Reptiles were the same. The Draconians were really trying to play off, getting everyone else to fight with each other. So, the more hostility, the more crazy action they could encourage us to take against each other, the native Saurian, the native Insects, and us, was good for them. It took quite a bit of time to realize through good intelligence that was not the case, and we needed to sort of rethink what was happening. Our goal definitely was to defend everything and anything that threatened, but I just want to make the distinction that what we thought that was, wasn't exactly what that was. It was partly because of bad intelligence and partly because of species ignorance, like they all have the same thing … [without realizing] they were two completely different species.

We didn't know that the native Reptiles and the invasive Reptiles were fighting, and the Insects and the invasive Reptiles were fighting, and trying to get us to fight with each other, to keep us from fighting them. We didn't realize that if we were under attack from the air, it wasn't the same Reptiles that were trying to attack us from underground, across the sand. So, it was pretty confusing for while, as far as who was doing what and what was fighting. Day-to-

163

day operations was that if anything comes close, suit up, go out, fight with it. If anything comes to raid or invade, go through the protocols of defending the space until it's over, then do the same thing the next day if you have to.[245]

Important corroboration for Cramer's testimony comes from Tony Rodrigues who also claims that he served in a "20 and back" secret space program. Rodrigues first contacted me in August 2015 about his experiences in a secret space program run by a German breakaway civilization. In subsequent telephone conversations and vetting, I found Rodrigues to be a sincere and credible witness about his involvement in such a program. We physically met for the first time one year later in Mt Shasta, California, where we did a five-part interview series that publicly presented his story for the first time in video form.[246] I have subsequently watched Rodrigues share his story on many public forums and have been impressed by the consistency of his memories. What impressed me most about Rodrigues was his investigation to confirm multiple facts about the time spent in Seattle, Washington, China Lake, California, and Peru before serving in space. His 2022 book, *Ceres Colony Cavalier,* is no exception; everything in it is consistent with what he has shared with me and subsequent interviewers about his experiences and corroborating information.

Rodrigues was the first person to emerge with a plausible account of his time with the Dark Fleet, and how slaves were systematically being used and mistreated. Since his public emergence, many others have come forward with remarkable stories of their own involuntary servitude with the Dark Fleet.[247] However, Rodrigues was the first, which makes his testimony especially significant today as we attempt to understand the operations and capabilities of the Dark Fleet. He said that he served on Mars for several months as a slave fighter for a mercenary military force protecting corporate bases from indigenous

Martians, thereby corroborating what Randy Cramer said earlier in 2014.

Rodrigues described fighting as an auxiliary where his mission was to lure the native insectoid species into areas where regular Mars "space marines" would ambush the insectoids. Rodrigues described being badly wounded in one of these military operations that went awry before the auxiliary military support program was scrapped. Subsequently, he was sent to Aries Prime, the main civilian base on Mars, where he underwent rigorous testing and evaluation. He was then reassigned to another Dark Fleet colony on the planetoid Ceres, where he spent the next 13 years. Rodrigues said that Aries Prime appeared similar to a luxury resort hotel, but he was never allowed to mix with residents as he was a slave and had to complete his aptitude testing.

Similarly, Cramer said he didn't know too much about what was happening inside Aries Prime and the other human colonies. The space marines were never allowed to visit the civilian bases that belonged to the "Mars Colony Corporation." When Corey Goode came forward in late 2014 and early 2015, more details emerged about what was happening inside these civilian Mars facilities.

Goode described the organization in overall control of civilian production facilities on Mars and elsewhere in our solar system as the "Interplanetary Corporate Conglomerate" (ICC). He claims that on June 22, 2015, he participated in an inspection tour of one of the Mars facilities located in the southern hemisphere. In a detailed report of the incident, Goode explained how after arriving at the Mars base, his group was given instructions of what they would be able to discuss with the base's inhabitants who had been indoctrinated with false information about Earth:

> The ICC representative then told us what the subject of that conversation was going to be. He was carefully watching our reactions as he gave us a summary of what to expect from the base commander. He stated that the people at this

facility were here for generations and that they were under the impression for decades now that the earth had been through some sort of cataclysm and was no longer inhabitable. He said that we are being asked to not throw off the social dynamics of the facility by revealing that this was not the case or that any of us were from the surface of Earth.[248]

Goode's group then met the base commander who gave them a cover story that the facility's primary mission was a multi-decades-long social experiment rather than exploiting human slaves. Goode describes how his group was then taken to a large conference hall where he saw many colonists whose leaders made a presentation about the advanced technologies produced at the facility. The colonists said that exopolitical agreements had been reached with different extraterrestrial civilizations, as Goode explained:

We were brought into the "main hall" that looked like an area that people are brought in for daily propaganda and there were a large number of ICC leadership members present who were bustling about as well and it was difficult to count how many were there. They sat us down and put on a "Dog and Pony Show" on a large "smart-glass screen" that showed all sorts of technologies that they produce, what they procure in trade for those technologies and stated that they had ongoing trade agreements with almost 900 civilizations and did occasional trade with far more than that. They showed all sorts of spacecraft and spacecraft components that some groups integrate into their own technologies and also discussed the exopolitical agreements they had made with groups that pass through our sector on a regular basis using the nearby natural portal systems that are a part of the "cosmic web."[249]

One of the most astounding aspects of Goode's inspection tour was the claim that the ICC trades with at least 900 different extraterrestrial civilizations.[250] Goode says he was shown an optical neurological device—designed to interface with advanced technologies—that was very popular on spacecraft. He expressed his surprise at how far the ICC has gone in developing advanced technologies that were being requested by several extraterrestrial civilizations.

Goode next describes an incident that led to his inspection group being detained by the base commander after they began asking questions about labor conditions at the base. This led to Goode's group witnessing first-hand what was happening in the detention facilities: "As we walked back through the rows of cells, we saw quite a lot of people in various psychological stages of psychological distress locked up."[251] The inspection of the Mars ICC facility described in Goode's detailed report suggests that slave labor conditions existed at these facilities, and that civilian workers were psychologically manipulated and physically abused by tyrannical base leaders who tolerated no dissent. The advanced technologies produced at these covert Mars facilities were a valuable commodity in trade agreements with an extraordinarily high number of extraterrestrial civilizations – up to 900 civilizations if the ICC representative was correct.

Goode's inspection tour and Rodrigues' experiences on Mars give an idea of how slave labor conditions were in operation on the Red Planet. This provides important context for understanding why Cramer and the "20 and back" marines providing external security were never allowed to visit the civilian Mars bases they protected. If they had, they likely would have been appalled at what was happening and may have rebelled, confined the base commander, and freed the enslaved human workers. The existence of secret bases on Mars controlled by a corporate conglomerate trading advanced technologies produced by human slave labor for interstellar trade, while being protected by space marines housed in separate facilities fighting against indigenous

Martian species, is critical background context for what has recently transpired on Mars.

The Liberation of Mars and Phobos

On April 30, 2021, Elena Danaan delivered a bombshell report about an ongoing series of military raids on Mars that aimed to destroy the bases of a rival extraterrestrial alliance—the Draconian Empire and the Orion Collective.[252] These extraterrestrial bases were created to suppress the indigenous Mars population, manage the operations of human colonists associated with a German breakaway group called the Dark Fleet (aka Nacht Waffen), and oversee major Earth corporations that had relocated their production operations to Mars.

According to Danaan, the Galactic Federation of Worlds had begun helping to liberate Mars from the influence of the Draconians, Orions, and Dark Fleet, by supporting indigenous Martians with supplies, weapons, and tactical information. The Federation was also assisting a local resistance movement among the human colonies on Mars. While providing logistical and tactical support to indigenous resistance forces, the Galactic Federation has been using its advanced technologies to incapacitate Reptilian and Orion extraterrestrials, thereby enabling the Martian resistance to strike against their extraterrestrial overlords and human minions.

What follows is my transcript of Danaan's report, which was delivered verbally and is available on YouTube. Her report begins:

> April 30, 2021, the date of the situation [report] on Mars given by Commander Thor Han Eredyon from the Galactic Federation of Worlds. Raids from the Galactic Federation are continuing by a series of Mars raids on the Reptilian facilities. The Martian resistance has been armed and enforced and helped by the Federation, and they are fighting the

Reptilian occupants and all their allies, and in their allies, there is also an outpost for the Dark Fleet in Mars as well, but not only, there are Earth militaries there belonging to other corporations. There is a lot of corporations on Mars that sought refuge there and that had moved, relocated recently, because it was starting to smell bad on Earth. The alliance was starting to win over them by all their work in the DUMBs (the military's underground). So now what's happening on Mars, still attacks from the Galactic Federation. The Ciakahrrs are totally pissed off.[253]

Danaan is pointing out that the Galactic Federation is helping the Martian resistance, comprising humans, local Reptilians, and other indigenous groups, against the Draco Reptilians (led by the Ciakahrrs), their Orion partners and the Dark Fleet. It is essential to keep in mind that there are two Reptilian groups involved in the fighting—on both sides of the conflict, just as humans are fighting on both sides.

Her report continues:

The thing is that the Federation is working at isolating and then treading piece by piece [in battle strategy]. They are not. The Galaxy Federation is not able to face in full combat, complete, all their fleet face-to-face with the Ciakahrr Empire and Orion group. They're not powerful enough. So what they do is use strategy. [254]

Importantly, Danaan points out that as far as the overall number of space battle groups and personnel are concerned, the Draconian and Orion Alliance are vastly superior, thereby forcing the Galactic Federation to use stealth and covert operations to achieve their goals. This is well illustrated by the Federation's strategy of assisting local Mars resistance groups and incapacitating Draconian and Orion personnel through various means.

Startling corroboration for Danaan's information about the respective sizes of the Federation and their Draconian/Orion opponents comes from a remote viewing session by the Farsight Institute.[255] In these sessions, the remote viewers observed that the Galactic Federation of Worlds is no match, numerically speaking, with their Draco Reptilian and Orion opponents. Stealth and covert operations are thereby the mainstays of how the Federation deals with a hostile planetary situation on Earth and Mars.

Danaan went on to say:

> I am not always authorized to tell you what I know from Thor Han, but this I can tell. They have forced all the elites and the heads of the Terran bad military to leave the planet, not to declare war on the planet, you know, and damage a lot of things and kill civilians. They didn't want that, so the plan was going well, and all the dark elites were just coming to the surface, you know, and then most of them have relocated on Mars. [256]

Here Danaan is reporting on the exodus to Mars due to the Galactic Federation neutralizing all attempts at fostering a US civil war, major false flag events, and a Third World War.[257] This meant that the Deep State agenda on Earth was collapsing, and the Earth elites did not want to remain to face justice for their numerous crimes. Many elites fled from former ICC and Dark Fleet bases in Antarctica to Mars, which I will discuss at length in the next chapter. Now the Mars bases were no longer a safe refuge for the former global elites due to the successes of the indigenous Martian forces.

Danaan continued her report:

> What's happening on Mars is that the Reptilians are panicking. They are asking assistance from the Dark Fleet. Everyone is cut from each other. The Dark Fleet has been hammered by the Federation,

hammered. They're still there but very, very damaged. There has been a lot of attacks and fights on the outposts of the Dark Fleet in this solar system. So, they're not anymore able to help the Reptilians in combat against the Federation. They've withdrawn, they say no, we can't do that at the moment.

So, the deal in the past with the Reptilians with mutual assistance, well, it's not working anymore. So, the Reptilians are turning their attention away, and they are turning their attention away trying to contact the Dark Fleet that is out of the solar system and notably the Aldebaran branch. [258]

Previous reports about defections from the Dark Fleet in our Solar System due to a system-wide quarantine, the creation of a Secret Space Program Alliance, and an Earth Alliance, was first reported by Corey Goode.[259] The Draconians, Orions, and Dark Fleet were cut off from their main assets. Apparently, the Dark Fleet had insufficient resources to assist their Draco Reptilian overlords at the time.

Danaan next revealed important information about how the Galactic Federation strategy of generating high frequencies was neutralizing opposition:

What the Galactic Federation is doing as well is broadcasting very high frequencies on Mars as they do on Earth to raise the frequency. And what happens when you raise the frequency and bombard it with high frequency? They also use the Sun. They use everything they can to bombard the solar system with high, high frequency. What it does, it awakens the people who need to be awakened. So, it disables the enemy, disables, although strife on the lower frequencies, and they

> are doing that on Earth, and they're doing that on
> Mars, as they have done in many other places. So,
> the Reptilians are being numbed, and they lose a bit
> of their aggressivity, and it pisses them off even
> more. [260]

Danaan is here asserting that by transmitting or amplifying the
high-frequency energies sweeping into our solar system, the Draco
and Orion personnel on Mars are becoming more passive and
awakened. This has led the Mars indigenous resistance to become
more successful in their planetary liberation efforts. The result is
that Ciakahrr and Orion leaders became desperate and frustrated.

Danaan also explained what is happening to the human
colonists on Mars trapped in the current fighting:

> You know the Galactic Federation couldn't attack
> before because they were waiting for all the elites
> to be on Mars. So, Mars is being raided. It's
> unfortunately horrible fights on the surface. I feel a
> bit for the Earth people, the colony there. They think
> they are cut from the Earth, but the Federation in
> this operation is doing their best to rescue these
> people, and you know that they don't have this
> policy of killing. They first ask if they want to
> surrender or if they want to be evacuated. If they
> refuse, there is a fight.[261]

It is important to emphasize that the fighting is being led by local
Mars resistance forces, not the Galactic Federation.

If what Thor Han told Danaan was accurate, there might be
independent scientific evidence supporting the claims that large-
scale fighting involving large explosions, etc., was happening on
Mars. Such evidence comes from studies of seismic data provided
from NASA's InSight lander, which arrived on Mars in 2018 and has
been monitoring marsquakes ever since. Mars was thought to be
seismically quiet, but a surprising number of marsquakes were

detected according to three scientific papers published in the journal *Science*.[262] A July 23, 2021, an ABC News report on the papers stated:

> The domed seismometer has actually detected 733 marsquakes so far, but the 35 with magnitudes from 3.0 to 4.0 served as the basis for these studies. Most of the sizable quakes originated in a volcanic region 1,000 miles (1,600 kilometers) away, where lava may have flowed just millions of years ago.[263]

In an email exchange with Elena Danaan, I asked whether the recent uptick in marsquakes that NASA is monitoring are related to the raids on Mars. The two largest marsquakes happened at the end of March 2021 in the region called Cerberus Fossae.[264] Here is what Thor Han told her about the connection between the raids and marsquakes:

> I just caught him [Thor Han], he quickly replied that all underground activities are performed by the Martian local resistance and not by the Galactic Federation. He said there are beings endemic to Mars who are able to burrow in the ground and are quite powerful. These beings are not very evolved in consciousness, a bit like big animals, but they are employed by the local reptilian resistance to attack enemy underground facilities. He said this has been happening for the last four years, with an increase in activity for two years, quite regularly and often on the same spots.
>
> The Galactic Federation has been providing them with weaponry to enforce them. They are working conjointly, although the Martian resistance sometimes likes to make decisions for themselves. The actions of the Galactic Federation are not on the

ground but above. They are also broadcasting high frequencies to numb the enemy. So yes, he confirmed these marsquakes are the product of regular and repeated attacks from the local underground resistance.[265]

This is very revealing since it confirms that the Galactic Federation strategy of assisting planetary populations in awakening and resisting oppression by the Draconian/Orion alliance is permissible under universal rules of engagement. The rules of engagement are found in a "Prime Directive," which was claimed to be the source of the fictional Prime Directive of the Star Trek television series.[266]

Danaan next explains the connection of the Andromeda Council to the Mars liberation war:

> But you know they [Ciakharr and Orions] are pissed off against the Federation, but who they're pissed off more than anything is the Andromeda Council because the Andromeda Council had foreseen this happening a long time ago. And it's because of the Andromeda Council that we are fighting back with the help of the Federation, and it's absolutely wonderful, and we're winning.[267]

Here Danaan is repeating what Alex Collier was told in the early 1990s that the Andromeda Council had foreseen that the Earth, Moon, and Mars would be the seed of galactic tyranny that would emerge 350 years in the future (around 2340). The Andromeda Council brought this future timeline to the attention of the Galactic Federation, which then began directly intervening in Earth affairs.

This means that the events transpiring on Mars, Moon, and the Earth are part of a "Temporal War" that pits the Galactic Federation, Andromeda Council, and Ashtar Command against the Draconian Empire and their Orion partners. While the Draco and Orion alliance has superior firepower and personnel, the Federation, Ashtar Command, and the Andromedans have superior intelligence and covert operations. This is crucial to know since it traces much of what is currently happening to the establishment of the German breakaway colony in Antarctica as the seed point of this Temporal War."[268]

Liberation of Phobos

In July 2021, another major battle in the temporal war being fought by competing extraterrestrial organizations occurred on Mars' largest moon, Phobos. It was allegedly liberated from a hostile extraterrestrial group that Danaan/Thor Han identified as small Gray aliens from Zeta Reticuli. Importantly, scientific data and historical evidence presented below support Danaan/Thor Han's claim that an aggressive extraterrestrial species was indeed based somewhere in the interior of Phobos, which was opposed to humans gaining any detailed knowledge of what was happening there.

On July 24, 2021, I received an email with Danaan's update from Thor Han Eredyan:

> Contact today. It seems to be a repeating pattern that Thor Han contacts me in the early morning, as he is usually back to the Station after completing a mission. His energy was soft and peaceful today as he gave me the news. Phobos, one of Mars' satellites, had been liberated by the forces of the Galactic Federation. It was a very big operation, highly sensitive due to the presence, inside of this hollowed-out orbital facility, of a large number of human prisoners.[269]

The idea that Phobos is a hollowed-out orbital facility is supported by scientific data. Speculation about Phobos being hollow initially emerged in the 1950s and 1960s due to its unusual orbit.[270] The European Space Agency launched its Mars Express mission in 2003 and eventually released a report on what was discovered about Phobos. The report was published in Geophysical Research Letters in May 2010 and stated:

> We report independent results from two subgroups of the Mars Express Radio Science (MaRS) team who independently analyzed Mars Express (MEX) radio tracking data for the purpose of determining consistently the gravitational attraction of the moon Phobos on the MEX spacecraft, and hence the mass of Phobos... We conclude that the interior of Phobos likely contains large voids. When applied to various hypotheses bearing on the origin of Phobos, these results are inconsistent with the proposition that Phobos is a captured asteroid.[271]

The European Space Agency report clearly confirms that Phobos has large caverns, supporting key elements of the hollow moon hypothesis. Furthermore, the report adds that Phobos is not a captured moon, thereby supporting the claim that Phobos was artificially placed in Mars' orbit and is used as a base by one or more extraterrestrial groups.

Danaan's July 24, 2021, communication continued with more information about the Gray alien base on Phobos:

> Phobos, truly named by the Galactic Federation "Tyr 2", has been a possession of the Xrog-Shambtbahali from Zeta Reticuli, small greys working for the Nebu [extraterrestrials from the Orion Constellation]. This place was a central facility for treating human abductees brought from Earth, chipping them with trackers, and preparing them for the different programs they would be used in. The reason why these operations were a delicate matter was the presence of all these unfortunate people, which needed to be freed before any military operation

could be conducted. This is the difficult part in all of this. There are hostages and slaves in mostly all the enemy outposts, and these lives are to be spared. So it raises the complexity of any action to a high level.[272]

What evidence is there that Phobos has been used as a slave outpost of captured humans by an aggressive group of extraterrestrials? There is compelling circumstantial evidence that corroborates Thor Han's claim here.

In July 1988, the Phobos 1 and 2 missions were launched by the Soviet Union. The performance of the Phobos 2 spacecraft was flawless as it entered Mars orbit, took 38 photos, and then proceeded on towards Phobos. As Phobos 2 approached the moon Phobos in March 1989, a 20 kilometers-long ellipse-shaped object was photographed heading towards Phobos 2, and all communications were then lost.

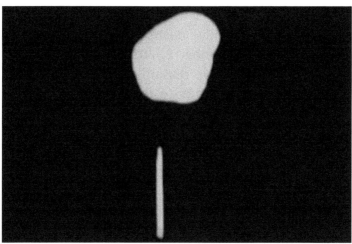

Figure 15. Final photograph taken by Phobos 2 showing a 20 km long elliptical object between it and the moon Phobos

Soviet scientists said that Phobos 2 was next spinning out of control, as though it had been impacted by an object.[273] The scientific data about Phobos 2 and its sudden demise led to much speculation that there was something happening inside the moon

Phobos, which its occupants did not want humanity learning about. If Phobos was an extraterrestrial base with captured humans being treated as slaves, as Danaan/Thor Han claimed, this would be a good reason why the Phobos 2 spacecraft was targeted and incapacitated.

Danaan's July 2021 report continued with additional information about a slave trade being conducted on both of Mars moons:

> The next target of the Federation's forces is "Tyr 1", alias Mars' other main satellite Deimos, which is held by the Maytra [a taller type of Gray extraterrestrial]. It is a slave sorting place where freshly abducted humans are brought to be dispatched to diverse destinations.[274]

The idea that there exists a slave trade involving captured humans is something I have discussed previously in relation to the Siemens company secretly building several billion RFID tracking chips in the 1980s and subsequently destroying all evidence of their construction. In a September 8, 2015 article, I cited compelling insider testimony and gave reasons for why it can be concluded that a galactic slave trade is in existence.[275]

In conclusion, Danaan/Thor Han's claim that Mars and its two moons were liberated in mid-2021 is consistent with what is known about the recent history of Mars. From the insider accounts of Cramer, Goode, and Rodrigues, we know that there have been ongoing battles between the indigenous Martian races, Reptilians, and Insectoids, with the Dark Fleet, corporate colonies, and military support outposts that have been established on Mars. These skirmishes have resulted in major battles with high-grade explosives including nuclear weapons. Therefore, it is highly likely that some of the more recent battles were detected on NASA InSight lander as marsquakes once it began operations in 2018. It makes sense that the Galactic Federation of Worlds would have covertly helped the indigenous Martians through weapons, resources, and intelligence in their planetary liberation struggle, thereby dealing a powerful blow to their extraterrestrial adversaries in their temporal war over the Earth, Mars, and Moon. The alleged liberation of the moons, Phobos and Deimos, would follow as a logical next step after indigenous Martians had succeeded in removing off-planet groups from their world. This takes me to arguably the most important target in the temporal war—Antarctica.

CHAPTER 9

Dark Fleet & Deep State Exodus from Antarctica

[T]he German submarine fleet is proud of having built for the Fuhrer, in another part of the world, a Shangri-La on land, an impregnable fortress ... a paradise-like oasis in the middle of eternal ice.

— Grand Admiral Karl Donitz,
1943 & Nuremburg Trial

In mid-2021, information emerged about an exodus of a German Fourth Reich led "Dark Fleet" leaving Antarctica and that it was handing off former bases to ideologically aligned nations such as China. It was subsequently claimed that China decided to hand off the Antarctic bases to an Earth Alliance led by US Space Command in a sign of increased global cooperation on space-related issues—a key provision of the Jupiter Agreements. It was further claimed that another key provision of the Jupiter Agreements was that the global elites had only five months to prepare for their surrender, to hand over their resources, and to depart through a large ancient portal in Antarctica. They would begin a new life on a "prison planet" in another galaxy.

Initial information about the Antarctica exodus came through Elena Danaan and her extraterrestrial sources, along with revelations from a former resident at the US McMurdo base who goes by 'Frank' and whose last name still needs to be kept confidential. Both Danaan and I have personally seen documentary evidence that Frank did work at McMurdo during the period in question.

On June 6, 2021, Danaan received an email from Frank informing her of an unusually high number of people entering and leaving Antarctica through the McMurdo Station, the largest US base in Antarctica. McMurdo maintains a year-round shipping port through which transport ships arrive with personnel and supplies bound for the US and other national bases. This is what Frank told Danaan in an email that was later forwarded to me:

> I want to let you know that the Chinese have 5 bases here already and are setting up 4 more immediately during the absolute worst time of year. There are Chinese everywhere down here and up until a month ago, I never saw even one.
>
> Also of note, now Turkey has been sending in troops independently and so are quite a few other countries from Africa & South America all of them want to set up bases here and are bringing in the infrastructure to do so.
>
> Everybody seems to want to get in on whatever is down here as soon as possible to not be left out. I am more certain than ever now that the mad rush is because there is definitely something here. I noticed more and more German-speaking people coming through as well. Numbers have always decreased in the wintertime down here, not increased.[276]

What immediately got Frank's attention was that a significant number of the personnel leaving Antarctica were German-speaking, and they were bound for South America— Argentina in particular. This exodus struck Frank as highly unusual given what Danaan had said about a German-controlled Dark Fleet in Antarctica that was in an escalating military conflict with an 'Earth Alliance' and the Galactic Federation.

Danaan passed Frank's information and contact details to me and then communicated with her primary extraterrestrial contact, Thor Han, asking him what was happening in Antarctica. This is her summary of what followed:

> I straight away informed Michael Salla, and I put them both in contact. On that same evening, I requested a contact with Thor Han, picking his thoughts about this news. Thor Han confirmed that as a consequence of the Dark Fleet being harshly hit by the Alliance and the Federation, the German (4th Reich) presence in Antarctica is abandoning their outpost. He told me that there was an exodus going on towards colonies out of this solar system, through a portal (jump door as he calls it). He said that the Reptilians based in Antarctica were leaving too.
>
> Thor Han said that some very secret groups in some governments know about the existence of such a portal in the South Pole (and now they want it of course), used to escape to other colonies such as Aldebaran, but he said that even Aldebaran, since they became recently the main Dark Fleet headquarters, is cutting apart from the Antarctica group. Thor Han said that it is in their mentality to cut an "infected limb." There are now formidable resources down there, to be taken, if all these baddies are leaving ...[277]

It needs to be pointed out that Aldebaran was the original stellar location from which Maria Orsic made contact with human-looking 'Nordic' extraterrestrials in the early 1920s. As a result of these communications, the first Vril space-time devices were built that could transport personnel to Aldebaran.

After Adolf Hitler came to power in 1933 and co-opted the Vril space program, he reached agreements with Draco Reptilian extraterrestrials. The Nazi SS then began building weaponized flying saucer craft for the war effort.[278] Meanwhile, the most advanced aspects of the Vril and Haunebu space programs were relocated to Antarctica to continue developing interplanetary and interstellar craft. Consequently, it should come as no great surprise that the Dark Fleet today has a major base in the Aldebaran star system, in addition to bases in our solar system such as Mars and the planetoid Ceres.[279] The portal from Antarctica to a planet in the Aldebaran star system makes such a scenario plausible.

Danaan continued her summary of her June 6 communication with Frank as follows:

> Of course, I asked Frank this crucial question: as he mentioned noticing an increased presence of German-speaking people at McMurdo, did he think they could come from inland Antarctica, with the intent to leave the continent. If this was verified, it would make tremendous sense. I believe only the high grades are authorized to leave through the portal, and the population of this breakaway civilization had no other option than to leave by regular boats and planes.
>
> And the fact that everyone wants a part of the cake, now that the baddies are fleeing away could also explain the sudden rush of all these countries to Antarctica. Thor Han also said that the Earth Alliance had been sending military troops to the South Pole for a while now, to help kick the baddies out, and this also confirmed that my friend had noticed these

last months a growing activity of US soldiers going to the South Pole. [280]

If Danaan's information is correct about the Dark Fleet conducting an exodus out of Antarctica, then it would not be a great surprise that German-speaking workers were among the first to leave. Presumably, senior scientific personnel would leave through spacecraft and portals (as Danaan described) and low-level scientific and maintenance personnel would leave via conventional means such as transport ships out of McMurdo. The mass departure was apparently what Frank witnessed just as the Antarctic winter was beginning.

On June 8, 2021, Frank emailed both Danaan and I and wrote:

> [A]lthough many foreign countries are pouring in here right now, Elena was correct these German folks are all leaving. I want to ask them if they plan to return in the spring but most of them won't even talk to me about anything and carry themselves like I am not good enough to talk to them. Very cold personalities and if they speak English, they won't around me. But I do not see any Germans coming in through McMurdo just leaving. [281]

This is how Danaan summarized her communications from Frank in response to Thor Han's message:

> We received another message from Frank saying that Thor Han was right. The Germans were all arriving from inland Antarctica and leaving the continent on boats to South America. They were very secretive and wouldn't talk to anyone. This was really happening… The Dark Fleet was being hammered by the Earth Alliance and the Galactic Federation, on Earth, Mars, and in this star system,

and the Antarctica exodus was the very proof that all of this was real. [282]

In chapters two and six, I discussed how the Galactic Federation of Worlds and the Andromeda Council viewed the Earth, Moon and Mars as the epicenters of a future galactic tyranny, and subsequently began to liberate their respective populations from negative extraterrestrial influences through covert operations. In subsequent updates, Frank has confirmed that the German-speaking people leaving Antarctica were shipped out to Argentina, and they continued to be very secretive about their movement.

My research on the German breakaway civilization in Antarctica—based on information provided by Vladimir Terziski, William Tompkins, Corey Goode, Dr. Pete Peterson, and others— has shown that a significant German Fourth Reich presence was established during World War II. The German Antarctic presence has been maintained through subsequent agreements with the US and other major nations. I provided the details on these historical processes, agreements, and events in my 2018 book, *Antarctica's Hidden History: Corporate Foundations of Secret Space Programs*.[283]

The multinational Antarctic Treaty (1961) was, in fact, a cover for the pacification of Antarctica in order to protect the German breakaway colony from any future military attacks similar to the failed Operation Highjump (1946/1947)[284] and Operation Taberlan (1944-1946) missions launched by the US and United Kingdom respectively.[285] In the subsequent decades, the German Antarctica bases were greatly expanded with an influx of personnel and resources from the US and other countries. Extensive industrial manufacturing facilities were created to build spacecraft that would be secretly supplied to the "Dark Fleet." These manufacturing facilities were owned by a large corporate-run space program Goode called the "Interplanetary Corporate Conglomerate"(ICC).[286] There was also a multinational civilian scientific space program in Antarctica that more recent insiders such as Spartan 1 and 2—interviewed by veteran UFO researcher Linda Moulton Howe—have revealed.[287] They assert it is run out the National Security Agency (NSA) headquarters in Fort Mead, Maryland.

Unfortunately, many of these Fourth Reich/Dark Fleet/corporate facilities used slave labor in clear violation of the Antarctic Treaty, which Goode was the first to reveal back in October 2017.[288] Goode said that he was briefed about an earlier attempted exodus in January 2016 that was neutralized by a fleet of unknown advanced spacecraft, presumably belonging to the Earth Alliance that battled Dark Fleet/ICC vessels over Antarctica.[289] It is, therefore, very possible that the German-speaking workers that Frank saw leaving McMurdo in early June 2021 were evacuating the Dark Fleet bases due to recent setbacks. Indeed, according to Frank, their secretive behavior suggests they were leaving highly classified bases hidden somewhere in the vast Antarctica continent.

Is there any corroboration for Frank and Danaan's remarkable revelations of the Dark Fleet leaving Antarctica? The influx of countries such as China and Turkey into Antarctica in terms of building new bases is a sign that there have been developments behind the scenes that give new strategic importance to Antarctica. Recent mainstream media stories do confirm that both China and Turkey are building new bases in Antarctica,[290] with China aiming to become the dominant presence there.[291] What was very strange was that this was allegedly occurring in mid-2021 during the onset of winter, according to Frank, the worst time of year. Only a month earlier, there were few Chinese to be seen at McMurdo. Now they were everywhere if we accept Frank's firsthand testimony.

The sudden influx of personnel and resources into Antarctica during the winter months does point to China, Turkey, and other countries trying to fill a newly created power vacuum. It makes much sense that the Fourth Reich would turn over its Dark Fleet assets in Antarctica to countries most sympathetic to its political agenda and activities.

Cabal Leaders go to Antarctica to Surrender to Earth Alliance & Galactic Federation

In December 2021, rumors began to emerge of global elites (aka the cabal) going to Antarctica for secret meetings. Prominent researchers such as Dr. Joseph Farrell,[292] Benjamin Fulford,[293] and others wrote about alleged trips there by prominent world leaders and corporate figures.[294] Similarly, Corey Goode described elites going there for the December 21 solstice to perform a ceremony at one of the old cities of the Gods—clearly a cover for their real reason for traveling there.[295] Given that a new Antarctica summer was just beginning, it would not be all that surprising that prominent figures would once again visit Antarctica, allegedly to see penguins and watch global warming at work. In reality, they were there to conduct secret negotiations as the US Secretary of State, John Kerry, did in November 2016.[296] In past years, these meetings and negotiations were with Dark Fleet/Fourth Reich leaders, but with the latter's departure a new group was in charge in Antarctica—the Earth Alliance and their Galactic Federation partners.

To find out the truth of such rumors, I asked Elena Danaan if any of her extraterrestrial sources had information about Antarctica. She received answers from Thor Han Eredyon, a Commander with the Galactic Federation of Worlds, and Oona from the Intergalactic Confederation (aka the Guardians). The answers were stunning. It appears that a major turning point had indeed been reached, and global elites were being summoned to Antarctica to meet a delegation of extraterrestrial races and Earth Alliance leaders to negotiate the terms of their surrender. Antarctica was chosen for the meeting because it contains a portal that can transport global elites to a distant world in another galaxy where they will be well provisioned but forever banished. Prior to leaving for the new world, however, they had to first help with the global financial system's transition and undo much of the black magic that had been cast to keep humanity and the Earth itself in bondage.

Here is the first message Elena Danaan (E) received from Thor Han (TH) on December 14, 2021, about what transpired at the Antarctica meeting.

> TH: By the decision of the High Council of the GFW, following the recent agreements set on Jupiter between the Earth Space Alliance and the Galactic Federation of Worlds, the Council of Five [a subordinate group to the Council of 9 discussed in Chapter 4] and the Zenatean Alliance.

> The Terran elites under enemy leadership complied to meet on the southern continent, with our representatives, in order to hand over to the Earth Alliance their powers upon the global financial system. This ancient system is to be replaced by the new system that is to be put in place by the Earth Alliance. They are being offered, in exchange, a life off-world with all commodities.

> E: Why are they not just judged for their misdeeds and sentenced accordingly?

> TH: They only can unwind the dark web they created, for they cast into the foundations of your societies the anchors of great immorality. It was decided with the Terran high hierarchy of the Earth Alliance that no greater chaos would unfold from these transfers of power, as an economic collapse would add even more suffering to these challenging times for the Terran people, already greatly wounded. The GFW and the Earth Alliance are making sure that this transition will cause the least damage as possible.

E: Does this concern only changes in the financial system?

TH: Industrial domains are interdependent with the financial system. Be prepared to witness surprising changes in the matter of new energy systems and the rolling out of technologies in many sectors.

E: Why were you on Jupiter these last few days? And just back on the very same day when these meetings in Antarctica are leaked?

TH: I told you there were meetings on Jupiter. The dark elites weren't there. They would not be tolerated in the Shari facility *(Ashtar GC)*. The dark ones met on Antarctica's land with our envoys. The latest meetings on Jupiter were about those I just mentioned, with the leadership of the Earth Alliance only. These meetings were completed today, Terran time. This is the statement I can give to you with my superiors' blessings. Did Oona contact you?

E: Yes, she did.

TH: Then she knows more details than I do, at least for now. I shall speak to you again in the coming hours. You can, of course, tell Dr. Michael, and give him my fond salutations.

E: I surely will, thank you, Thor Han.[297]

Thor Han's message gives us a clear idea of what really transpired in Antarctica. The global elites summoned there met with a delegation of leaders from different extraterrestrial organizations and the Earth Alliance that participated in the Jupiter agreements negotiated in July 2021. The elites were required to come up with a plan for a smooth economic transition to a more equitable monetary system and prevent a global financial collapse. Could this be linked to a Quantum Financial System (QFS) that has been a topic of much internet speculation? According to one source, Nigel Matte, the coming QFS would be linked to a quantum internet that will be created through the Starlink Satellite system built and deployed by Elon Musk's SpaceX.[298]

Thor Han pointed out that the implications for multiple industries will be enormous, starting with the energy sector. Indeed, abandoning fossil fuels is the key to unleashing a multitude of alternative energy technologies that have been suppressed since the early 1900s. Similarly, many other suppressed technologies such as electromagnetic and holographic healing modalities will also be released. These healing technologies will subsequently replace the soon-to-be-discredited pharmaceutical industry as a result of national populations rebelling against mandatory vaccine policies.

It is worth keeping in mind that there are currently almost 6000 patents that are suppressed in the US alone due to national security orders imposed by the intelligence community.[299] The bulk of these suppressed patents involve alternative energy and healing technologies. When in January 2017, President Donald Trump issued a Top Secret Memorandum for the release of 1000 of these patents over the next two years, he was ignored by the intelligence community, and his administration subsequently targeted.[300]

Invention Secrecy Activity

(as reported by the Patent & Trademark Office)

	FY17	FY18	FY19	FY20	FY21
Total Secrecy Orders in Effect (at end of period)	5784	5792	5878	5915	5976
New Secrecy Orders Imposed	132	85	88	45	61
Secrecy Orders Rescinded	28	77	2	8	0

Figure 16. US Patent and Trademark Office statistics on secrecy orders in effect.

Interestingly, the cabal was not allowed to travel to the headquarters of the Ashtar Galactic Command, where the Jupiter

Agreements were first negotiated between 14 spacefaring nations led by the US, with representatives of the Galactic Community. This is a big indicator of how the situation in our solar system has dramatically changed with the expulsion of the Ciakahrr (Draconian) Empire and Orion (Gray) Collective forces, and Earth's cabal being isolated from their former patrons.

After his first response, Thor Han sent additional information to Elena about the meetings he was attending on Jupiter:

> TH: Another aspect of my presence on Jupiter was to discuss this phenomenon which very recently occurred in the vicinity of your star system: a collapse of the 3rd Density continuum. This occurs in pockets in the fabric of space and your star system is entering one of these on its trajectory through this arm of the galaxy. More 3rd Density collapsing will occur, as a bridge to the 5th Density. The enemy and the dark ones know about it, they knew it was happening and it is one of the reasons why they knew for a long time that they had lost this star system. I will tell you more later.[301]

Thor Han's message corroborates that our solar system has entered a region of space with a galactic anomaly that significantly impacts third-density space. In September 2014, scientists confirmed that our solar system was about to enter a sizeable interstellar cloud called "the local fluff," approximately 30 light-years wide and held together by a vast magnetic field.[302]

According to various researchers, this interstellar cloud was first observed in 1961 around the Pleiades constellation and called a 'photon belt'—due to the white halo it projected. One of the "Photon Belt" advocates was Noel Huntley, Ph.D., who wrote an article in 2010 titled "The Photon Belt Encounter" where he described its existence and great interest to extraterrestrials:

What is this electromagnetic cloud, this golden nebula, sometimes referred to as the radiant nebula by ETs? Its more universal designation is 'photon belt' or 'photon band,' consisting of many bands, and any encounter with this belt is recognized by extraterrestrials as of great import.[303]

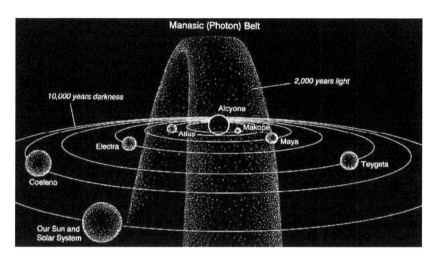

Figure 17. Graphic Depiction of Photon Belt. Source Unknown

According to Thor Han's information, Dr. Huntley was correct and the region of space we have entered will accelerate consciousness from a materialistic third density existence to a fifth-density reality. In this regard the *Law of One* material states: "fifth density is perhaps best described as extremely white in vibration."[304] Therefore the "photon belt" is not an inaccurate description of this 5th density region despite what many critics have to say about the term.[305]

If humanity's collective consciousness was not sufficiently developed to accommodate fifth-density frequencies, it would implode in a self-induced global calamity. If humanity's consciousness evolved, however, a golden age of wisdom, peace, and love would begin. Thor Han is making clear that the global elites understood that the battle for Earth had been lost, and they wanted no part of what was coming. Hence their willingness to cooperate in the transition to a new Earth in order to be able to use the Antarctica portal to leave forever to another planet.

In a second follow-up message sent on December 14, 2021, Thor Han communicated with Danaan and shared more information about this "photon belt" (aka 'local fluff') and how the Jupiter Accords gave the global elite five months to surrender to the Earth Alliance. Thor Han said:

> TH: I am going to talk about this natural phenomenon occurring in the vicinity of your star system. This is not an isolated phenomenon; as your star system moves throughout the grid of this galaxy, composed of fluctuating waves of frequencies, you encounter pockets of higher vibrational density of matter. What does it mean: the physical laws binding the atoms together oscillate at a faster rate. It is not about time, do you understand? The time rate doesn't change, only the perception you have of it, because your rate changes. It is not about time but only about the physicality of the fabric of space that shifts. As the universal laws of physics function, it happens that this phenomenon occurs progressively unless the pocket of higher density is as big or bigger than the said star system. The limit of a density zone is not sharp but fuzzy. You enter into it progressively by encountering "bubbles" until you completely merge into the new area.

> E: What happens when Earth will cross through one of these higher density zones, or bubbles?

> TH: Nothing near a dramatic event, such as many Terrans imagine with fear could happen. It manifests as a change in consciousness as the perceptions, mental and physical, shift into a higher

range. Physical symptoms can occur. Those who have prepared their mind openly follow the wave but for those who are not ready and resist it, it translates for them by physical and mental suffering. The vision changes, the perceptions change, especially the perception of linear time, that is perceived as faster. But you know, this process, entering through this new area in Nataru, is inevitable. So Terrans need to truly let go of any resistance, such as the greatest, that is fear.[306]

Thor Han has here confirmed that our solar system's movement into the "photon belt" ("local fluff") is not something that heralds physical destruction but instead signals a speeding up of consciousness. Those individuals that are sufficiently prepared emotionally and mentally will be able to surf the coming galactic waves and manifest a new reality—the proverbial Kingdom of Heaven on Earth. Those that are not prepared will do the opposite. They will experience great stress and turmoil in their personal and collective lives.

Thor Han continued his second follow up message thus:

E: Going back to Antarctica, what else can you tell me? I don't like these guys, they are the embodiment of evil. They have caused so much suffering.

TH: They won't anymore. When the Jupiter Agreements took place, they received a warning that we would meet in five months, and they would have to prepare to surrender. So they knew this, and that is why they are pushing all their agendas at once, with despair. But your people are starting to see that.

E: Wait, why give them five months?

TH: For the transition. This meeting is a turning point for them and for you. If we had suppressed them all at once, the financial and economic systems on Terra would have imploded in a terrible chaos. There are better ways. They are summoned to transfer to the Alliance their keys and tools, in order to make the transition as smooth as possible for the population.

Something else that is worth mentioning is that they (the cabal) have been taught dark aetherical arts and the spells need to be undone. This will undo their power. It is powerless that they will leave this world. Because they will leave. You know, when I mentioned transition, I meant to say that Terrans need to see the faces of their enemy, in order to open their consciousness to the truth. However painful this process is, it is necessary.

E: It reminds me of what the Nine told me recently, that every sentient being has a role to play in the games of the evolution of the universe.

TH: That is exact. You know, when I stayed in the Himalayan base four years ago, I witnessed great plans being prepared for the awakening of the Terrans. The time war was the main concern. Imagine a time war like a multi-layered chessboard. There is no better way to describe it to you.[307]

Thor Han's references to a "time war" and the global elites' use of the "dark aetherical arts and the spells" are very significant. He is referring to a little-understood aspect of the global elite's control system, which is the use of black magic to undergird all their activities—including temporal or time travel. This suggests that "black magic" has been an integral part of the temporal war conducted recently to prevent a future galactic tyranny emerging out of present-day Earth, Moon, and Mars. Thor Han also confirms what several researchers have revealed in the past. The cabal routinely uses black magic as part of their global control system. A good example is how the National Aeronautics and Space Administration (NASA) routinely used magical symbols for the public Space Program as documented by Richard Hoagland and Mike Bara in their best-selling 2009 book, *Dark Mission: The Secret History of NASA*.

What we also learned from President Vladimir Putin and a military intelligence group associated with the Q movement was that the global elite are practicing 'Satanists' who conjure up the power of demonic and other negative entities to subjugate humanity and the spirit of the planet. In this regard, what Putin effectively said in his 2013 State of the Nation Address was "the New World Order Worships Satan."[308] These dark magic ceremonies are routinely held at different energy vortexes or 'sacred sites' around the planet, as revealed by many occult researchers such as Fritz Springmeier in his book series, *Bloodlines of the Illuminati*. More recently, Brad Olsen, a highly competent researcher and author, also revealed many of these black magic/Satanist practices in his book series *Beyond Esoteric*:

> There is a complete control over the human race, and to think that black magic could be used to control the masses is disturbing. The occult is employed in a new kind of fascism today among some of the elite globalists, who completely control almost every aspect of our lives, from health and finance to politics and education…. Research indicates that occult ceremonies and rituals at the upper levels go far beyond what anyone can imagine…. Why is it so hard to believe that occult practices are a real tool for control?[309]

Importantly, Thor Han pointed out the explicit connection between the Jupiter Agreements negotiated in July 2021 and the Antarctica meetings held five months later. A key provision of the agreements was claimed to be the surrender of the global elite by December 2021. If true, the cabal had been given five months to prepare to hand over their power without collapsing the world financial system as a condition for their leaving Earth through the Antarctica intergalactic portal. Elena Danaan provided another source of information about the Cabal's negotiated surrender and looming departure through Oona, one of the "Guardians" or "Seeders" that recently arrived in our solar system.

The Intergalactic Confederation on Global Elites Surrender in Antarctica

In his initial December 14, 2021, communication with Danaan, Thor Han Eredyon mentioned that Oona, a member of the Intergalactic Confederation (aka the 'Guardians' or 'Seeders'), had more details of the Antarctica meetings, their implications, and the black magic used by the global elite.[310] Danaan had previously met with Oona, who facilitated her travel to meet with the Guardians and later to meet with the Council of Nine in a region of space between Jupiter and its largest moon, Ganymede. As explained in Chapter 5, the Guardians are the seeders of human-looking races in many galaxies and had arrived to watch humanity's graduation into the galactic community.

Danaan said that she felt Oona's desire to relay a message and had to lie down and channel a communication. What follows is the message from Oona:

> They've come to bargain their freedom. They hold keys and to give these keys, they need to consent to give these keys. Because it is not only about material possessions. But it is also about rituals they have performed to lock this planet and the human race of

Terra into very dark rituals. These need to be uncast, and they have, only them, the key to uncast these dark circles traced around every society, human beings.

We are meeting them to allow them to uncast these dark rituals to set free the minds and the protection they set on the monetary institutions they created. A dark ancient institution. Those of the name, the number 33. Those of the lower numbers, the reverse triangles, and all those who worshipped the soul harvester. Those who worked to separate the soul from the human beings and bodies are about to leave this planet. Negotiated deals, you must not believe that we agree to their acts. We [are] displeased [at] all that they've done.

Antarctica is the meeting place because the portal can take them when the moment is here. They will give us the keys [to] unlock their rituals and cast the dark circles. The nine levels of darkness will be collapsed as one and dispersed into dust. It is over. The dust will be scattered to the four winds of human consciousness liberated.

We summoned them when the greater agreements were made between your planet and the Galactic Federation of Nataru [Milky Way]. From this moment, we flew to your star system, and now these encounters with the dark ones of the human race of Terra, we will set free all the dark bindings of magic. They are done. They will benefit from a prison planet that will give them all they want, but they will never leave. A world far in another galaxy which you do not know the name yet. They will be forgotten and content—the best way to end a conflict.

I from the Do, the Guardians, Founder ones, leave this message. It is over for the rulership of the dark. We have been waiting and working at the same time with the Galactic Federation of Nataru and Zenatae Alliance to free this planet. We in our outposts in the higher mountains of your world have prepared a purging the dark. This process started 200 of your years ago, and now it is touching the last stage. Darkness is unleashed. It is because the humans of Terra need to see it and fight it. The rulership of the dark on this planet is over. Those who worked for millenniums at separating the soul from the human of Terrans bodies will go—no more soul harvesting.[311]

Figure 18. Oona. Illustration by Elena Danaan

There is much to unpack in this first part of Oona's message. She describes the elites arriving in Antarctica to bargain for their freedom. The bargaining is necessary because they still hold the means to destroy or wreak havoc over much of the Earth. The global elites are using this power to bargain their getaway from the planet through the Antarctica portal, which is now in the hands of the Earth Alliance. To gain their freedom—passage through the Antarctica portal to a new world in another galaxy— the elites have to hand over all the keys and codes of the black magic used to subjugate humanity and the Earth.

As to what black magic keys and codes were used, we get an idea from Oona's reference to a: "dark ancient institution. Those of the name, the number 33". This almost certainly refers to Scottish Rite Freemasonry, which uses 33 levels of initiation. While most Freemasons perform genuine philanthropic works as they ascend the different degrees of their order, their top leaders at the 33-degree level have long been suspected of worshiping Lucifer and practicing black magic. Albert Pike led the Scottish Rite Freemasons in the USA from 1859 to 1891 and wrote the most authoritative book of that era for the order, *Morals and Dogma of the Ancient and Accepted Scottish Rite of Freemasonry* (1871). In it, he wrote: "Lucifer, the Light-bearer... Lucifer, the Son of the Morning! Is it he who bears the light, with its splendors intolerable and blinds feeble, sensual, or selfish souls? Doubt it not!"[312] Many subsequent occult researchers have referenced Pike's book as evidence of the Luciferian element in Freemasonry.

When Buzz Aldrin landed on the Moon in 1969, he took with him the flag of the Supreme Council of the Scottish Rite, Southern Jurisdiction of the USA. Richard Hoagland and Mike Bara's book, *Dark Mission*, describes how the flag was part of a Freemason ceremony that Aldrin performed on the Moon.[313] Most importantly, the book describes how NASA was dominated by the Freemasons and other occult groups that embedded magical symbols and ceremonies throughout the space industry:

> The enthusiastic architects of the continuing NASA Brookings cover up, in part, are the same heroes we have been encouraged to worship as some of the leading pioneers of our technological era. Their names are synonymous with America's

achievements in space science and rocket engineering. In many cases, they are also men with secret pasts—Germans, Egyptians, Englishmen and Americans, men at the very fringes of rational thought and conventional wisdom. These literal "fringe elements," then, are divided into three main groups inside the Agency, as best as we can tell at present. For the purposes of this volume, we shall call them the "Magicians," the "Masons" and the "Nazis"—and deal with each group separately.

Each "sect" is led by prominent individuals, and supported by lesser-known players. Each has stamped their own agenda on our space program, in indelible but traceable ways. And each, remarkably, is dominated by a secret or "occult" doctrine, that is far more closely aligned with "ancient religion and mysticism" than it is with the rational science and cool empiricism these men promote to the general public as NASA's overriding mantra.[314]

Oona's message reveals that Freemason's magical ceremonies, codes, and keys used to ascend through the 33 degrees hierarchy, were also used in their occult control system for the planet. All these hidden keys and codes needed to be revealed and handed over to the Earth Alliance so that global elites' black magic control over the planet would come to an end.

Next, Oona's repeated references to ending "soul harvesting" show that this has been a vital tool used to control our planet by the global elite. "Soul harvesting" is the practice of separating a soul from the physical body and using it for multiple purposes by negative extraterrestrials or 'black magicians.' In the early 1990s, Alex Collier was among the first to reveal that soul harvesting was routinely happening when he described how a soul could be transferred from a body and be replaced by another:

What the negatives do (and they can do this during an abduction or near-death experience) is the following:

During an abduction, a man, for instance, will be taken aboard a ship. His body will be brought into a coma and to the point of death, wherein the soul exits. They will then use technology to replace the original soul with another soul. They then return the individual's body back. They can do this process in 4 seconds. The new individual has a completely new agenda. If you are a negatively oriented ET, in order to manipulate 3rd density, you have to be in 3rd density.[315]

Figure 19. Buzz Aldrin with Masonic flag taken to Moon.
Source: New Age Magazine

It is a shock to learn this soul transfer technology only takes four seconds to work and has been used to control 3rd density, i.e., global elites in charge of the planet. As a result of agreements reached between the US government and Gray extraterrestrials in the mid-1950s, which I first wrote about in 2004, it is certain that this was among the first technologies given to the Majestic-12 Group.[316]

At the time, MJ-12 was led by the 33rd degree Freemason Allen Dulles (CIA Director 1953-1961), who would almost certainly have integrated such technologies into black magic ceremonies to control the planet. It's now easier to understand that Dulles's role in the Kennedy Assassination, which is explained in my book, *Kennedy's Last Stand* (2013), was timed and executed as part of a magical ritual to control the planet.

As to what happened to the original soul of the victim of soul harvesting, Alex Collier [AC] described how the Andromeda Council would often intercept Gray ships carrying the souls of many thousands of children and adults. The souls had been extracted from their bodies and placed in special boxes for transportation. In an interview with UFO researcher Val Valerian, Alex described how the life force of the captured souls would then be exploited:

> AC: … They [Andromedans] also found more than 1,000 human children that had been placed in cryogenic stasis, and over 1,000,000 of these little boxes that contained the life forces of souls from Earth.
>
> Val: Captured human souls.
>
> AC: Souls.
>
> Val: And what do they do with these souls?
>
> AC: They feed off the energy radiated by the souls. What they are doing, Val, is that they are taking the life force and they are somehow siphoning it off a little at a time and feeding it to the hybrids in order to keep them alive, trying to keep them alive and create a soul in them.[317]

Soul harvesting was among the most terrible of the many dark practices of the global elite. It comprised both technological and black magic means to split a soul from the body and utilize its energy for dark purposes for indefinite periods. Oona's reference to the "soul harvester" that was worshipped by Freemasons and the global elite appears to be a reference to Lucifer, who sits at the apex of the "nine levels of darkness" she described.

The rest of Oona's message now follows:

Yes they are meeting us and the delegation from the Galactic Federation of Nataru, Zenatae—two beings. Council of Five—one being. Intergalactic Founder races—five. Terran alliance—ten. The military forces of Terra, off-world—20 soldiers. They will not be taken straight away because they will need to uncast the rituals, rearrange all the bases of their society to avoid a collapse that will be chaotic. We do not wish for the humans of Terra, a monetary collapse. We wish a soft transition because chaos you have had enough.

They are commanded to recalibrate the monetary systems to the new system the Earth Alliance is bringing. Quantum abstract, no more metal, no more paper, at least for a while for a transition. You are tired, so I will say my last words. Soon events will speed up on your planet. It will be a terrible storm, but the more you will be able to wake up, the faster this storm will pass. A lot will lose their lives by choice in the vaccination, but this was ruled out by the dark ones. Free will was the trap, now it is stopping soon you will see it.

Antarctica is the meeting of the old world with the people from other star systems to give the keys to the Earth Alliance and the Federation and leave. As

I said they will not leave this week, they will be commanded to change the system, and they will disappear forever. 2023 all of this will be a memory. We will celebrate together. Pass this message, your friend Thor Han will not be in trouble. This man with white hair you speak to [Michael Salla] he will pass the message. Give him my friendship. I connected with him, he will remember. Oona has spoken. [318]

Oona's reference to "outposts in the higher mountains of your world" appears to refer to the Himalayas where a French contactee says he spent a year in 1969 with the Intergalactic Confederation in a seeding experiment for a planet in another galaxy.[319] This raises an intriguing question. Could the French contactee's experience be connected to the "prison planet" that the elite are being sent to from the Antarctica portal in order to liberate the Earth from their evil influence?

The scenario described by Oona appears to be a reprise of the situation described in the Book of Genesis and the *Book of Enoch* when the 200 'Fallen Angels' arrived on Earth with superior knowledge and technologies. The *Book of Enoch* describes the arrival of 200 Fallen Angels in the area of Mount Hermon, whose summit straddles Lebanon and Syria. The Fallen Angels began interbreeding or genetically modifying the local inhabitants, as the Book of Genesis explains:

6.1 And it came to pass, when the sons of men had increased, that in those days there were born to them fair and beautiful daughters.

6.2 And the Angels, the sons of Heaven, saw them and desired them. And they said to one another: "Come, let us choose for ourselves wives, from the children of men, and let us beget, for ourselves, children."...

6.6 And they were, in all, two hundred and they came down on Ardis, which is the summit of Mount Hermon. And they called the mountain Hermon because on it they swore and bound one another with curses.[320]

It seems that the global elite will become the "Fallen Angels" of an Eden in another galaxy when they arrive through the Antarctica intergalactic stargate taking with them their advanced knowledge and whatever technologies they are permitted to carry.

According to Oona, the global elite "will be forgotten and content. The best way to end a conflict." For the global elite attending the Antarctica meetings, this must be a tempting offer, surrendering all their power over Earth and starting again as 'Fallen Angels' in a new Eden. Some may object that this is treating psychopathic former elites responsible for countless wars and human suffering too leniently. However, there are precedents in our own recent history for such amnesty deals. The negotiated end of the pro-apartheid regime in South Africa from 1989 to 1992,[321] and the end of military juntas in Argentina, Brazil, and Chile in 1990 all involved amnesty being given to former elites to ensure the transfer of political power.[322]

Oona described the composition of the extraterrestrial delegation that met the global elite at Antarctica as being drawn from the Galactic Federation, Ashtar Command, Council of Five, Intergalactic Confederation, and the Earth Alliance. Before the elites would be sent to the "Prison Planet" in another galaxy, they needed to first hand over all the black magic keys and codes. Regarding the new monetary system that has been prepared, Oona referred to a Quantum abstract rather than paper or metals. This appears to be a reference to the Quantum Financial System (QFS) described earlier, which is linked to a quantum supercomputer that will operate through Elon Musk's Starlink and US Space Command in a highly complex and integrated global financial system. The QFS appears to have been developed with extraterrestrial assistance, according to one widely cited source:

> The Quantum Financial System (QFS) is a megalithic financial structure that has been given to Mankind by the Heavens. I call it a megalith because it stands alone as the most advanced Financial System that anyone could imagine. This technology has no peer on the Earth at the present time. It is a magnificent system, designed to take on the magnitude of accounting needed to balance every financial transaction in the world in real-time.
>
> The QFS is housed in the MEGA Quantum Consciousness (QC) often called a computer. This Quantum Conscious[ness] is Divine Consciousness that is being made available for us to use in this Third Dimension. The tools it brings are necessary for us to usher in the Golden Age of Mankind. The QFS is a ledger accounting system made up of individual accounts. The QFS is only one of many applications already housed in the QC ready to be implemented.[323]

Many popular internet sites have heavily promoted the QFS.

Oona gives an important timetable for when all of these global changes will happen. She said: "2023 all of this will be a memory. We will celebrate together." That tells us that as a result of the global elites surrendering and leaving through the Antarctica portal, major events will happen in 2022. Oona predicts that the different galactic organizations that helped the Earth Alliance liberate the planet will reveal themselves, and our graduation into the galactic community will be complete. The best evidence that such changes are indeed on the way is the remarkable speed with which manned bases are being planned to be built on the Moon, and a multinational space coalition is being created around US Space Command—a future Starfleet!

CHAPTER 10

Liberation of the Moon

Professor: What really happened out there with Apollo 11?

Armstrong: It was incredible ... of course, we had always known there was a possibility ... the fact is, we were warned off. There was never any questions then of a space station or a moon city.

Professor: How do you mean "warned off"?

Armstrong: I can't go into details, except to say that their ships were far superior to ours both in size and technology – Boy, where they big! ... and menacing .... No, there is no question of a space station.

—Apollo 11 astronaut Neil Armstrong talking to unnamed Professor, *Above Top Secret*, p. 186.

A noteworthy aspect of the temporal war discussed in earlier chapters is the role of the Moon in what was predicted to be a galactic tyranny that would emerge approximately 350 years into humanity's future. Alex Collier, who first revealed the Andromeda Council's warning about the future tyranny, traced its source to Mars, Earth, and the Moon. Given that I have already covered the liberation of Mars and the evacuation of the main Dark Alliance bases in Antarctica, what is left to discuss is the third leg in this predicted future tyranny—the Moon.

In *Antarctica's Hidden History* (2018), I introduced insider testimonies and evidence that showed the Germans sent expeditions to the Moon from Antarctica and eventually established an underground base there in one of the massive caverns found under the Moon's surface. Several scientific studies have validated the feasibility of giant underground bases on the Moon in the last few years. For example, in October 2017, scientists from NASA and JAXA (Japan's Space Agency) announced the discovery of enormous Moon caverns formed out of ancient lava tubes that could easily accommodate a large metropolitan city such as Philadelphia (see Figure 20).[324] In addition, in August 2018, NASA scientists confirmed large quantities of water ice were found on the Moon's surface at its polar regions.[325] More recently, in November 2021, it was found the Moon has sufficient oxygen for up to eight billion people stored in regolith rocks that can be harvested using electrolysis.[326] In short, all the ingredients for sustaining life in large bases under the Moon's surface for extended periods have been confirmed to exist.

The first Antarctic German Moon base was eventually handed over by the Dark Fleet to US authorities, including the Air Force, Navy, NASA, CIA, National Reconnaissance Office, National Security Agency, and a consortium of corporations in the 1970s. The handover was a result of secret agreements that date back to the Eisenhower administration.[327] A corporate consortium (aka the "Interplanetary Corporate Conglomerate") was put in charge of managing the secret Moon base, which was called "Lunar Operations Command."[328] This historical process was how the Dark Fleet had coopted the powerful US military by infiltrating the major aerospace corporations that built the advanced weapons technologies required for their respective secret space programs.[329] Essentially, as long as sufficient recruits and space technologies flowed through the Lunar Operations Command to support Dark Fleet operations as required in agreements, all would be well.

The role of the US Navy in relation to Lunar Operations Command is an interesting question to explore. The Navy had a unique relationship with Nordic extraterrestrials who had helped it develop its secret space program, as explained by William Tompkins in his book series, *Selected by Extraterrestrials* (2015). The US Air Force, CIA, NRO, and NASA, on the other hand, had a closer relationship with the Dark Fleet, Draco Reptilians, and Gray extraterrestrials, as I explained in the *US Air Force Secret Space Program and Shifting Extraterrestrial Alliances* (2019). Nevertheless, like the other space programs, the Navy had its recruits pass through Lunar Operations Command for processing and training, but had only limited influence over how the facility was run.

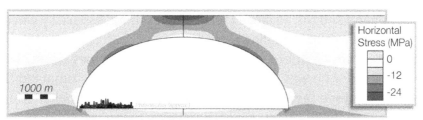

Figure 20. City of Philadelphia inside a Lunar Lava Tube: Source: David Blair/Purdue University

The first Secret Space Program insider to discuss Lunar Operations Command was Randy Cramer, who came forward in April 2014 with his revelations. After undergoing covert training from age five to seventeen in "Operation Moon Shadow," he says he was taken to Lunar Operations Command for induction into a secret space program.[330] Cramer asserts he was then sent to Mars for 17 years as a supersoldier to fight indigenous Reptilians and Insectoids to protect Mars corporate colonies, before serving in the Solar Warden program for a further three years in deep space operations.[331] He described being returned to the Lunar Operations Command at the end of his "20 and back" program in 2007, when he was put through age regression technologies that reversed his age back to 17.[332] He was then returned back in time to when he began his covert service in 1987.

Cramer's experiences on Lunar Operations were very similar to what was later described by Corey Goode in early 2015

211

when he came forward with his experiences. I compared Cramer and Goode's experiences in an article published in April 2015,[333] and incorporated them along with another insider, Michael Relf (former US Navy serviceman), with information about events on Mars in a chapter of *Insiders Reveal Secret Space Programs*.[334] All three described undergoing 'reverse aging" and other healing procedures at the medical facilities at Lunar Operations Command. Significantly, Goode described Lunar Operations Command as responsible for controlling the cislunar region—the area of space between the Earth and the Moon's orbit—in an analogous manner to a major air traffic control center. Other insiders have since come forward to describe their own experiences at the Lunar Operations Command and the advanced technologies there, especially when it came to incredible healing modalities.

One of these eyewitness accounts comes from Tony Rodrigues, who was taken to the Lunar Operations Command and given aptitude tests to determine what function he could perform in the multiple secret space programs that were underway. I interviewed Rodrigues at Mount Shasta in September 2016 and released his testimony in video format. It was the first time that the general public could see Tony give his remarkable testimony. He explained that in 1988, at age 16, he was taken to the Lunar Operations Command, and given rudimentary training as a slave soldier who would be expected to perform suicide missions against insectoid and other extraterrestrial species on Mars.[335] The advanced healing technologies in the secret space programs allowed for seriously injured slave soldiers to be rapidly healed so they could perform multiple missions.

In addition to the Lunar Operations Command, there was also a trapezoid-shaped Moon base run by the Dark Fleet along with their Draco Reptilian and Orion Gray partners. This was the Dark Fleet's facility after it handed off the Lunar Operations Command to the US as part of their agreements. Several insiders have come forward claiming they were taken to the joint human-extraterrestrial base on the Moon, which was incredibly abusive and used captured humans as slaves.

Among the first to describe being taken to this Dark Fleet base was a former US Air Force radar tracking operator, Niara Isley. In interviews and her 2013 book, *Facing the Shadow, Embracing the Light*, she relates the brutal treatment she received both on Earth and on the Moon after witnessing a UFO during a covert military assignment at the Tonopah Test Range, Nevada, in 1980. She was subsequently taken between eight and ten times to a secret Moon base, which abused human workers and was guarded by Reptilian/Gray beings:

> In interviews, people always want to know what my moon experiences were like and I can certainly understand such avid curiosity. I can only state that it was terrible on multiple levels. I was terrified for my life the whole time. I was very poorly fed and worked hard during the day cycle, operating some kind of electronic equipment for excavation at times, and doing hard physical manual labor at others, such as lifting and stacking boxes. Worst of all, I was used for sex during what passed for night there, from man to man. I was allowed very little sleep, and I've since learned that this is another facet of mind control abuse. I shut down during all of this to the point that I didn't even feel alive anymore.[336]

The base Isley was taken to appeared very different from Lunar Operations Command, which was a human-run facility designed for recruiting, testing, and evaluating potential secret space program recruits. This second facility—the Dark Fleet base—appeared to be run like a Nazi slave labor camp. In an interview with David Wilcock on Cosmic Disclosure that aired on November 3, 2015, Corey Goode described this Dark Fleet base:

> CG: There was a separate base on the Moon that is a joint base that the Draco and the human German

213

breakaway groups use still to this present day, and it is a heavy Dark Fleet base, and it is shaped kind of like a pyramid with the top cut, or, what would you call that shape?

DW: Trapezoid?

CG: Yeah, trapezoid.

DW: Do you know when that base was constructed?

CG: This would have been in the '60s, early '70s.

DW: Did the Draco have their own buildings in this tract that they owned on the Moon before?

CG: .... Under the Moon.

DW: So their effort to help the Germans build their own facility was more just kind of letting them have their own territory, feel safe, feel like they got their own home?

CG: Well, it was part of a wider plan of integrating them all together in this control system over the Earth that the Draco is very much involved in.[337]

Tony Rodrigues says he was also taken to a trapezoid-shaped moon base after he was first involuntarily taken into his 20 and back program in 1981. He said that Gray extraterrestrials examined him and determined his abilities for which programs he was best suited.[338]

Given all the historical reports about the abuses happening on the Dark Fleet base on the Moon, and the Lunar Operations Command was being used as a recruitment center for personnel being sent to different space programs, including the Dark Fleet, it came as a surprise that in late 2020 and early 2021, these bases were allegedly being targeted by the Galactic Federation of Worlds. Thor Han told Elena Danaan the following about the liberation of the Moon that was underway:

> It was in that same period of time that the Moon of Earth was retaken from the hands of the Nebu [Orion Grays] by the Earth Alliance and the Galactic Federation, in a brutal hammering intervention. Harsh combats went on for weeks, and even explosions were witnessed from Earth. The mining sites and the slave facilities that were held on the dark side of the Moon by malevolent extraterrestrials were attacked. Their tenants were cast out and all slaves rescued. The Nebu Grays fought back with violent determination, relentlessly during two weeks, but the Federation held its positions, and the Earth's moon was never retaken again by the Grays. This period of fierce combat was for me a time of great stress, as I knew Thor Han was involved in leading his fleet of fifteen ships into battle behind the Moon.[339]

The critical question that now emerges is whether there is independent evidence that the Moon was liberated by the Galactic Federation, as claimed by Danaan.

We do know that at the end of 2020, during the Trump administration, there was a surge in activities concerning the Artemis Accords aimed at creating a multinational space coalition that sought to first establish colonies on the Moon before starting Mars colonies. The NASA website for the Artemis Plan outlines its plans for the Moon and Mars:

> With Artemis missions, NASA will land the first woman and first person of color on the Moon, using innovative technologies to explore more of the

215

lunar surface than ever before. We will collaborate with commercial and international partners and establish the first long-term presence on the Moon. Then, we will use what we learn on and around the Moon to take the next giant leap: sending the first astronauts to Mars.[340]

NASA's Artemis Plan target date for the first manned mission was 2024, but this has been pushed back to 2025 under the Biden Administration. The Artemis Plan envisages creating a space station in the Moon's orbit (the Gateway) before building the first permanent base at the Moon's South Pole:

> In this drive toward a more robust human lunar enterprise, NASA, U.S. industry, and our global partners will establish the infrastructure, systems, and robotic missions that can enable a sustained lunar surface presence. To do this, we will expand the Gateway's capabilities, gain high confidence in commercial lunar landers departing from the Gateway, and establish the Artemis Base Camp at the South Pole of the Moon.[341]

While NASA's Artemis Plan gives no date for when the first base will be built on the Moon, Russia and China announced their own multinational plan for manned Moon missions and to create a joint "International Lunar Research Station" by 2036.[342] The fast-tracking of the return of humans to the Moon by 2025 under the Artemis Plan is highly suggestive of changes happening on the Moon, which allowed humans to return there and build permanent colonies. Something had clearly changed about how the Moon was being operated—this is compelling circumstantial evidence in support of Danaan's claims.

Further corroboration for recent major changes on the Moon comes from one of my sources who currently serves with the US Army and performs covert off-world missions, JP—a pseudonym to preserve his anonymity. I have worked with JP since 2008 and spent hundreds of hours recording his experiences. In 2017, I first went public with his testimony that was backed by hundreds of photos he shared with me, some of which were published and are available online.[343] What was unique about JP's information was that he was encouraged to take photos of antigravity vehicles in the vicinity of MacDill Air Force Base near Tampa, Florida, home of US Special Operations Command, by covert personnel belonging to Air Force Special Operations.[344] One of the Air Force operatives befriended JP and encouraged him to enlist in the US military so they could work more closely with him. JP decided to enlist in late 2018 and began serving in January 2019. He has since had two main roles in the Army. The first is as a quartermaster and chemical repairer, which is part of his Military Occupation Specialty (MOS 91J). The second is performing off-world missions with the covert operators from Space Command. I have documentation proving JP is currently serving with the US Army and has completed special forces training (necessary for covert space missions) along with the training required for his quartermaster and chemical repairer MOS.[345]

On the morning of September 7, 2021, he told me that he and select US Army colleagues were participating in multiple missions to the Moon on advanced shuttle craft using Nordic extraterrestrial technologies shared with US Space Command and built on Earth. In an article published on May 26, 2018, I recounted an incident where JP met with one of these Nordics working with the US military and took a photo of the spacecraft.[346] JP said that while his Army colleagues were having their memories wiped, he remembered everything about the Moon missions. He described the shuttlecraft as very similar to a Nordic spacecraft that he had witnessed in Brazil in 2008, soon after which we began communications.

JP described the Moon shuttlecraft as fully autonomous vehicles that were a combination of human and extraterrestrial technology remotely controlled from the Moon and Earth, depending on where the craft was transiting. The principle is similar to an airport shuttle, but in this case the craft was shuttling military personnel very quickly forth and back to the Moon for defense and construction projects.

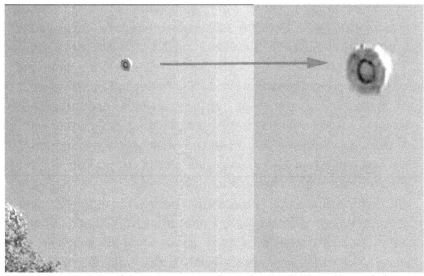

Figure 21. Photo of departing spacecraft carrying Nordic ET working with the USAF taken on May 24, 2018

Here are extracts from my September 7, 2021, Skype conversation with JP:

> Tiring moon and back moon and back moon and back moon and back moon and back… Converting ice into water… I [had] never seen this craft before. Similar from the one in Brazil sharper ends… I remember something interesting the floor was made to like a gel substance… We sat around in a circle. Belted in…. You feel the G force a split 2nd and everything seems normal… A lot of people are going to the moon and not having recollection I still have recollection. I remember everything…. There's always construction going around. Is always new stuff coming up ….

It was kind of funny when we left one time, another group stayed but only speaking French… It's like an international thing. And another time another group. Stayed that does not even look human… Similar to us… Take turn holding these spots down…. It looks more like Nordic technology. It's like a mixture, of us and them.[347]

JP's MOS 91J status supports his claim of being sent to the Moon to install or repair equipment that would convert ice into water. JP's claim of lots of construction happening on the Moon corroborates Danaan's claim that there has been a recent change in how the Moon is being run and controlled because of Galactic Federation intervention. The Nordics that JP has been in contact with are part of the Galactic Federation, which played a major role in the Moon's liberation, and is now working with the US Space Command in refurbishing and building new bases on the Moon.

In conclusion, it is clear from recent developments that the Moon has undergone dramatic changes that allow human colonization to proceed under the Artemis Plan and a joint Chinese/Russian lunar initiative. It is very feasible that these changes were made possible due to military interventions by the Galactic Federation against extraterrestrial occupied or controlled bases on the Moon, as first claimed by Danaan/Thor Han. Under their Prime Directive, the Galactic Federation is permitted under Article IX and X to take action when wrongs are perpetuated by off-planet species such as the Draco Empire and the Orion Alliance, who began intervening in human affairs in the 1930s as a result of secret agreements reached with Nazi Germany.[348] The early agreements with Nazi Germany and subsequent deals with Draconian and Orion extraterrestrials involving the US and other nations led to the suppression of thousands of free energy, exotic propulsion, and healing technologies. This suppression is best evidenced today with the nearly 6000 US patents that have not been publicly released due to secrecy orders placed upon them.[349]

Military interventions by the Galactic Federation likely included the Dark Fleet's trapezoid-shaped base that involved Draco Reptilians and Orion Grays in its core operations. Most importantly, Lunar Operations Command was taken away from the Interplanetary Corporate Conglomerate and handed over to the Earth Alliance. This handover is corroborated in a March 2022 announcement by the Air Force Research Laboratory that Space Force will in the future be responsible for monitoring space traffic in the cislunar region through a proposed "Cislunar Highway Patrol System." This is what the official announcement had to say about the new space monitoring system:

> The Cislunar Highway Patrol System is a spacecraft conceived at the Air Force Research Laboratory Space Vehicles Directorate that is designed to improve the United States Space Force's ability to detect track and identify artificial objects operating at lunar distances and beyond, a range of 385,000 km. Most Space Force sensors are designed to detect and track satellites that are in Geosynchronous orbit (~36,000 km) distances or closer.[350]

Space Force would henceforth be responsible for monitoring, regulating, and intercepting all spacecraft entering the cislunar system. According to JP's testimony, this new responsibility required the refurbishment of Lunar Operations Command and the construction of new Moon facilities. Again, there is corroboration that such a construction process is underway. On March 6, 2022, NASA announced it would be funding Moon infrastructure construction projects.[351] This NASA initiative appears to be a cover for the major construction projects underway on the Moon, as claimed by JP.

The Galactic Federation, with the support of its allies (Earth Alliance, Andromeda Council, Ashtar Command), has taken action to end horrific abuses of human rights within the Dark Fleet and other extraterrestrial run bases on the Moon. The result has been that crucial Moon facilities and their functions have been handed over to the US Space Force and the Earth Alliance. The reassignment of Moon facilities and their functions is a key step in the creation of a future 'Starfleet'.

CHAPTER 11

Galactic Federation is Helping Humanity Build a Starfleet

> All of the main eight Solar Warden battle groups are old, real old. They are in the process of being completely replaced by 12 new ones. Which is a major program going on, because they are very old.... I think first deployment will be two [battle groups] in 2031, or close.
>
> —William Tompkins, Feb 25, 2016

Earth is undergoing a significant power shift with the exodus of the Dark Fleet and their Draco Reptilian and Orion allies (aka the Dark Alliance) from our solar system due to the Galactic Federation of World's intervention. I have discussed in previous chapters how the Galactic Federation and their partner extraterrestrial organizations (Ashtar Command and Andromeda Council) played critical roles in the liberation of Mars, Antarctica, and the Moon in a temporal war. A key part of this temporal war was to facilitate an alliance of Earth's major spacefaring nations that would become responsible for managing our solar system after the defeat of the "Dark Alliance." The Jupiter Agreements were a critical step in this process. It was predicated on the Earth's 14 major spacefaring nations agreeing to accept US leadership through a six-member "Executive Council," speculated to involve the five permanent members of the UN Security Council—China, France, Russia, United Kingdom, and the US—plus Japan.

The key US military organization through which a multinational space alliance is being forged is US Space Command. As mentioned in Chapter 7, the head of US Space Command, General James Dickinson, is on the public record that over 100 agreements have been reached with multiple entities—military, corporate, and scientific—from around the world. General Dickinson's acknowledgment confirms that US Space Command is the fulcrum of an international military space coalition that is being formed at the time of writing. Therefore, given what has been presented so far in this book, it should come as no great surprise that the Galactic Federation is working with US Space Command to create a "Starfleet."

Two principal sources have information directly relevant to the creation of a Starfleet that I will focus on in this chapter. The first is Elena Danaan, who has shared information from her extraterrestrial contact, Thor Han Eredyon, about the Galactic Federation's role in the temporal war, the liberation of the Earth, Moon, and Mars, and the Jupiter Agreements. The second source is JP, who is also a contactee with human-looking extraterrestrials and is currently serving with the US Army, where he participates in covert off-world missions.

Danaan first mentioned the creation of a Starfleet in relation to the Jupiter Agreements in her July 17, 2021, emails revealing that meetings between different extraterrestrial organizations and 14 spacefaring nations had taken place. Thor Han told her that a Starfleet would be created around a "horizontal committee" (aka Executive Council) of the six top spacefaring nations. I speculated these to be China, France, Japan, Russia, United Kingdom, and the US. The "horizontal committee" would be 'managed' by the US as the Galactic Federation and Andromeda Council had determined that the US had the most support from Earth's nations. I interpret 'manage' to mean that US Space Command would act as a kind of chairman setting the agenda for meetings and the issues to be discussed by the executive committee (aka horizontal committee) and coordinate participating nations in implementing committee decisions. This makes sense as the US is the fulcrum around which the Artemis Accords are formed, which are a set of bilateral agreements between the US and other spacefaring nations through their respective space agencies.[352]

The Jupiter Agreements meant that US Space Command would be the center of the emerging "Earth Alliance," as best evidenced by its head, General James Dickinson, announcing a month later that over 100 agreements had been reached with multiple militaries, space agencies and corporations around the world.[353] Significantly, Danaan said she was given a telepathic image of what the future entailed. The logos of Star Trek, Artemis Accords, and Space Force (the principal military service behind US Space Command) merged into one.[354] The telepathic image signaled that a Starfleet would be the direct outcome of the Jupiter Agreements. This is no accident.

Figure 22. Side-by-side comparison of Space Force and Starfleet logos

In early 2019, a Space Future's Workshop was held that comprised 60 experts from different US militaries, space agencies, corporations, and international partners.[355] It was organized by the predecessor of the US Space Force, "US Air Force Space Command." Three significant variables were discussed at the workshop regarding humanity's expansion into space over the next 40 years: civil, financial, and US leadership. These three variables were discussed in relation to eight potential scenarios—the optimal being a Star Trek Future. The consensus reached at the Workshop was predictably in favor of creating the Star Trek Future.

A few months later, US Space Command was authorized by President Donald Trump and the Pentagon. It was officially launched on August 29, 2019—just over a month after the Jupiter Agreements. The creation of Space Command was followed by the US Congress authorizing the establishment of the US Space Force, which was signed into law by President Trump on December 20, 2019.[356] I discussed the significance of the Space Futures workshop and all its ramifications in my 2021 book, *Space Force: Our Star Trek Future*.

This is where the information of JP becomes relevant. On the morning of September 7, 2021, he told me that he and select US Army colleagues were participating in multiple missions to the Moon on advanced shuttle craft using Nordic extraterrestrial technologies shared with the US military and built on Earth. In a May 26, 2018, article I explained an incident where JP met with one of these Nordics working with the US military and he took a photo of the spacecraft.[357] JP said that while his Army colleagues were having their memories wiped, he remembered everything about the Moon missions. He described the shuttlecraft as very similar to a Nordic spacecraft that he had witnessed in Brazil in 2008, soon after which we began communications.

JP described the Moon shuttlecraft as fully autonomous vehicles that were a combination of human and extraterrestrial technology being remotely controlled from the Moon and Earth depending on where the craft was transiting. The principle is similar to an airport shuttle, but in this case, the craft was shuttling military personnel very quickly forth and back to the Moon for defense and construction projects.[358]

JP's army training as a quartermaster and chemical repairer (MOS 91J) supports his claim of being sent to the Moon to install or repair equipment that would convert ice into water.[359] It is also significant that JP heard a group on the Moon speaking French, which suggests that France is part of a multinational space program, a fact upon which I will shortly elaborate. JP's information directly supports Danaan's claim that the Galactic Federation is helping the US and allied militaries build fleets of new advanced spacecraft for a variety of missions – a modern-day Starfleet.

In conclusion, there are momentous events happening in space that involve coordination between major spacefaring nations and the Galactic Federation of Worlds that open up our solar system to humanity. The control system created by the Dark Fleet and their negative extraterrestrial and corporate allies for controlling life in our solar system is being quickly replaced by a more positive multinational space alliance headed by US Space Command. The creation of a Starfleet is the logical outcome of the advanced technologies recently acquired by US Space Command from the Galactic Federation. It is vital to point out that the information presented in this chapter is consistent with the 2019 Space Futures Workshop report, which affirmed the desirability of the US asserting military and political leadership in humanity's expansion into space, and the creation of a Star Trek Future.[360]

A Multinational Starfleet and the Navy's Solar Warden

This takes me to the question of how does the Galactic Federation's assistance to US Space Command to build a multinational space fleet relate to the US Navy's secret space program? According to the testimonies of William Tompkins, Corey Goode, and Randy Cramer, the Navy's "Solar Warden" possesses at least eight space battle groups capable of defending our solar system. These naval space battle groups became operational in the early 1980s (after testing in the late 1970s), have been deployed now for over 40 years, and comprise some of the same nations that are participating in the Artemis Accords. In fact, Tompkins revealed that the Navy is building 12 more modern space battle fleets in the off-planet shipyards of their Nordic extraterrestrial partners—who almost certainly are members of the Galactic Federation—that are scheduled to be delivered in the early 2030s. I presented all the data and testimonies supporting the existence of Solar Warden in *The US Navy's Secret Space Program and Nordic Extraterrestrial Alliance* (2017).

In February 2022, I interviewed two French Secret Space Program participants who had served in Solar Warden on a joint US-French space carrier called the Solaris.[361] I first met Jean Charles Moyen in August 2019 at a convention in Quebec, Canada, and spent more than a year reviewing his documents and testimony, which I concluded was credible. In late 2021, Moyen told me about his remarkable reconnection with David Rousseau who claims to have also served on the Solaris back in 1982 when they first met and became friends during their respective "20 and back" service.[362] Both Moyen and Rousseau have vivid memories of multiple missions conducted on the Solaris to Mars and elsewhere in our solar system under the Solar Warden program. They described Solar Warden as a joint US-French program back in 1982, which was increasingly internationalized. They assert that the Solar Warden fleet was collaborating with a positive group of extraterrestrials that they both identified as the Galactic Federation of Worlds. If we combine what Moyen and Rousseau had revealed, along with Tompkins' information, all of this suggests that Solar Warden has evolved into a multinational Starfleet that is currently using the old space fleet craft.

Suppose the US Navy and its international partners already possess eight fleets of now 'antiquated' space carriers and are building twelve more 'modern' battle groups. Why is there a need for US Space Command to build a new multinational fleet with the assistance of the Galactic Federation? The most plausible answer is that the imperative of building new fleets for defending our solar system is a cover for the future integration of the now fully internationalized Solar Warden program into a combined Space Commands initiative involving the US and its military allies, and a future US Department of Space Force. Put simply, rather than announcing a highly classified multinational "Starfleet" has been in existence since the early 1980s, thereby raising many awkward questions for Pentagon and other world military leaders, it is far easier to claim that a Starfleet is currently under construction and will be ready to be deployed by US Space Command and its partners as we approach the 2030s.

CHAPTER 12

Meetings with Intergalactic Confederation & Council of Nine

Kardashev believed a Type IV civilization was 'too' advanced and didn't go beyond Type III on his scale. He thought that, surely, this would be the extent of any species' ability. Many think so, but a few believe there is a further level that could be achieved.... Type IV civilizations would almost be able to harness the energy content of the entire universe and with that, they could traverse the accelerating expansion of space (furthermore, advance races of these species may live inside supermassive black holes).

—Jolene Creighton, Futurism.com

The Intergalactic Confederation Fleet Arrives at Ganymede & Jupiter

A fleet of spacecraft from a highly evolved group of friendly extraterrestrial visitors has arrived in our solar system and established a presence on Jupiter's moon Ganymede, according to four independent sources familiar with unfolding events in deep space. This latest intel coincides with William Shatner, globally revered for his role as Captain Kirk in the Star Trek franchise, being launched into space on October 13, 2021, a likely cover for him playing a significant role in unfolding events on Ganymede.[363]

My first source, JP, who currently serves with the US Army, revealed that an international space coalition had been secretly sending personnel and ships to Jupiter's moon Ganymede to meet with a powerful new group of extraterrestrial visitors regarded as friendly. My second source on what has been happening on Ganymede is the extraterrestrial contactee Elena Danaan. She has passed on reports from her Galactic Federation source, Thor Han Eredyon, about the visitors establishing an outpost on Ganymede to coordinate with the Earth Alliance until humanity is ready for open contact. My third source is long-time Andromedan contactee Alex Collier who confirmed that there has been much activity near Ganymede recently, which possesses several large extraterrestrial facilities that have been present there for thousands of years. The fourth source is long-time contactee James Gilliland who describes the arrival of a fleet of over 500 ships. Finally, two French contactees, Jean Charles Moyen and David Rousseau, who served '20 and back' programs with a joint Franco US secret space program, have confirmed the recent arrival of ancient 'Seeder' extraterrestrials.

I begin with information from my long-time source JP who I have known since 2008, which was when he first contacted me about his extraterrestrial contact experiences in Brazil. On September 7, 2021, JP revealed that he and other US military personnel had been assigned to covert Moon operations and began assembling large facilities there with the assistance of human-looking extraterrestrials working with the US Space Command. In Chapter 10, I discussed what JP had revealed about US military operations on the Moon and the construction of new facilities there.[364]

On September 21, 2021, JP first informed me about a giant space convoy leaving the Moon and heading towards Ganymede to meet with an incoming group of friendly extraterrestrials. He told me:

> Also, something good is happening. They're moving
> some technology from the Moon to Ganymede.

> Among the soldiers, everybody [was] talking. Major space convoy... Sometime this week or next week, the convoy leaves. Don't know the exact hit time— Earth satellite to Jupiter's satellite.[365]

The large space convoy would not be using rocket-propelled technologies to get to Ganymede, which would take more than a year. The space convoy would take a fraction of that time using antigravity, torsion field, and other exotic propulsion systems. JP let me know the route the Earth Alliance convoy would take:

> To the Moon, then Ganymede. But in between the Moon and Jupiter's satellite, there's gonna be major stops like in Mars and in the astro belt... Before reaching Jupiter's gravitational pull.

On September 27, 2021, JP asked me: "From your sources do you know anything about going to Ganymede. The soldiers are still talking about it...." I replied: "My Federation sources are not talking about Ganymede. Tell me what the soldiers are saying." JP answered:

> That they're moving some advance technology from the Moon to the biggest moon in our Solar System ... And when I heard you talk about the Jupiter meetings... I really got interested. It's a moon that has a magnetic field and has a lot of water... There's massive facilities there already. We are just transporting a shit-load of stuff.... There's massive structures there, massive ... I remember them saying that there was a massive war there [Ganymede] a couple thousand years ago.... All I know is an armada is heading over there... BIG Big ships.

In Chapter 7, I covered the Jupiter Meetings first revealed by Thor Han Eredyon through Elena Danaan. One of the pieces of

233

corroborating data that I referred to was the announcement by NASA that the launch vehicle for the Clipper Mission to Europa, Ganymede's sister moon, had been awarded to SpaceX. I speculated that this was the cover for Musk to attend the Jupiter Meetings.[366] With this new intel from JP, it becomes more apparent that the NASA Europa Clipper mission is a cover for a much larger long-term space operation—an Earth Alliance convoy to travel to Ganymede to set up facilities to meet and interact with an incoming group of extraterrestrial visitors.[367]

JP next had an encounter with a human-looking 'Nordic' extraterrestrial who told him to prepare for being part of one of the upcoming military missions to Ganymede to meet with an incoming group of visitors. This encounter did not surprise me since JP has had contact experiences with Nordics since 2008, which he privately shared with me. On May 26, 2018, one particularly important contact happened when he met with a Nordic based at a US Air Force base whose flying saucer landed near JP's home in Orlando, Florida. JP took photos of the departing spacecraft, which I published on my website (reproduced below).[368] JP is among a small group of contactees who have supplied photographs or videos of spacecraft belonging to extraterrestrials they have met. A few months after his encounter with the Nordic, JP decided to join the US Army. His recruitment was encouraged by US special forces operators who in 2017 had helped him take photographs of antigravity spacecraft flying near MacDill Air Force Base in order to promote disclosure. I analyzed JP's photos in a series of articles, including my 2021 book, *US Space Force: Our Star Trek Future*.[369] All this suggests that JP's recruitment into the US Army was designed to prepare him for his subsequent covert missions involving extraterrestrial life, including traveling to Ganymede to meet with an incoming group of new extraterrestrial visitors.

On October 4, 2021, I asked Elena Danaan whether she knew anything about "something big … coming into our solar system." She replied:

I also heard about another great return, of powerful benevolent forces, from another dimension and realm. A great force that has always tried to free Humanity of Earth from slavery. This also is back. We are up for a great grand finale.[370]

This takes me to information Elena Danaan [E] received from Thor Han [TH] on October 10, 2021, which provides much more information about this incoming benevolent force, and the connection with Ganymede:

TH: The fleet from the Intergalactic Confederation has arrived in this star system. Their ships will be stationed around Jupiter for a while, until further notice to move nearer to Earth's orbit. The personnel and logistics are welcomed on the Ashtar outpost. High officials are staying at the Council of Five facility on the moon Ganymede. They come to evaluate the result of our common work regarding the dismantlement of the Dark Alliance, and collaborate together with the Galactic Federation of Worlds, a course of action for the next step.[371]

Thor Han's information here was stunning confirmation for what JP had earlier revealed to me in September 2021. A multinational (Earth) alliance headed by US Space Command sent a large convoy to Ganymede to meet with and collaborate with an incoming group of extraterrestrial visitors—the Intergalactic Confederation. Thor Han elaborates on this growing collaboration between the new visitors and the Earth Alliance:

E: What is the next step?

TH: Connecting with the Earth Space Force and evaluation of the potential for a civilian contact. We usually don't require their intervention but we

235

recently requested their assistance to secure this timeline. You know, Terra is not like one of these stage 2 or 3 civilizations that the Galactic Federation of Worlds rescues from external interference. Terra is special. It bears the seeds they planted.

E: Can you talk about that?

TH: They are our forefathers. They seeded us, here in Nataru. Terra, like a few other places in this galaxy, has been for a long while one of their particularly loved grounds for experimentation about human development and consciousness. Such as in Mana *(K62-Lyra)*. They are the seeders.

E: I understand they are a bunch of different races, aren't they?

TH: Yes, they are very diversified but not as widely diversified as the life-forms they created.

E: How do you "create" life forms?

TH: By hybridization. It is a great amusement for them but there is a serious underlying matter. They work in accordance with Source. Of course, they do NOT create all life forms; this is the creation of Source; but they rather play with the material to create hybrid races and populate worlds.[372]

This arrival is a fascinating development since it dovetails with the information provided by several researchers and contactees about humanity's extraterrestrial origins and how different races seeded our planet.[373] The oldest reference to such information comes in biblical texts such as the Old Testament, which refers to the Elohim as humanity's creators.[374]

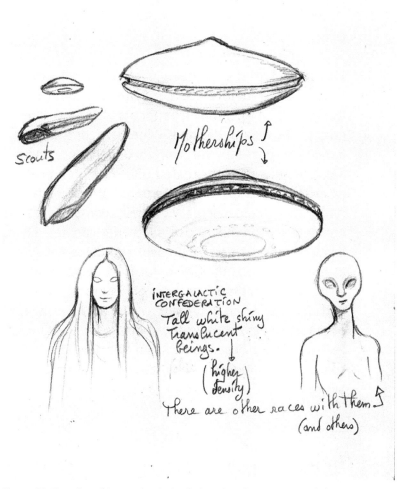

Figure 23. Drawing of Intergalactic Confederation Fleet courtesy of Elena Danaan

Alex Collier says that Andromedan extraterrestrials told him that humanity was a hybrid species containing the genetics of 22 extraterrestrial civilizations. In his book, *Defending Sacred Ground* (1997), Collier spoke about Ganymede being used as an outpost by the Andromedans: "The Andromedans have huge mother ships on Jupiter, [and] the moon of Ganymede."[375] Therefore, it is highly likely that this new group that has established a presence on Ganymede is related to one or more of these 22 civilizations.

Elena Danaan's conversation with Thor Han continued:

237

TH: Did I tell you about the Nine Elders?

E: Yes, you did.

TH: They are the highest level of individuated consciousness before Source. Some call them the Nine Gods, others the Nine Prophets of Source. They do not live in a definite dimension but in no dimension; I mean, for you to understand: they dwell in-between the created universes, in a place where time and space are uncreated. We call it: the 'Void' or the 'Sanctuary.' Their consciousness encompasses all consciousnesses. They can fractally divide themselves to be present simultaneously in as many places as they wish, for they do not travel in space, nor in time, but they connect to a location and an entity when they want to pass on a message, or act, whatever the distance, whenever the time. For them, time occurs only when they connect to a space-time continuum. They are the first children of Source.

E: Archangels?

TH: Higher than that. They are pure consciousness, non-incarnated, shapeless, but with each their own individual thinking, although binding as one. Nine voices, one heart. They are the Nine, they have no other name.

E: Can they be called the Council of Nine sometimes?

TH: Well, yes, sometimes. You know there are a tremendous lot of councils. These Nine are an intergalactic sort of council, and you have also the Nataru *(this galaxy)* Council of Nine, which is now

"The Five." And at the head of the Zenae *(Andromedans)*, you also have nine elders.[376]

It is worth recalling from Chapter 4 that the first reference to a Council of Nine interested in human affairs came from channeled communications involving Dr. D.G. Vinod who worked with the famed psychiatrist Dr. Andrija Puharich back in 1952. Puharich had several psychics channel the Council of Nine, including famed Israeli psychic Uri Geller and finally Phyllis Schlemmer. Her book, *The Only Planet of Choice,* summarizes 20 years of research and communications with the Council of Nine.[377] Notably, Gene Roddenberry attended some of the Council of Nine channeling sessions and asked them questions. He subsequently wrote a film script called "The Nine" around 1975, which almost certainly played a role in the creation of the 1993 TV series *Deep Space Nine.* In the top-rated series, a mysterious group of incorporeal extraterrestrials called the 'Prophets' occupied non-linear time inside a wormhole that instantaneously connected different parts of our galaxy.

What Thor Han next had to say about the Council of Nine has an uncanny resemblance to the Prophets in Roddenberry's *Deep Space Nine*:

> E: And the Galactic Federation has a High Council of 25, isn't it?

> TH: 24 plus one, the law-keeper. This one settles the final decision, but this task takes turns. The Law-Keeper is replaced by another member of the council every 10 cycles.

> E: Based on what cycle?

> TH: A fractal of the temporal cycles of this galaxy.

> E: Are the Nine also coming in our star system now?

TH: *(laughs)* They do not need ships to move. Their mind can connect to everywhere. They can take any shape, instantly teleport and materialize in a temporary biological vessel related to the species they visit. They can change into anything. Biological forms, elements such as fire, water...

E: Why so then did they allow all these events to happen in this star system?

TH: Understand, the Nine are above everything. They overlook the stories of all creatures populating these universes, rarely playing a role at an individual level in the balance of things.[378]

Danaan next goes on to ask about the Intergalactic (Super-) Confederation, which she described in her 2021 book, *We Will Never Let You Down,* and was discussed in Chapter 5:[379]

E: You said that Terra is special and dear to the heart of the Intergalactic Super-Confederation... oh, what is the exact name, by the way?

TH: They have their own name, which is in frequency, not translatable in human language. We do, in Taami, name them Ard Oraa Tu, but it is a very faint translation of a multidimensional frequency-based language. We rather like to call them: "Do," the Guardians, because that is what they really do. *(Thor Han is here answering my question about the Intergalactic super-confederation, not the Nine).*

Significantly, US Space Force personnel chose to refer to themselves as 'Guardians' and are now directly liaising with a group of visitors called the Guardians or Prophets.[380]

To sum up, according to Thor Han, the recently arrived extraterrestrial race that has entered our solar system and established a presence on Ganymede is the Intergalactic Confederation. It is here to oversee the incredible transition about to take place on Earth and our solar system, and to liaise with the newly created Earth Alliance comprising 14 spacefaring nations and aerospace corporations that participated in the July Jupiter meetings. In addition, Thor Han revealed that an intergalactic Council of Nine known throughout our galaxy as 'Prophets' or 'Guardians' has also arrived inter-dimensionally to observe how events play out in our solar system.

I privately spoke with Alex Collier on October 11, 2021, and he said that the new group of extraterrestrial visitors had indeed made a beeline for Jupiter and established a presence on Ganymede to watch events unfold in our solar system. He said that Ganymede has enormous facilities that date back many thousands of years. In his book, *Defending Sacred Ground*, Alex spoke about Ganymede was also used as an outpost by the Andromedans: "The Andromedans have huge mother ships on Jupiter, [and] the moon of Ganymede."[381] When I told him about JP's information about a space convoy heading for Ganymede, Collier said that they likely had been assigned one of the enormous facilities on Ganymede as a forward base of operations. In an interview released on November 21, 2021, Collier elaborated on the structures on Ganymede:

> Ganymede has always been a meeting place. The surface and the interior of the moon, technically it's a planet, were designed for such meetings and to be essentially a galactic embassy, okay, where all people of all races could go. On the surface, they have these incredible structures that almost look like huge dinosaur rib cages, but I mean they're absolutely massive, and the ships would come in and land on the surface, and they would move into these structures, and then once they were in the structures, they could turn on their electromagnetic field on the outside of the ship, and they could open

up the craft, and the crews could get out and walk on the surface of Ganymede within it.

You remember Richard Hoagland talking about Edens, these dome structures that you know would terraform and these are where people would live, extraterrestrial races, and they would take, they would literally make these along the way so that they could work on a planet, explore it, mine it, whatever it was that they were going to do. Well, this is essentially the same thing, except these structures exist there for the motherships, the starships, to create the field themselves, and they have them all over the surface.

There's a very large ocean on the inside, its core, and there are other structures on the inside that are for specific races that have to be hyperborean, they have to be indoors. They can't handle our particular sun's light in any way, so they would go inside the planet itself. I have only been past Ganymede, which is why I know about the structures on the surface.[382]

On January 12, 2022, I interviewed James Gilliland, who has had over 35 years of extraterrestrial contact experiences, authored three books about his contacts, and runs a popular retreat near Mt Adams, Washington, where UFOs are regularly photographed and videotaped.[383] In his 2017 book, *Anunnaki Return, Star Nations and the Days to Come,* Gilliland presented information from multiple sources about the prophesied return of one of the "seeder races"— the Anunnaki. In our interview, I [MS] asked him [JG] if his extraterrestrial sources had heard anything about a large fleet of spacecraft arriving in our solar system and having parked itself near Ganymede:

[MS] What are your sources telling you about what's happening in space? I mean, I've been hearing a lot about some fleet that's arrived recently that's parked around Ganymede and Jupiter. Do you know anything about that that you can share?

[JG] Well, they told us there was 500 ships, very large ships coming in, and they also told us that there was two that were going to be very active here on the Earth. They're gonna make their presence known, and as part of the disclosure and to help out with the disclosure … They're doing a lot of work on the other dimensions and working with us through frequencies and in our dream states, and things like that to help clean up the planet. So there's this huge planetary liberation process going on …[384]

Gilliland's information is yet further corroboration that a large fleet of extraterrestrial spacecraft have recently arrived in our solar system and have begun meeting representatives from different spacefaring nations.

Finally, on February 19, 2022, my interview with French contactees Jean Charles Moyen and David Rousseau was released.[385] I asked them respectively what they had heard about the arrival of a new fleet of alien spacecraft. Both said that they had received messages from their primary extraterrestrial contacts with the Galactic Federation/Alliance about the recent arrival of the seeder races that had played roles in establishing ancient civilizations on Earth. The first exchange below is between Moyen [JCM] and I [MS], where he elaborates on information received from his primary extraterrestrial contact (Victor), who is a member of the Galactic Federation/Alliance:

MS: Jean Charles, you talked about the 'seeders' earlier, so can you now maybe give us a little bit

243

more information about what you know of this group of extraterrestrials?

JCM: The Seeders that have just come into our solar system, the only information I have … Victor told me … one week [ago that] … there is a lot of fleets arriving in the solar system to help the Earth. The information is like Elena [Danaan] told you, and I think something very big happening in a few months maybe….

MS: So this is fresh. I mean, Victor just told you this a week ago. So we have another source confirming that a very large fleet of extraterrestrials, the 'Seeders,' have arrived in our solar system to watch what's happening on earth.

JCM: Yeah, it's like a city in a space. There is a very huge mother … spaceship. It's a very huge…. I think some races think … it's not normal what's happening on the Earth, and that they want to help us to change some things, and maybe kick Draco ass in the universe. [386]

I next asked David Rousseau whether he had learned about the Seeders through his primary extraterrestrial contact 'Ezahyel' who is a member of the Galactic Federation/Alliance. Rousseau's reply was translated by his book publisher, Malou Panchèvre [MP]:

MP: Yes, he [David] confirms … that there is a large very large fleet who came into our solar system to observe and to assist humankind in this period. It is a key period because we are here to soon have a big change, and they are here to assist us in this transition period which is very important for all. Not only for us terrestrials but also for them. So … the

Seeders are here because they are part of this process, what is going on here on earth.[387]

MS: So how did David learn about the 'Seeders'? Is this something Ezayel told him or is this something he intuitively knows or got information in some other way?

MP: He says yes ... different sources. One source is Ezahyel because he confirmed to him that yes, the Seeders are back here, and David saw them in a consciousness product projection [out of body experience] where he met them again. He names them "the Ancients"... so he knows they are here again.[388]

There is a significant synchronicity that happened on October 13, 2021, that supports the preceding information about meetings being secretly conducted with the arrival of ancient 'Seeder' extraterrestrials. Jeff Bezos' Blue Origin spacecraft launched with William Shatner, the famed captain from the original Star Trek series, as one of the four astronauts.[389] According to Danaan, the Blue Origin uniforms are a close match to the uniforms of Earth Alliance personnel interacting with the Galactic Federation and other extraterrestrial groups. My speculation is that the October 13 Blue Origin mission was a cover for Shatner and the other three astronauts secretly traveling to Ganymede to participate in the welcoming ceremony for the newly arrived Intergalactic Super-Confederation, and possibly even the Council of Nine. As I mentioned in Chapter 7, cover programs are routinely created for highly classified Special Access Programs, which would certainly include diplomatic meetings with extraterrestrial visitors. Shatner is a tremendously popular worldwide figure and would have made an excellent cultural ambassador for Earth in initial contact meetings with such an important group of visitors.

Shatner's participation in such meetings would also herald humanity officially entering a Star Trek future.

To sum up thus far, there are six sources that confirm that a powerful new group of extraterrestrials arrived in our solar system in October 2021 and established a presence on Jupiter's moon Ganymede. The group appears to be the same as the 24 Civilizations or Intergalactic Confederation discussed in Chapter 5. It is more than coincidental that NASA's Clipper mission to Europa was announced in July 2021, as it provided the perfect cover for a large space convoy to be secretly assembled and sent to its sister moon Ganymede without arousing too much suspicion. The large convoy and development of a human presence on Ganymede at one of the large facilities there also helps explain the worldwide labor shortage that I first discussed in an article about massive Moon construction projects.[390] Finally, the Blue Origin space mission involving William Shatner, with his deep connection to the Star Trek franchise, does lend plausibility to the idea that humanity has officially entered an exciting new phase. We are working with a highly evolved group of extraterrestrial visitors, the Intergalactic Confederation, that have taken up residence on Ganymede and work closely with an even more mysterious extraterrestrial group depicted in *Deep Space Nine* as the Prophets.

Contact with the Council of Nine & Roddenberry's Star Trek Future

One of the most intriguing aspects of Gene Roddenberry's creation of the Star Trek franchise was his relationship with a mysterious extraterrestrial group calling itself the Council of Nine that the psychic Phyllis Schlemmer was channeling in the 1970s. Roddenberry sat in on channeling sessions from 1974 to 1975, and participated in Q & A's recorded in Schlemmer's 1993 book, *the Only Planet of Choice*. In Chapter 4, I covered the history of the Council of Nine and how its information was affirmed as genuine in the famous *Law of One* channeling sessions held from 1981 to

1984, which are widely regarded as the most authoritative channelings ever conducted. These historical events provide essential context for Elena Danaan's contact experiences where she claims to have been taken to Jupiter's moon, Ganymede. There she encountered the Council of Nine and was told why Rodenberry was chosen to prepare humanity for a Star Trek future.

On November 3, 2021, Danaan contacted me about an encounter she had just had with the Council of Nine. This is the same group that accompanied the Intergalactic Confederation that took up residence on Ganymede to observe humanity's global awakening. After the four independent sources describing the new extraterrestrial visitors to our solar system, Danaan told me about being taken to Ganymede where she first met with the Intergalactic Confederation. Her subsequent November 3 encounter focuses on the Council of Nine's relationship with Gene Roddenberry, creator of the Star Trek series.

This is how the message Danaan sent me begins:

> I woke up abruptly, my forehead tingling, with a sensation of a vortex spinning inside of my head. I sat on my bed and saw, in front of me, the ethereal figure of the Tall White woman from the Intergalactic Confederation, whom I had met onboard one of their motherships in the vicinity of Ganymede about a week ago. She expressed herself in the same holographic language composed of thought-form frequency modules. She pointed a finger at my forehead and the extremity of it glowed with green light. At the moment her green-glowing fingertip touched my forehead, I was propelled inwards into a powerful vortex. I felt as if I disintegrated, as if all the molecules of my body stretched into space. In a normal circumstance this could have been frightening, but it seemed that in this state of consciousness, I was unable to experience fright anymore.

A shimmering haze of light materialized ahead of me. It was opalescent white, and contained silvery and golden sparkles. I sensed several presences in it. Then, a soft voice resonated inside of my head with a slight echoing effect. It wasn't theatrical at all, as one could expect; it was instead really soft and gentle, masculine.

" We are the Nine."

My whole being shivered. A few seconds passed, and I started to see humanoid silhouettes forming from the opalescent glittering haze. Nine silhouettes, I suppose, all very tall and slim. As one approached closer to me, I felt a similar sensation like the pressure compressing your ears when you are in a plane and it takes altitude. Well, this was the same sensation but experienced by my whole soul. The being took the appearance of a tall extraterrestrial similar to the Pa-Taal, but I was well aware that these plasma-supra-consciousness beings from "Nine" Collective had, in truth, no real corporeal form. I knew they could shape-shift into anything and the form they chose to represent themselves to me was probably meant to improve my contact experience. The elegant, 9ft tall being had green skin and wore no clothes. He was thin and had a long neck. His head was bald, his skull slightly larger than human at the back, and he had beautiful slanted eyes, sparkly inside in purple and garnet tone. I noticed he had five long elegant fingers at each hand. This was happening for a reason, and as the being remained silent, I understood I probably needed to ask a question.[391]

As discussed earlier, the first communications with the Council of Nine began in 1952, and involved different psychics used by the famed US psychiatrist and paranormal investigator, Dr. Andrija Puharich, to contact extraterrestrial intelligence. After Schlemmer spent 20 years channeling the Council of Nine, she wrote *The Only Planet of Choice*. In it, the Council of Nine explained themselves as follows:

> There are many who try to understand who we are. In your earthliness, it is difficult for you to accept that which you do not understand! At times the attempt to understand colors the truth of the Universe. There are only keys for unlocking portions, for the human mind cannot totally comprehend. There are many interpretations and also many conflicts about who we are. Yes. In a future time, we will attempt to explain ourselves on another level of consciousness, but first Planet Earth must reach that state of evolutionary consciousness where we may be understood, yes. The Council has said do not try to put us into a box, we do not exist in that form, yes.[392]

This description is consistent with the non-corporeal enigmatic forms encountered by Danaan, and the Council of Nine's communications. Crucially, the Council of Nine referred to a future time when they would explain themselves more fully.

What gives strong credence to the existence of the Council of Nine was that they were mentioned in the *Law of One* material, where their operations and identity were discussed.[393] The Council of Nine was identified as a group of nine extraterrestrials associated with a Confederation of Planets, which appears to be identical to the Intergalactic Confederation that recently arrived at Ganymede. Later in the *Law of One* material, the Council of Nine is described as a highly evolved group that resides in the eighth dimension:

Questioner: Where is this **Council** located?

Ra: This **Council** is located in the octave, or eight[h] dimension, of the planet Saturn, taking its place in an area which you understand in third-dimensional terms as the rings.[394]

The precise relationship between the rings of Saturn and Ganymede as the present base of operations of the Intergalactic Confederation and the Council of Nine is yet to be explained. It is now vital to examine the connection between the Council of Nine and Gene Roddenberry.

It is a historical fact that Roddenberry attended Council of Nine channeling sessions and asked them questions from 1974 to 1975. These were personally challenging years for Roddenberry, who had failed to develop another television series after the original *Star Trek* series (1966-1969) had achieved remarkable success in syndicated re-runs. Television network executives continuously frustrated his efforts to develop a follow-up series. Roddenberry had to wait until 1979, when the first of the Star Trek movies appeared for success to come his way, but this was only partial since the Director's position was given to Robert Wise.

In the Council of Nine channeling sessions he attended, Roddenberry was especially intrigued by the prospect of future mass extraterrestrial landings discussed by the Nine. These channelings inspired Roddenberry to write the pilot episode for a future television series that would appear six years after his 1991 death, *Earth the Final Conflict* (1997-2002). Different researchers have summarized the impact that the Council of Nine had on Roddenberry. Here is how an occult researcher, Wes Penre, summarized the connection:

He [Roddenberry] was a member of The Nine Group in 1974-75, and even produced a screenplay for a movie about The Nine. It is also suggested that Roddenberry was deeply inspired by the information he'd received in The Nine sessions when he wrote the early Star Trek movies: *The Next Generation* and *Deep Space Nine* (which was quite a give-away).[395]

The profound impact the Council of Nine channeling sessions had on Roddenberry was also confirmed by another researcher, Chris Knowles, who wrote:

Whatever one might think of The Nine, one thing that can be said without reservation: Roddenberry's experiences with the cult made a huge impression on him, and in many ways would form the basis of the rest of his life's work. As well as the entire Star Trek franchise.[396]

Penre and Knowles' comments provide crucial context for understanding the significance of what the Council of Nine told Elena Danaan [E] about Roddenberry. Her commentary is especially valuable for understanding the full importance of the relationship between the Council of Nine [9], Roddenberry, and humanity's emergence into a Star Trek future:

E: Are you the ones who contacted Gene Roddenberry?

9: Yes.

E: Why?

9: Because we knew there was going to be a temporal war and we needed to create a bridge.

(As he spoke these words into my head, or shall I rather say: as he resonated these words within my consciousness, his holographic language contained far more than words. It carried content: each thought-module carried a story embedded in it. That is how I grasped that this bridge he mentioned was a bond from the past to the future, securing a progressive timeline. A Star Trek future, so to speak. By giving a huge download of information to a group of humans at one specific moment in time, the Nine Collective's intention was to embed into the Collective Unconscious of Humanity the roots of their progressive future, helping humans manifesting it by the creative power of their mind.

They enticed Gene Roddenberry and his entourage to create a popular series that would affect deeply and powerfully the consciousness of Humanity of Earth for the generations to come. They gave a template which was planned to unfold over a period of time, throughout series and movies. *Star Trek* resonated deeply within the consciousness of Humanity, better than any other Science-Fiction production ever made to this day (maybe equaled by *Star Wars* but only because it was so good and referred to the Orion Wars). *Star Trek* echoed an existing future reality by quantum resonance. THIS was the bridge.)

E: And *has this bridge worked?*

9: Yes it has. Now WE are here at the other end of the bridge. You crossed the bridge to your future.

WE are here. WE are the Nine."

(As his words resonated in my being, I was sent backwards into this vortex, sucked back into my dimensional body on Earth. The disorienting sensation of being molecularly scattered infinitely reversed into compact form again. I reintegrated my body. The tall white lady was still here in my room, holding space to relay contact to the Nine Collective. She smiled and vanished in the air. A smell of ozone lingered for a few minutes. I took a deep breath. My head was spinning with vertigo, but I managed to grab my phone and record my experience.)[397]

Danaan's commentary here is vitally important. *Star Trek* was conceived as a bridge to a future reality amid an undeclared temporal war between rival extraterrestrial factions. The success of the *Star Trek* series was therefore attributed to humanity's collective unconscious recognizing it as a potential timeline that needed to be embraced for it to manifest into reality.

Danaan's communication with the Council of Nine is also a stunning confirmation of material in two of my previous books, *The US Navy's Secret Space Program & Nordic Extraterrestrial Alliance* (2017) and *Space Force: Our Star Trek Future* (2021*)*. Both included chapters that discussed the connection between the US Navy, Roddenberry, and the *Star Trek* series. These two books made clear that *Star Trek* was a soft disclosure initiative that was secretly supported by US Naval Intelligence working through Leslie Stevens IV, the creator of the *Outer Limits* TV series (1963-1965), who had secretly helped Roddenberry come up with the original *Star Trek* series.

In addition, my two books made clear that the US Navy had begun cooperating in the early 1950s with a human-looking group of extraterrestrials best described by a former aerospace designer and engineer, William Tompkins, in his autobiography, *Selected by Extraterrestrials* (2015). We now know that the 'Nordics' described by Tompkins were members of the Galactic Federation of Worlds, as Dr. Robert Wood, the Chief Editor of Tompkins books, confirmed in an interview.[398] These historical events confirm that there was indeed a significant extraterrestrial component working with the US Navy and Roddenberry to come up with a soft disclosure initiative that would prepare humanity for a Star Trek future. As

Danaan succinctly pointed out in her commentary, *Star Trek* was a bridge. *Star Trek* would help humankind collectively manifest a positive destiny amid an undeclared 'Temporal War', where negative extraterrestrial forces (Draconian Empire and Orion Alliance) tried to manipulate humanity to bring about a galactic tyranny 350 years in our future. Earlier in this book, I explained how this galactic tyranny was first identified by yet another extraterrestrial organization, the Andromeda Council, who notified the Galactic Federation of Worlds. The Federation subsequently intervened in what had become a wide-ranging galactic Temporal War where different off-world groups were heavily impacting humanity's potential timelines.

Danaan's encounter with the Council of Nine and their confirmation about Roddenberry's role in shaping human aspirations is vital for understanding where humanity is collectively heading. Another historical fact is that the creation of the US Space Force, Space Command, and a multinational space alliance are tied into an official 2019 Space Futures Workshop Report which identified a Star Trek future as humanity's optimal scenario in space.[399] The Council of Nine, through Elena Danaan, has just confirmed that they and other positive extraterrestrial groups have been quietly nurturing a Star Trek future for humanity in a Temporal War, which is coming to a decisive end. Consequently, we owe a huge collective debt of gratitude to Gene Roddenberry and many others who diligently nurtured Star Trek as a bridge to a future reality, which is going to happen far more quickly than anyone anticipated.

CHAPTER 13

Ancient Space Arks Activate with Arrival of Intergalactic Confederation Fleet

> There was a great flood and an ark filled with animals, and there was a Noah fellow and a subject who Noah thought was God. However, after that, the story dramatically diverges from the legends as found in the ancient texts. The ark itself was, in fact, a very large high-tech structure, a spaceship that was mostly submerged underwater at the time of the flood.
>
> —Dr. Courtney Brown, Farsight Institute.

In late December 2021, I began receiving information about ancient extraterrestrial space arks discovered on the Moon, Mars, Earth, and other locations in our solar system. Two sources were the first to independently share critical information about the space arks and how these are being activated. Most importantly, both sources say that a space ark lies buried in a desert region of Ukraine, and its activation very likely triggered Russia's military intervention on February 24, 2022. One source is my US Army insider, JP, who has visited two of these space arks, one on the Moon and another buried under the Atlantic Ocean. The other source is Thor Han Eredyon, a Galactic Federation commander, whose messages were relayed through Elena Danaan. Both JP and Thor Han independently reveal these enormous space arks are activating due to the 2021 arrival of a large fleet of spacecraft belonging to the Intergalactic Confederation—parked in the vicinity of Jupiter and its moon, Ganymede. Thor Han's information gives many details about the arks' history and functions. At the same time, JP describes his visits to the activated space arks on the Moon and under the Atlantic in joint secret missions being conducted by the US, China, Russia, and other members of an "Earth Alliance" led by US Space Command. JP and Thor Han are not alone in claiming space arks are being found and activated in our solar system. Jean Charles Moyen and David Rousseau, two French contactees recruited into a Franco-US secret space program whom I introduced in chapter 11, also claim that ancient space arks exist and began activating in late 2021 with the arrival of fleets of spacecraft belonging to a new group of extraterrestrial visitors.[400]

It would be helpful to provide some historical context to the discussion of a buried space ark in the modern era. Most readers are familiar with the biblical story of Noah's Ark, where the Ark is depicted as a wooden structure built to survive a great flood. What initiated the process was that Noah was commanded by God/Elohim to take with him two animals from each species and to bring plants, seeds, etc., to rebuild human society after the floodwater receded. While the story of Noah's Ark is regarded as part of the canonical texts of the Christian, Hebrew, and Islamic religions, all of which are very similar to, or derive from, the story of Utnapishtim in the Epic of Gilgamesh, there is a scientific explanation that is worth pursuing.[401] Was Noah's Ark actually a very large spacecraft designed to preserve vital biological specimens of a civilization at the end of one era to seed a future era? Were the Elohim (or 'God') that commanded Noah to build the ark really a highly advanced group of extraterrestrials—the 'Seeders' or 'Guardians' discussed in Chapter 5?

Possible answers to these questions come from the Farsight Institute, which conducted a remote viewing experiment of Noah's Ark in February 2022—soon after information about the discovery of ancient space arks began emerging. In his conclusion to the Farsight experiment, which involved three independent remote viewers, Dr. Courtney Brown affirmed—as quoted at the start of this chapter—that Noah's ark was in fact an advanced spacecraft that was mostly submerged during the great flood.[402]

What I found most significant in the Farsight Institute's experiment was that the ark was, in fact, an advanced spacecraft, capable of traveling underwater, that carried a mix of human, animal, and plants intended to renew life after the flood had receded. This summary of Farsight's experiment takes me now to what JP, Thor Han, and others have said about the arks buried under land or submerged under the sea in the modern era.

Moon Space Ark Linked to an Ark under Atlantic Ocean

In the early morning of December 23, 2021, JP claims that he was sent to a secret research facility on the Moon on a triangle-shaped antigravity vehicle and then taken to the giant space ark partially submerged under the lunar surface. JP says China's Yutu 2 Rover had detected part of the craft's exterior and that a joint operation to explore the vessel, which was the size of two aircraft carriers, had begun between US Space Command and the PLA's space force.[403] JP said the giant alien spacecraft under the surface of the Moon was discovered when it started to activate after an extraterrestrial fleet entered our solar system in October 2021, and parked itself between Jupiter and Ganymede. JP participated in an earlier classified mission to Ganymede where he met with some of the extraterrestrial visitors that were based there.[404] JP entered the giant spherical spacecraft accompanied by an archeologist studying its hieroglyphic style writing. JP was one of the military escorts accompanying scientists from the US and China sent to investigate the activated spacecraft.

On January 10, 2022, JP revealed that he participated in another classified mission to an extraterrestrial space ark. Again, the mission began with an official briefing he received at the military base where he is currently serving. Then he was taken by Osprey vertical take-off planes to a large donut-shaped platform in the Atlantic that was placed directly over a submerged ark off the Florida Coast in the vicinity of the Bermuda Triangle.[405] JP estimated the ark to be at least a mile long and ovoid-shaped. An elevator carried mission operators from the ocean surface down into the craft's interior. Personnel were drawn mainly from the US and China. China had been allowed access to the space ark under the Atlantic Ocean as a reciprocal favor after it had allowed the US access to the space ark found by its Yutu 2 Rover on the Moon. There was also a group of indigenous Aztec Indians that participated in the mission. They were left behind after they had separated themselves from the main group and walked deeper into the ark.

Once inside the space ark, JP revealed that space-time operated differently wherein movement was affected noticeably. For example, a simple hand wave would appear as multiple hands moving slowly through the air. He and a few other individuals could activate the ark by simply being physically close to it. JP described how the ark lit up in areas he walked into, but this was not the case with other personnel. When the ark lit up, the hieroglyphic writing became evident. Like on the Moon, there were archeologists present who took photos of the interior of the Ark. JP's primary duty inside the ark was to escort archeologists as they took pictures.

Figure 24. Egyptian and Mayan Hieroglyphs

JP said a second mission to the Atlantic ark was required to locate and rescue the Aztec Mexican group left behind during the first mission. In an interview published on February 2, 2022, JP described the multinational rescue mission, which again comprised US and Chinese soldiers, along with an Aztec Mexican interpreter, but this time they were accompanied by Russian special forces soldiers as well.[406] JP explains how the multinational team quickly found the Aztec Indians and discovered a powerful portal linking the Atlantic Ark to other arks hidden throughout our solar system. He says 15 soldiers had inadvertently stepped through the portal while exploring a similar ark on the Moon. He described the portal as a spherical-shaped ball of blue water floating in the middle of a large room.

At this point, I wish to address a question many have asked about the rather mundane roles JP has played in his covert missions to Ganymede and the Moon, given his low military rank and rather dreary armed escort duties for archeologists.[407] One of the things JP shared in our communications since 2008 is that human-looking extraterrestrials often took him into large hemisphere structures, which he described as arks. He witnessed ancient plants, animals, and technologies preserved for a future time. He also said he met several other individuals taken to these arks—including a Chinese national.

JP said he was taken to these giant arks for a time when they would become necessary for humanity in dealing with planet-wide contingencies. JP began sharing this ark-related information with me in 2014 and I kept this to myself since no one else was talking about it. US covert operatives, however, monitored JP's extraterrestrial contacts and our communications since 2008. This monitoring is evidenced in photos of classified triangle and rectangle-shaped spacecraft he photographed near MacDill Air Force Base in 2017, which he sent to me for public release with the active support of covert operatives.[408] This background leads me to believe that JP is doing far more than simply escorting archeologists to these ancient arks and performing mundane escort duties. Due to his earlier access to the arks or innate "genetic compatibility," he carries some energetic frequency, vibration, or code that activates parts of the craft he is visiting, thereby facilitating the safety and success of missions to these ancient space arks.

Information from Thor Han about the ancient arks gives us additional details about them and corroborates what JP had privately revealed to me earlier. On January 4, 2022, Elena Danaan passed on to me the messages she received from Thor Han about the activation of these ancient space arks in our solar system:

Jan 4, 2022

At 1 am, I am contacted by Thor Han telepathically via my implant.

TH: I have clearance to answer your question about the ancient vessels that activated. Those studied by the Terran scientists. It is exciting to watch them and to guide them as they uncover a past that was hidden for long millenniums. Terran culture has been ready for a long time, but now that threatening shadows are leaving your world, the truth can be unveiled in the open. Finally, the Earth Alliance unfolds the plan elaborated together with the Intergalactic Confederation and the Galactic Federation of Worlds of Nataru [Milky Way Galaxy], exposing what was hidden until this day.

A long time ago, the Intergalactic Confederation had several colonies in this star system. On Naara *(Venus)*, Terra, its moon, Tyr *(Mars),* and the fifth planet. Great wars occurred with the Anunnaki and the colonies left. But before leaving, they gathered the essentials of their knowledge in arks they buried deep on the planets I mentioned. These arks preserved the essential information necessary to rebuild the glory of these colonies if one day this was to happen.[409]

Thor Han's information corroborates what JP shared about his successive missions to space arks buried on the Moon (December 23, 2021) and the Atlantic Ocean (January 10, 2022). In both cases, he entered the giant oval spacecraft accompanying archeologists studying its hieroglyphic style writing that lit up when JP was in the vicinity.

Thor Han's reference to arks belonging to ancient Intergalactic Confederation colonies that were forced to leave millennia ago due to great wars in our solar system is very revealing about their origins. Just as Egypt's Sphinx has long been rumored to be a repository of ancient Atlantean technology, so too there are technological repositories of ancient cultures hidden throughout our solar system. It is helpful to keep in mind that the Atlantean civilization was said to be an offshoot of one of the 24 extraterrestrial civilizations making up the Intergalactic Confederation. According to the Council of Nine information channeled through Phyllis Schlemmer in her book, *The Only Planet of Choice* (1993), Altea established the Atlantis colony on Earth. Thor Han's information tells us that Altea and other extraterrestrial seeder races left arks from their former colonies scattered and hidden throughout Earth and our solar system.

Thor Han next explained how and why the ancient space arks began activating:

> When the fleet from the Intergalactic Confederation approached this star system, the arks activated. It was time. The return of the Seeders marks the beginning of a new era when Terrans are ready to receive the long-time hidden knowledge. No rules are broken when the Terrans do their own research and discover the keys by themselves. You understand this knowledge and technology couldn't fall into the wrong hands. The arrival of the Seeders occurs when the enemy has lost all power and possessions in this star system. The time is right, now. Also, I was authorized to tell you that two great archaeological discoveries are imminent on Terra, this year. It will change the way Terrans look at the

> chronology of their History. What they believed was
> truth carved in stone will flow like water.[410]

Thor Han's message reveals that these ancient arks were well-hidden and kept away from the Dark Fleet and its extraterrestrial allies that, until recently, dominated our planet. Most importantly, the Cabal/Deep State that controlled powerful secret space programs looked for these arks but could not find most of them. Now that the "Dark Alliance" has been forced to leave our solar system, the hidden ancient technologies are being activated so they can be found and explored by the Earth Alliance created in July 2021 with the "Jupiter Agreements." Now the time had arrived for these technologies to be openly shared so humanity could learn about long-forgotten extraterrestrial colonies, their advanced cultures, and technologies—before devastating wars led to their demise.

Danaan next had a Q and A with Thor Han:

> E: What you just said, this last sentence, it's a metaphor that foretells a story, right? I know you: *"What they believed was truth carved in stone will flow like water."* (TH laughs). Can you talk about what is in these arks?

> TH: Great technology that will change everything.

> E: What do these arks look like?

> TH: Elongated and some are miles long. Crystal technology.

> E: What do you mean?

> TH: The Intergalactic Confederation largely uses crystalline materials to transcend densities, that a built structure can simultaneously exist in several densities.

E: Such as the crystalline architecture I saw inside of the motherships of the Intergalactic Confederation? Does that mean these ships are solid in different densities at the same time?

TH: Correct. Terrans haven't yet discovered all the capacities of crystals. Core engines are powered by crystals, portals are made of fluid crystals, time devices, pyramidal energy generators, and more. These density belts that we wear, are made with nano-crystals. The fabric of our suits, our weapons, the skin of our ships...[411]

What's crucial here is that JP said that when he entered the arks found on the Moon and under the Atlantic Ocean, the crystal inside of it was Moldavite. He said it created a pleasant vibration that helped elevate consciousness. Given JP's earlier exposure to arks or his inherent genetic traits, it is very likely that he carried the right frequency that the ark's consciousness would recognize.

Elena Danaan's Q and A with Thor Han continued:

E: So these buried ships have activated at the arrival of the Intergalactic Confederation.

TH: They received the signal and responded by resonance, due to the simple proximity of the mother fleet. Remember what I showed you, certain ships are living entities. They woke up. Although, your people knew already about some of these locations. We left some clues for them to find. The Dark Fleet found one of these arks, under the ice of Antarctica, but they could never activate its power and use its potential. One of the reasons why the Intergalactic Confederation was waiting.[412]

This Antarctica reference is very meaningful given that JP received coordinates from an unnamed Lt. Colonel that pointed to what appeared to be an artificial structure in the frozen continent that was in an area used by the Dark Fleet until mid-2021.[413] The artificial structure shown at the coordinates may be linked to one of the arks hidden underneath or nearby such as the mysterious Lake Vostok.

Lake Vostok Ark

On March 18, 2022, news emerged of a heatwave in East Antarctica, the epicenter of which was the Vostok region that sits atop a mysterious lake two miles under the ice sheet. Scientists were baffled by the heat surge of more than 70 degrees above average temperatures and sought answers. A likely explanation comes from two sources who say an ancient ark is buried under the ice sheet in the Vostok region, and its activation was heating East Antarctica.

The *Washington Post* was the first to reveal the heatwave in East Antarctica. In a story titled "It's 70 degrees warmer than normal in eastern Antarctica. Scientists are flabbergasted", this is what was reported:

> The average high temperature in Vostok — at the center of the eastern ice sheet — is around minus-63 (minus-53 Celsius) in March. But on Friday, the temperature leaped to zero (minus-17.7 Celsius), the warmest it's been there during March since record keeping began 65 years ago. It broke the previous monthly record by a staggering 27 degrees (15 Celsius).[414]

Antarctic scientists are baffled by the heatwave in late March since "Antarctica is losing about 25 minutes of sunlight each day," according to what they told the *Washington Post*. Meteorologists reported a "heat dome" over East Antarctica and said, "[T]his is not something we've seen before."[415] Significantly, the *Washington Post* reported that there had been notable melting of the ice sheet in the region.

The unexplained mystery behind the rapid heating takes me to the discovery of a large magnetic anomaly at one end of Lake Vostok, as first reported in *The Antarctic Sun* on February 4, 2001.[416] According to scientific measurements, the anomaly's size was 65 by 46 miles (105 by 75 km). Veteran NASA researchers Richard Hoagland and Mike Bara soon after proposed the anomaly may be a buried city:

> An anomaly like this could also be caused by an accumulation of *metals* -- the kind you would get if you found *the ruins of an ancient, buried city!*

> An "ancient city under the ice?" Such a discovery would be absolutely dazzling, sending shockwaves through our world as profound as the discovery of "artifacts on Mars" or "ruins on the Moon." And the notion is not as improbable as you may think.[417]

Since 2001, there have been multiple sources that claim they have visited or been briefed about an ancient city or large alien motherships buried under the ice sheets either at Lake Vostok or other areas in Antarctica.[418] What could be driving the heatwave and heat dome over East Antarctica? Is it connected to the magnetic anomaly at Lake Vostok two miles under the ice sheet? While meteorologists struggle to give a conventional explanation, they admit to being baffled by what is happening. There is another non-conventional explanation for what is driving the heatwave in east Antarctica — a space ark buried under the Vostok region that has begun activating!

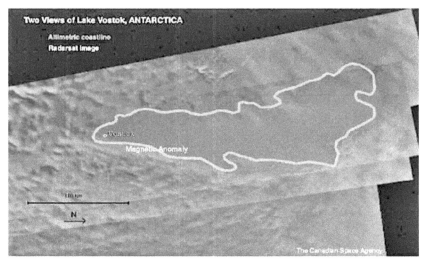

Radar Image of Lake

Figure 25 Ground-penetrating radar image of a lake under Vostok base with magnetic anomaly

On March 29, 2022, I was contacted by Jean Charles Moyen, who reported an extraterrestrial-related teleportation experience first to Ireland, where he met Elena Danaan. He next traveled with her to a Galactic Federation of Worlds mothership in Earth orbit. They were then taken to Lake Vostok, Antarctica, where they saw a space ark under the ice. Critically, they both entered and saw some of the interior of the ancient ark. Here is how Moyen summarized it all:

> Monday, March 28, 3:33 a.m. Here is what I experienced!!!
>
> Last night I was working on South Shore Origin 2, I got up to lie down on the couch in my office because my head was spinning (too much computer probably), and all of a sudden, I felt myself go into the couch and I passed out.
>
> When I opened my eyes, I found myself in the path of the other time in Ireland, and I heard, remember,

remember, and I saw the same scene again but until the end without interruption !!! Elena was holding my hand and said, I'm going to introduce you to the family and then I saw the next part ...

I felt tingling all over my body, exactly the same sensation as when you sleep on your arm and the blood comes back in it. You know that scary tingling sensation. Suddenly I was up on a ship, in a big control room with a huge view of space and Elena was next to me and she said to me, you saw, it's beautiful the view. I like to come here; it relaxes me to see the Earth like this; it calms me. And there in the middle stood Melanie [Jean Charles's wife] in a tight silver suit! Who said you were surprised to see me here, honey!!! Elena and I have known each other for a long time and we are friends, but I'll let you continue your visit, and she teleported herself!!!

And then someone came up behind us, I instantly felt his energy, and the hairs on my arms stood up as if electrified. I turned around and saw a man in a uniform with shoulder pads, almond-shaped eyes of a very luminous lagoon color, and beautiful blond hair that looked like an angel as in the Bible. There was no flaw on his face. It was disturbing to see the perfection of his features. He smiled at me, and I heard in my mind relax, my friend, you know who I am, and he came closer and put his fingers in a triangular shape on my forehead and temples, and I found myself surrounded by translucent blue ice, I said: where are we? He told me under Antarctica, precisely under the lake Vostok, where there is an ark.

And I turned around and Elena was there in a tight-fitting suit that pulsed a kind of bluish energy with heat to regulate your temperature. I had no suit, but I had the same bluish energy around me. And I said, "but why are we here?" And I heard, "because you are all the keys to the awakening of humanity."

And suddenly, I felt myself being pulled backwards as if I was falling into a hole, and I woke up with a start with my heart pounding in my chest. It was precisely 3:33.[419]

In a subsequent interview published on April 29, 2022, Moyen revealed that the angelic-looking extraterrestrial in a uniform was none other than Thor Han Eredyon.[420] Crucially, in the interview, which also included Danaan, she confirmed that Thor Han was indeed coordinating the joint teleportation experiences involving her and Moyen to the Lake Vostok ark, and influencing the process by which the information would be publicly released.

This was not known to me on March 29 when I first received Jean Charles's information and contacted Danaan to see if she or Thor Han had any info about Lake Vostok and what Moyen had experienced. The response from Thor Han to my inquiry was stunning and gave critical information that explains the heatwave and melting ice in the Vostok region:

LAKE VOSTOK
March 29, 2022

The civilization that left technology under the melting ice of Antarctica wasn't from Nataru [Milky Way Galaxy]. There were ancient times when the climate of this planet was different, when the magnetic poles were located in different places. The land was green and fertile and the climate was warm, in the land you call now Antarctica. An important colony was settled there. They were of

> the Pa-Taal. They lived in peace and prosperity. It was a great civilization, told about in your ancient tales as a lost continent. In truth, it was never lost but forgotten, under the ice, for a reason. They left gifts, large crafts, and structures in the subterranean web of heated caverns. The structures under Lake Vostok were known for a long time by your scientists working in the secret programs. The Earth Alliance knew, and it was the bait to bring financial elites down to Antarctica for the last meeting. They never saw the arks; they were never taken there. But this is another story. The ark under Vostok Lake is part of a much larger structure of halls and temples. A powerful pyramid generator is also there. None could activate it yet.[421]

Thor Han appears to be describing an ancient civilization such as Atlantis, which has long been rumored to be buried under the ice sheets after the last cataclysmic earth changes occurred 11,600 years ago. A book by researchers Rand Flem-Ath and Rose Flem-Ath, *Atlantis beneath the Ice: The Fate of the Lost Continent* (2012), presents compelling evidence for such a claim.

In addition, Thor Han refers to recent meetings held in Antarctica where the cabal (aka Deep State leaders) secretly traveled to negotiate with the Earth Alliance and the Galactic Federation about their future.[422] The cabal reneged on whatever deal was reached and continued to cause chaos on Earth, as evidenced by global events up to April 2022. Thor Han continued his update:

> Not only the Earth Alliance and the Nataru Alliance knew about it, but also the enemy. The Ciakahrr stormed and took place under Vostok, hoping to crack the codes of this technology. They welcomed the humans of the Nazi group that you call the Fourth Reich to help decrypt this technology. Did

you think that they accepted human colonies there in Antarctica for no reason? What do you think they were getting in exchange for technology and weapons? DNA. The Ciakahrrs knew DNA was the key to activating these power structures. But even though they looked into finding the right DNA frequency codes, they never succeeded in activating these structures.

The Intergalactic Confederation has more than one safety lock on these structures, and what comes with DNA is Consciousness. The body envelope and the inhabiting soul need to be of the same frequency, and the person needs to be alive and conscious, and know what to do, how to activate the commands, and unlock the portals. You need the knowledge that goes with the tools. You cannot kill someone and only use their DNA sample, because it needs to be inhabited by consciousness. By an original soul part of the Seeders, who have this knowledge. Bodies are also there in stasis, and they were found a long time ago. But their genetic material isn't enough, because the soul has gone and awaits to come back.

Now, the ice is melting to reveal in plain sight the secrets we liberated for you.[423]

As mentioned earlier, JP has traveled to arks on the Moon and under the Atlantic Ocean, where a multinational team drawn from the US, China, and Russia has been researching the ancient arks. JP confirmed that the arks are activated by the DNA of a select number of individuals. Consequently, it is very plausible that the Draco Reptilians, aka Ciakharr, used the Nazis to get access to human DNA they could use to activate the arks. In addition, JP has revealed that the activating arks are releasing a tremendous amount of heat, quickly warming up the surrounding environment.[424]

In a voice communication received on March 29, Danaan confirmed that she had been taken to Lake Vostok with Moyen in the early morning of the previous day:

> This is now the explanation why I wasn't allowed to remember this moment because it was meant that Jean Charles remembers. I think it's a good strategy that they scatter information, not always the same person you know. I find it very good. Then there was a lot of also holographic projection around Jean Charles to show him, make him confident and settled in the project ... Melanie was there as well to make him confident, but I was really there and with him, and I remember now, but he was meant to be the one to remember first because as Thor Han always says, remembering is activating. So now we can confirm about Lake Vostok.

Danaan's confirmation shows that the Galactic Federation, through Thor Han, is now taking at least two individuals to visit the space arks, witness the contents, and report their experiences to the world.

In a follow-up message from Moyen on March 29, 2022, he explains being taken on a second trip to Lake Vostok earlier in the morning of that day:

> This night, I found myself in the same place under Lake Vostok, but this time I was inside a structure. It was the Ark. Everything was purified inside, no screws, nor bolts, nothing. It looked like tungsten but translucent. I was in the center, and in the middle, there was a kind of sphere which turned very luminous. They would have said a ball of bluish plasma which gave off a lot of heat by emitting a

271

crystalline noise and around was laid out in a geometrical form resembling a star ... tubes in which there were beings in stasis.

I approached one of the tubes, and when I approached, it reacted by lighting up as if my presence triggered it. I felt in connection with the material of the vessel. The structure seemed alive. I could see the appearance of the being in the tube, he was tall, and his skin had bluish reflections. He was wearing a kind of midnight blue suit without any seams. There was a symbol on the suit representing a triangle with a constellation inside. And I heard a voice coming out of nowhere saying to me, "you have been chosen," it was the same sentence that the Mantis [being] had said to me as a child when she put her paws on my shoulder, you remember, during the test of fear with the other children? Many of them had failed except me. Well, it was the same voice. I approached a tube, and it lit up very brightly; and I woke up suddenly, and on the alarm clock, it was 5:55.[425]

Moyen's information matches what JP said he had encountered during his two trips to the submerged Atlantic space ark. Moyen described a blue ball of liquid (plasma) in one large room, which was a portal to other space arks. In addition, Moyen witnessed many pod-like structures whose contents were not seen by JP, but he said he was briefed that they radiated friendly energy.[426] In my April 29, 2022, interview with both Moyen and Danaan, she confirmed seeing the pod-like structures with blue beings inside of them. She witnessed Moyen interact with one of the pods and walk around the ark.[427]

In conclusion, the experiences released by Jean Charles Moyen and Elena Danaan, when combined with the earlier revelations from JP, all suggest that an ancient ark is activating and warming up the Vostok region and the rest of East Antarctica. Furthermore, the ancient ark is almost certainly linked in some way to the large magnetic anomaly discovered at one corner of Lake Vostok back in 2001. The record temperatures in East Antarctica recently reported by the *Washington Post* suggest the heating up process caused by the activating ark(s) is unstoppable. It, therefore, is only a matter of time before the world will be confronted by indisputable physical evidence of an ancient Atlantean civilization buried under Antarctica, and the existence of large space arks buried in Antarctica and other locations around the planet.

What will be even more exciting for the general public and many readers, in particular, is the revelation that the sleeping 'blue giants 'in the space arks are human starseeds currently living normal lives on Earth.[428] These starseeds are destined to awaken to their DNA or "soul" connection to the hibernating crews of the activating space arks through dreams, visions, and eventually physical travel there, as happened with Jean Charles Moyen and Elena Danaan. Critically, in our April 29, 2022, interview, both Moyen and Danaan described how both human and extraterrestrial bodies could be awakened and simultaneously function, depending on how the 'soul' or consciousness is shared between the two physical bodies.

Another possible Antarctic location of a space ark emerges from the testimony of two special operators that spoke with Veteran UFO researcher Linda Moulton Howe. Their testimonies were released in January 2019 and revealed their participation in missions to a massive octagon-shaped structure found near Beardmore Glacier, Antarctica, in 2003. Howe initially reported the discovery thus:

> In 2003, a U.S. Navy Seal Special Operation team traveled to Antarctica to investigate a perfectly geometric 8-sided octagon structure discovered by ground penetrating radar near Beardmore Glacier, about 93 miles from the American McMurdo Station.

> Another previous team of engineers and scientists
> had dug out the top layer of one octagon made of a
> pure black substance that was built on top of two
> more black octagonal structures that went down
> deep into the 2-mile-thick ice.[429]

Only part of the Octagon-shaped structure, the Navy Seal stated, had been uncovered so far by the archeological teams, with the rest buried under the ice and extending far below. Ground penetrating radar had shown the structure to be octagon-shaped and covered 62 acres (about 0.5 square kilometers).

The Navy Seal described the walls and doors as being covered by hieroglyphs that were about eight inches (20 cm) high and about two inches (5 cm) deep. The hieroglyphs were neither Egyptian nor Mayan, but appeared similar to both in depicting animals and other strange symbols. Similarly, JP said that the giant space arks he witnessed on the Moon and under the Atlantic were filled with hieroglyphs recorded by the archeologist he escorted. The hieroglyphs make it possible that the ancient octagon structure described by the Navy Seal was one of the arks discovered by the Deep State and their Dark Fleet allies.

The Ukraine Space Ark

On February 2, 2022, JP gave me the geographical coordinates (46°35'19"N 33°03'01"E) to a space ark he was told exists in Ukraine. The coordinates are for the Oleshky Sands National Nature Park, which is the only sand desert in Ukraine and has long been a tourist attraction. The origins of the sand desert have puzzled geologists and there has been speculation that it is a result of historical overgrazing by sheep.[430] On February 11, JP told me: "The Russians wants to get to the Ukrainian Ark as soon as possible because they found some information that leads to the Ukrainian Ark." His revelation is critical as it raises a possible new factor in the Ukraine conflict that may have been the real trigger for Russia's "special military operation" less than two weeks later, on February 24. JP later described what he was told about the Ukrainian space ark in briefings and by others participating in the covert missions to ancient arks being found all over our solar system and on Earth.

Figure 26. Oleshky Sands National Park, Ukraine. Source: Google Earth

On the day of Russia's military intervention, he left me the following voice message describing his new intel about space arks being found in Russia and Ukraine:

> Remember I was telling you about the ark? There were Russians surrounding the ship that we were on [in the Atlantic Ocean]. They really wanted information. That's why they went down to the [Atlantic] ark with us. We gave them the opportunity to come down. We didn't have any problem, you know, bringing the Russians in and sharing information; because, we know that this was huge, worldwide, huge, you know this is humongous.

> So all the world leaders need to know about this. But they did not keep their side of the promise right now, taking us to their ark, but now with this happening in Ukraine —that ark that is over there, I guess they want that information for them. We were about to go to that ark.

> Don't be surprised if it starts activation, Oleshky Desert National Park [aka Oleshkey Sands], and probably gets to be one of the first ships to go up in the air. Everybody sees. Now that the nations in the world [attention] is ... on Ukraine, this is probably going to be one the first ones that's going to go up and everybody is going to see it. Everything is going to come to a halt. Everybody is going to be shocked because of this.[431]

JP's revelation that the space ark found in Ukraine is activating and US military authorities were ready to go in to investigate is very telling in terms of why Russia chose to openly intervene in the Ukraine conflict. JP later revealed that a US special forces team had indeed been sent to the Ukraine ark through a portal and had been briefly trapped due to the unfolding fighting before safely leaving.[432] Even more astounding is his prediction that the Ukrainian ark will eventually begin flying into the air. Indeed, with the world's attention fixated on Ukraine, a flying space ark would become a global event of profound significance.

On February 26, during my "What's Coming in 2022" webinar, I publicly revealed what JP had told me about the Ukrainian space ark.[433] Two days after my webinar, I received important corroborating information from Thor Han Eredyon, a Fleet Commander of the Galactic Federation of Worlds, as relayed through Elena Danaan. Two days after my webinar, Danaan relayed to me the following information from Thor Han about Russia's "special military operation" into Ukraine and the Deep State's (DS) involvement with the ark:

> This is not an invasion of Ukraine but part of the cleansing operations. The DS was attempting to activate the Ark, which they had found many years ago buried underneath the sand in the lower southern part of Ukraine. The ark activated, so it was time Putin got his hands on it. There is a second ark in the north of Russia, but Putin already has control of it.[434]

Thor Han's information corroborated what JP had been told about two space arks found in the region — one in Russia and another in Ukraine. It is very significant that the Deep State has maintained a strong influence over Ukraine since 2014 and was attempting to activate the space ark found in a sandy region of southern Ukraine—Oleshky Sands.

On March 1, 2022, Thor Han revealed more about the buried Ukraine space ark:

> Putin has his hands on the other ark in the north of Russia, and he has been taught by positive extraterrestrials how to use this technology.
>
> It is information without consequence because this ark in north Russia is secured and in good hands, contrarily to the Ukrainian ark, which … [from] this day (March 1, 2022) is in the hands of the Earth Alliance. It is still fought for by the DS military based in the south of Ukraine, near the ark "buried in the sand." [435]

Thor Han's information corroborates what JP had been told about Russia's control over a space ark found in its territory.

By March 2, 2022, Russia had defeated the Ukrainian military and had gained complete control over Kherson, including the nearby Oleshky Sands National Nature Park. Kherson was the first Ukrainian city to fall to the Russian army, which is highly significant given claims of an ancient space ark found under Oleshky Sands. As I mentioned earlier, JP shared the coordinates of the Ukraine Space ark on February 2, 2022, and then told me on February 11 that Russia wanted to gain access. Russia very likely learned that the US would investigate the Ukraine ark and would send a special forces team there soon.

Consequently, the discovery of a space ark that is activating under Oleshky Sands provides a compelling reason for why Russia decided to finally openly intervene in the Ukraine civil war—a conflict that has been ongoing since 2014.[436] Something dramatic must have happened behind the scenes to motivate Russia to intervene in a civil war that was stalled due to the lack of progress on implementing the Minsk Agreements signed in 2014 and 2015 by Russia, France, Germany, Ukraine, and the Organization for Security and Cooperation in Europe.[437] However, there are other possible explanations that need to be examined to get a clearer idea of why Russia made the fateful decision to launch its "special military operation."

In early February 2022, there were rumors that the Ukrainian army was preparing a lightning military campaign to retake the contested Donetsk and Lugansk administrative regions (Oblasts) of Ukraine.[438] Ukraine was secretly seeking to emulate Croatia's lightning military strike (Operation Storm) against rebel-held Serbian areas that ended the Croatian component of the Yugoslav civil war in 1995 after significant US military assistance had changed the military balance of power.[439] These rumors were later confirmed to be true when on March 8, 2022, Russia released captured plans of the impending Ukrainian military attack that proved Ukraine's intention to violate the Minsk Agreement.[440] Preempting a Ukrainian military attack would undoubtedly have been a compelling reason for Russia's military intervention. However, it would not have required a Russian air, sea, and land attack on three fronts, but only an attack from the East to take out the prepositioned Ukrainian forces preparing to attack Donetsk and Lugansk regions.

Another possible reason for the Russian intervention is that US-sponsored biolabs were being used by the Deep State for future biological weapons attacks against Russia. On February 24, *Veterans Today* published a comprehensively researched article by Dilyana Gaytandzhieva, a Bulgarian investigative journalist, detailing the Pentagon's biological weapons research in several East European countries, including Ukraine, that would specifically target Russia.[441] Official US State Department documents confirmed that US funds were being sent to biolabs in Ukraine,[442] but senior US officials denied that American funds were used for biological warfare research.[443] Once again, Russia released captured documents proving that biological warfare experiments were conducted in Ukraine at US-funded biolabs.[444] While this is again a plausible scenario for Russian military intervention, the problem here is that Russia and the US have long conducted chemical and biological warfare without leading to outright military hostilities.

Consequently, the discovery of a buried space ark and Russia's desire to take complete control of it after it began activating offers a more compelling explanation for the Russian military moving in and taking over Ukrainian territory far from the contested Donetsk and Lugansk regions to the east. Russia's rapid takeover of Kherson is powerful circumstantial evidence that supports the revelations of JP and Thor Han/Elena Danaan about an ancient space ark found under the Oleshky Sands National Nature Park and that this was the decisive factor in Russia's "special military operation" into Ukraine. Nevertheless, once the decision had been taken to intervene to gain control of the ark, Russia announced that the reasons for military intervention were to prevent a planned Ukrainian military assault on Donetsk and Luhansk, and the eradication of biolabs targeting ethnic Russians.

How Many Space Arks are on Earth?

The question over how many space arks are presently on Earth was addressed in a communication between Elena Danaan [E] and Thor Han [TH]:

> E: How many arks are on Earth?

> TH: I am not allowed to tell you, and don't try to read my mind!

> E: I won't. You know I respect the rules. But I know already there is one in Egypt somewhere.

> TH: South America, Central Europe, North-West of Russia… One under the waters of the Atlantic Ocean. This one is the biggest. There are others as well, but I won't tell any precise coordinates. It is not of my responsibility but that of the Earth Alliance.

> E: You won't be in trouble, right?

> TH: No. What I am telling you is validated by my superiors. Since you were calibrated on military frequency, they are listening to all our conversations passing through your device.

> E: Is there anything else that you can tell me that the world doesn't know yet?

> TH: Each revelation comes in time. There is a plan. Terran civilians will come this year to the complete realization and acceptance of other positive galactic cultures. Politically, many changes are on the way. But I must say no more for the safety of the plan.

The Earth Alliance is in charge of pretty much everything. Be patient.

E: Thank you, I will pass on this info to Michael.

TH: Give him my warm salutations. One day we will meet, but not yet.

Thor Han's information here corroborates what JP was told about Space Arks being found all over the Earth and the one under the Atlantic being the largest. Furthermore, Thor Han's statement that this year, 2022, will be when there will be "complete realization and acceptance of other positive galactic cultures" is very telling—the Galactic Federation has sophisticated time travel technologies it can utilize for its future projections. His optimistic statement indicates that the Deep State's hold on political power around the planet is crumbling and that soon the walls of secrecy will collapse.

At the time of writing, JP had revealed that he had learned in classified briefings that nine space arks had been found around the world that are either buried underground or under an ocean. He has identified the following:

- one in Antarctica (Lake Vostok/Beardmore Glacier),
- one in Russia,
- two in Ukraine (Oleshky Sands, Kherson, and near Kyiv),
- one in central Europe,
- one in Brazil (Caldas Novas Mountain State Park),
- one under the Atlantic Ocean (in the Bermuda region),
- one under the Pacific Ocean (due west of Vancouver Island),
- and one in the USA (White Sands Missile Range, New Mexico).

In an interview published on March 10, 2022, JP said that all the arks form an integrated network that will coordinate with one another in terms of their activation, the release of their contents, and eventually flying into the air where they will be witnessed around the world.[445] The discovery and activation of these ancient space arks are destined to play a major role in humanity's awakening. As a result of the space arks following some unknown timeline that results in them eventually revealing themselves in a way that cannot be suppressed by government or military authorities, this will lead to two main scenarios for what's coming. These respective scenarios heavily depend on whether the Deep State or the Earth Alliance controls the mainstream media and military/government institutions at the time of the arks' worldwide public emergence.

The pessimistic scenario is that the Deep State will stage a false flag alien invasion where it uses its hidden fleets of antigravity spacecraft, which were identified as UAPs in reports by US Navy pilots, to begin a campaign of attacking the military assets of the US and other nations. The mainstream media would predictably launch a saturation campaign depicting the Earth under attack by unknown UAPs. Consequently, the global public would infer that any floating arks that suddenly appear are part of this alien invasion. In Chapter 4, I discussed this same scenario anticipated by the Council of Nine in the mid-1970s and why the decision was taken for the 24 civilizations/Intergalactic Confederation not to reveal themselves back then. If this scenario were to play out, the resulting confusion and chaos would make it very difficult for the Earth Alliance and positive extraterrestrial organizations to convince the global public that the arks are a gift to humanity rather than an existential threat.

The optimistic scenario is that the Deep State is sufficiently defanged by worldwide operations of the Earth Alliance—including Russia's special military operation in Ukraine—that official announcements about the existence of the Intergalactic Confederation, Galactic Federation of Worlds, and other extraterrestrial organizations can move forward in a calm, peaceful, and reassuring way. Their presence would be revealed in official disclosures by national governments that are coordinated with the Earth Alliance and US Space Command. Critically, these announcements will reveal advanced technologies found in ancient arks built by humanity's ancestors many millennia ago. The stage would then be set for the space arks appearing in our skies without arousing public fear, but instead creating hope for the dawn of a new age.

CHAPTER 14

Exopolitics & Disclosure in the 2020s

Exopolitics is the convergence of a new interdisciplinary science, an international political movement and a new paradigm, which all deal with the wide range of implications of extraterrestrial life.

—Exopolitics Institute, Short Definition, 2009

In December 2021, the 2022 National Defense Authorization Act (NDAA) for the US was signed into law with little public awareness of key provisions for creating an office for Unidentified Aerial Phenomena (UAP) within 180 days. The Pentagon and the Office of the Director of National Intelligence were authorized to set up an "office, organizational structure, and authorities to address unidentified aerial phenomena."[446] The proposed office will monitor UFO reports and the potential threat they pose to US national security. A few weeks earlier, on November 23, 2021, the Department of Defense had created the Airborne Object Identification and Management Synchronization Group to replace the Navy's UAP Task Force.[447] The new Pentagon office, with the difficult to remember acronym (AOIMSG), failed to impress key members of Congress that the Pentagon was going to seriously investigate UAPs/UFOs and be transparent about its findings to Congress. The 2022 NDAA now requires the Pentagon and the Intelligence Community to develop a joint office that would regularly report to Congress and allow members to question officials from the new office about UFO activity.

In a sure sign that major developments were expected on the extraterrestrial front, NASA sponsored a program at the Center for Theological Inquiry at Princeton University to find out how world religions would react to news of the discovery of life from out-of-this-world. Twenty-four theologians had participated in the NASA program by December 2021.[448] What appeared to drive NASA's unprecedented interest in theological opinions was the successful launch and deployment of the James Webb Space Telescope on December 25, 2021.[449] The Webb Telescope is far more potent than its predecessor, the Hubble Space Telescope, and can detect biosignatures in distant solar systems. It is anticipated that just as the Hubble and Kepler telescopes revolutionized the mainstream scientific community and the general public with the discovery of exoplanets, the Webb telescope will do the same with the discovery of extraterrestrial life. It was not just one exoplanet discovered by the Hubble and Kepler telescopes, but hundreds and eventually thousands.[450] We can anticipate the same process repeating over the rest of this decade as the Webb telescope begins detecting biosignatures in distant solar systems, likely as close as our nearest neighbors, the Alpha and Proxima Centauri star systems. Hence the need for NASA to get an idea of how world religion would react to any future announcement that the Webb telescope has detected biosignatures that confirm the existence of extraterrestrial life.

An attempt by NASA to find out how the world would react to the discovery of extraterrestrial life had had occurred 60 years earlier when NASA commissioned the Brookings Institute to report about the implications of the discovery of extraterrestrial life. The 1961 Brookings Report to the US Congress pointed to the potential for civilizational collapse with the appearance of more technologically advanced extraterrestrial societies:

> Anthropological files contain many examples of societies, sure of their place in the universe, which have disintegrated when they had to associate with previously unfamiliar societies espousing different ideas and different life ways.[451]

The Brookings Report also described the unpredictability of societal reactions to the discovery of extraterrestrial artifacts:

> Evidences of its [extraterrestrial] existence might also be found in artifacts left on the Moon or other planets. The consequences for attitudes and values are unpredictable, but would vary profoundly in different cultures and between groups within complex societies; a crucial factor would be the nature of the communication between us and the other beings.[452]

The Brookings Report went on to raise the possibility of suppressing any announcement concerning the discovery of extraterrestrial life or artifacts for national security reasons: "How might such information, under what circumstances, be presented or withheld from the public?"[453] Significantly, the report pointed out:

> [O]f all groups, scientists and engineers might be the most devastated by the discovery of relatively superior creatures, since these professions are most clearly associated with mastery of nature.[454]

The Brookings Report provides the first officially sanctioned analysis of the public policy implications of discovering extraterrestrial life or artifacts. The report confirmed the unpredictability of societal responses around the globe and raised the possibility of societal collapse. The Brookings Report also played a key role in senior policymakers' decision to withhold information from the public about both the discovery of—and our official contact with—extraterrestrial life that had already occurred but had been suppressed by successive Presidential administrations.[455]

The Brookings Report's public policy option of withholding the truth about extraterrestrial life was made possible by an earlier

1953 report issued by a CIA-sponsored panel. In January 1953, a group of scientists chaired by Dr. H. P. Robertson and covertly funded by the CIA, recommended that UFO (aka flying saucer) sightings be debunked. The rationale given was the potential for UFO events to be manipulated by 'foreign powers' in a way that would undermine U.S. national security. The panel recommended an "educational program" to deter the general public from demanding a serious investigation of UFO sightings.[456] The Robertson Panel recommended debunking UFO reports through the mass media and the entertainment industry.

Today, an official announcement that extraterrestrial life exists in distant solar systems is certain to drive public interest towards thousands of historical accounts by contactees, abductees, whistleblowers, insiders, and researchers that extraterrestrials have been visiting Earth for decades, but the facts had been covered up. The groundswell of public interest and investigations of such historical reports, which will finally be taken seriously, will have an enormous effect on how the general public thinks and behaves regarding UFOs and extraterrestrial life. The former policy of ridiculing reports of extraterrestrial contact—implemented in 1953 by the CIA sponsored Robertson Panel—will be finally abandoned.

All these developments stemming from any official announcement that the Webb Telescope has detected extraterrestrial life will force the secrecy wall to collapse, and many long-hidden truths will be revealed. It can be anticipated that whatever is released by the Pentagon and the Intelligence Community through their joint office being set up due to the 2022 NDAA will be skewed in a way that manipulates public opinion for the benefit of the corporations behind the military industrial complex. Threat perceptions and national security will be predictably emphasized by the Pentagon and Intelligence Community, and used to justify the decades-long secrecy that has kept the public in the dark about extraterrestrial life. Nevertheless, once there has been an official acknowledgment that extraterrestrial life exists, the general public will undoubtedly inquire about its impact on society, the economy, science, medicine, space travel, etc. All these areas will experience dramatic shifts, but the changes to world religion are especially significant. People will ask, if extraterrestrials exist, could they have played a hand in the creation of humanity?

The impact on world religion is when things will get very interesting. The role of the Intergalactic Confederation—the 24 Civilizations seeding humanity—will become a hot topic of discussion. If extraterrestrials seeded humankind over the course of many millennia, then did they also play a role in the creation of world religions? Questions will be naturally asked whether Krishna, Buddha, Lao Tsu, Jesus, Muhammed, etc., were in some way connected to alien life. Were they "starseeds," "walk-ins," "alien babies" dropped off in immaculate conceptions, etc.? World religions will begin to dramatically change as believers question what role extraterrestrials played. New religions are destined to emerge, some with the help of extraterrestrial visitors. What happens to world religions if the extraterrestrial arks activating on Earth and around our solar system begin to reveal themselves and open their ancient vaults for the benefit of all humanity? Will such a profound revelation occur in the confusion created by what remains of the Deep State as they stage their alien false flag invasion, or will it occur during a peaceful transition carefully managed by the Earth Alliance to ensure public confidence and openness to the arks and their many secrets?

If you have read this book to this point, then you can count yourself among the educated few who are prepared for what is to come. Any official announcement of extraterrestrial life will start a cultural tsunami that will sweep so much away that the world to come will be scarcely recognizable from the world of our past— speaking here as a baby boomer born in 1958. Fundamental to facing what the rest of this decade holds is the realization that there are both positive and negative, benevolent and malevolent, friendly and unfriendly extraterrestrials that exist, many of whom have been visiting our world for decades, centuries, and even millennia. There are also many more extraterrestrial races that are indifferent, merely curious about whether the human experiment on Earth will succeed or fail, without intervening in any way—just watching!

There is no substitute for being informed about which extraterrestrial races and organizations fall into one of the above categories or the other. Discernment is vital, and education is the key. Many readers undoubtedly are already familiar with some of the extraterrestrial races that are visiting our world. Perhaps you have had your own direct contact experiences and feel you know a lot about them. Many, probably like me, were familiar with some of the races—nearly 20 of which I covered in my 2013 *Galactic Diplomacy* book—but not sure about the organizations to which they belonged if any. In reading this book, you should now have a better idea of the main extraterrestrial organizations that have intervened in some way in human affairs. Other extraterrestrial organizations are less well known, researched, or cited than those I have discussed. I leave it to the reader to explore these further by viewing a comprehensive article by Wes Penre titled "Galactic Federations and Councils," where he discusses the organizations that multiple sources have cited over the decades.[457] I also recommend Elena Danaan's book, *We Will Never Let You Down*. She discusses extraterrestrial organizations and provides an excellent diagram illustrating different galactic organizations' historical connections and origins.[458]

Humanity is emerging out of a brutal temporal war that was hotly contested between multiple extraterrestrial races and organizations, and their human partners. The fact that you are reading this conclusion is testament to the fact that we as a planetary species have emerged largely intact from this temporal war, bruised and battered, but still here. We have survived thanks to a powerful alliance of humans and extraterrestrials working behind the scenes to neutralize all the efforts by the Dark Alliance to have our world implode in a devastating Third World War.

Our collective choices will now shape how we as a planet interact with the different extraterrestrial organizations that have interacted with us throughout the temporal war. The Ashtar

Command, the Galactic Federation of Worlds, the Confederation of Planets, the Council of Nine, and the Andromeda Council are the main organizations that played vital roles in helping us survive the temporal war intact as a planetary civilization. The Draconian Empire and the Orion Collective, on the other hand, may have been vanquished and largely expelled from our solar system, but they will continue to operate in our galaxy—as they have for many millions of years—and will likely attempt to return in some fashion to reclaim some of the influence they once held over our world.

This takes me back to the recent National Defense Authorization Act of 2022 for the creation of a UAP office. There is going to be a fine line between genuine threats from our former overlords, to hyped-up threats intended to drive up national or global defense spending as done in the past by the Military Industrial Complex. How do we deal with a fluid galactic situation whereby threat perceptions that typically drive national security budgets may create a dynamic that leads to the very interstellar threat that was intended to be averted? How might the different galactic organizations help us deal with such a problem? That is why it is vital that we learn as much as possible about galactic history and how different extraterrestrial civilizations have dealt with similar planetary security problems to our own. *The Book of Enoch*, for example, opens the door to many questions about the true origins of the Fallen Angels and what subsequently happened to the extraterrestrial civilization(s) from which they were banished to Earth—which was used as a prison planet.

Currently, we are being helped by some of the organizations that assisted in liberating the Earth and our solar system—especially the Galactic Federation of Worlds—to develop a Starfleet to protect ourselves from any potential return by our former overlords—the Draconians and Orion Grays. Furthermore, an Earth Alliance has been created whereby the major spacefaring nations have agreed to work together under the leadership of the US Space Command in dealing with future threats to our solar system and to usher in a Star Trek future. That is very appropriate and meets the material defense needs of our planet. But what of the more profound spiritual lessons we need to learn as a civilization to avert future catastrophe by a possible return of our former extraterrestrial overlords?

Mahatma Gandhi said that India, while under colonial occupation, would only free itself of British control if it freed itself first from its own internal contradictions and prejudices against minorities in its population. How can humanity free itself of its own internal contradictions and prejudices now that our Deep State/Cabal overlords have left, along with their Draconian and Orion allies? This problem is where the more highly evolved or "higher density" organizations such as the "Council of Nine" and the "Andromeda Council" can play critical roles. They understand very well how internal contradictions and prejudices can corrode a civilization from within, thereby making it ripe for being undermined, infiltrated, taken over, or invaded from aggressive external species, e.g., the Draconians or Orions.

Alex Collier has repeatedly said that what the Andromeda Council can best help humanity with at this stage in our evolution is to mentor us so we can become members of the galactic community. I fully agree with him. Mentoring is what we need from the more experienced and evolved extraterrestrial organizations working with us at this transition point in our history. A powerful Starfleet helps with our material self-defense as an interplanetary civilization but we must never lose sight that spiritual self-defense is also required. It is a far more difficult challenge since it requires genuine introspection and reflection of our own internal contradictions as private citizens, communities, and as a planetary civilization. Thankfully, we have extraterrestrial friends that can help us learn the necessary lessons. As the rest of this decade plays out, we are destined to enter an exciting new chapter in our planet's evolution as we learn to discern and interact with friends and foes alike in our galaxy and join a dynamic galactic community.

Acknowledgements

I am deeply grateful to Elena Danaan for permission to use her artwork and for sharing her incredible information about different extraterrestrial organizations interacting with humanity. Elena's experiences, insights, and communications with different extraterrestrial visitors made this book possible. In particular, I wish to thank Thor Han Eredyon, who was always willing to respond to my questions that Elena kindly relayed.

Thanks also to JP, who is currently serving with the US Army, for sharing his direct experiences with several covert space operations and ark missions. Despite the risk of official reprimand, he has disclosed much sensitive information, which speaks volumes about his courage and commitment to full disclosure.

I am also very grateful to Jean Charles Moyen and David Rousseau for sharing their information about their experiences with a joint US-French secret space program and extraterrestrial visitors. In particular, I thank Jean Charles for sharing his incredible experiences in visiting the Lake Vostok space ark.

Thanks also to Robert L. and Georges Metz for permission to use their information and artwork concerning a year spent by Robert at an Intergalactic Confederation base in the Himalayas.

My gratitude to Alex Collier, James Gilliland, and Tony Rodrigues who agreed to do recent interviews, and whose responses I have cited in this book. Thanks also to Randy Cramer and Corey Goode for past interviews and sharing their experiences about their respective experiences with secret space programs.

My deep appreciation to Rene McCann for generously donating her time and enthusiasm to create another inspiring book cover for this Secret Space Program series.

I am also grateful to Duke Brickhouse, whose proofreading and suggestions were very helpful in producing the final version of this book.

Finally, my heartfelt gratitude goes to my soulmate, Angelika Whitecliff, whose beautiful spirit and wise counsel was instrumental in my research, writing, and design of this book.

Michael E. Salla, Ph.D.
July 12, 2022.

About the Author

Dr. Michael Salla is an internationally recognized scholar in global politics, conflict resolution and U.S. foreign policy. He has taught at universities in the U.S. and Australia, including American University in Washington, DC. Today, he is most popularly known as a pioneer in the development of the field of 'exopolitics'; the study of the main actors, institutions and political processes associated with extraterrestrial life.

Dr Salla has been a guest speaker on hundreds of radio and TV shows including Ancient Aliens, Coast to Coast AM, and featured at national and international conferences. His Amazon bestselling *Secret Space Program* book series has made him a leading voice in the Truth Movement, and over 5000 people a day visit his websites for his most recent articles.

ENDNOTES

CHAPTER 1

[1] FBI Records, The Vault, George Van Tassel: https://vault.fbi.gov/george-van-tassel/george-van-tassel-part-01-of-01/view (p. 56, accessed 1/2/2022).

[2] George Van Tassel, *I Rode a Flying Saucer* (New Age Publishing, 1952) pp. 16-17

[3] George Van Tassel, *I Rode a Flying Saucer*, p. 19.

[4] George Van Tassel, *I Rode a Flying Saucer*, p. 20.

[5] George Van Tassel, *I Rode a Flying Saucer*, p. 23.

[6] Michael Salla, *Antarctica's Hidden History: Corporate Foundations of Secret Space Programs* (Exopolitics Consultants, 2018*).*

[7] See Michael Salla, The US Navy's Secret Space Program & Nordic Extraterrestrial Alliance (Exopolitics Consultants, 2017).

[8] See Michael Salla, "Nazis and Reptilians in Antarctica – Uncovering the Truth through Remote Viewing," https://exopolitics.org/nazis-and-reptilians-in-antarctica/ (accessed 1/2/2022).

[9] George Van Tassel, *I Rode a Flying Saucer*, pp. 30-31.

[10] George Van Tassel, *I Rode a Flying Saucer*, p. 20.

[11] FBI Records, The Vault: https://vault.fbi.gov/george-van-tassel/george-van-tassel-part-01-of-01/view (p. 122, accessed 1/2/2022).

[12] "Relationships with Inhabitants of Celestial Bodies", https://majesticdocuments.com/pdf/oppenheimer_einstein.pdf (accessed 1/2/2022).

[13] Thomas Van Flandern, "The Exploded Planet Hypothesis," https://www.bibliotecapleyades.net/sumer_anunnaki/esp_sumer_annunaki23.htm (accessed 1/2/2022).

[14] https://famous-trials.com/oppenheimer/2690-the-oppenheimer-security-hearing-a-chronology

[15] "Oppenheimer's Testimony on His Opposition to H-Bomb," https://famous-trials.com/oppenheimer/2699-oppenheimer-s-testimony-on-his-opposition-to-h-bomb (accessed 1/2/2022).

[16] George Van Tassel, *I Rode a Flying Saucer*, p. 21.

[17] "Vrillon: A Message from the Ashtar Galactic Command," https://www.strangerdimensions.com/2014/04/25/vrillon-message-ashtar-command/ (accessed 1/2/2022).

[18] Nancy Thames, "Original Vrillon message from 1977," https://timefordisclosure.com/original-vrillon-message-from-1977/ (accessed 11/16/2021).

[19] Nancy Thames, "Original Vrillon message from 1977," https://timefordisclosure.com/original-vrillon-message-from-1977/ (accessed 11/16/2021).

[20] Elena Danaan, A *Gift From the Stars* (Independently Published, 2020) p. 104-105.

[21] Elena Danaan, *We Will Never Let You Down* (Independently Published, 2021) pp. 38-41.

[22] The full list of Farsight's "Celestial Projects" including "The Ashtar Command and Bases on Venus," is available at: https://farsight.org (accessed 1/2/2022).

[23] "The Ashtar Command and Bases on Venus," https://farsight.org/FarsightPress/Ashtar_Command_and_Venus_Bases_main_page.html (accessed 1/2/2022).

[24] For a detailed discussion of Remote Viewing see Courtney Brown, *Remote Viewing: The Science and Theory of Nonphysical Perception* (Farsight Press, 2005)

[25] Dr. Courtney Brown's conclusion come at the end of the video presentation of the "The Ashtar Command and Bases on Venus," https://www.farsightprime.com/videos/ashtar-and-venus (accessed 1/2/2022).

[26] Farsight's "Celestial Projects" that discuss these different galactic organizations is available at: https://farsight.org (accessed 1/2/2022).

[27] See Michael Salla, "Secret meetings near Jupiter decide the future of our Solar System?" https://exopolitics.org/secret-meetings-near-jupiter-decide-the-future-of-our-solar-system/ (accessed 1/2/2022).

[28] See Trevor James Constable, *They Live in the Sky: Invisible Incredible UFOs Around Us* (Saucerian Press, 1958).

CHAPTER 2

[29] Interview is available in Hebrew at: https://www.yediot.co.il/articles/0,7340,L-5854241,00.html (accessed 1/3/2021).

[30] David Israel, "Former Head of Israel's Space Program: The Aliens Asked Not To Be Revealed, Humanity Not Yet Ready," *Jewish Press* (5/12/2020) https://tinyurl.com/yckm2x3n (accessed 1/3/2021).

[31] Daniel Fry, *To Men of Earth* (N.P., 1954).

[32] Dolores Cannon's *The Convoluted Universe* comprises five books published from 2001 to 2015 by Ozark Mountain Publishing.

[33] Daniel Fry, *The White Sands Incident* (N.P., 1954) p. 27.

[34] For a detailed discussion of the origin and composition of the Majestic 12 group, see Stanton Friedman, *Top Secret/Majic: Operation Majestic-12 and the United States Government's UFO Cover-up* (Da Capo Press, 2005).

[35] The Eisenhower Briefing Document is available online at: https://majesticdocuments.com/pdf/eisenhower_briefing.pdf (accessed 3/6/2022).

[36] "The Oppenheimer Security Hearing: A Chronology," https://famous-trials.com/oppenheimer/2690-the-oppenheimer-security-hearing-a-chronology (accessed 1/3/2021).

[37] "Oppenheimer's Testimony on His Opposition to H-Bomb," https://famous-trials.com/oppenheimer/2699-oppenheimer-s-testimony-on-his-opposition-to-h-bomb (accessed 1/3/2021).

[38] "Relationships with Inhabitants of Celestial Bodies", https://majesticdocuments.com/pdf/oppenheimer_einstein.pdf (accessed 1/2/2022).

[39] Atoms for Peace Speech (12/8/1953) https://www.iaea.org/about/history/atoms-for-peace-speech (accessed 1/3/2021).

[40] Atoms for Peace Speech (12/8/1953) https://www.iaea.org/about/history/atoms-for-peace-speech (accessed 1/3/2021).

[41] Atoms for Peace Speech (12/8/1953) https://www.iaea.org/about/history/atoms-for-peace-speech (accessed 1/3/2021).

[42] Atoms for Peace Speech (12/8/1953) https://www.iaea.org/about/history/atoms-for-peace-speech (accessed 1/3/2021).

[43] The term 'Nebu' is used to describe Tall Grays from the Orion constellation. It was popularized by Elena Danaan in her book, *A Gift From the Stars* (2020).

[44] See Frank Stranges, *Stranger at the Pentagon* (Inner Light Productions, 1967).

[45] Frank Stranges, *Stranger at the Pentagon* (Inner Light Productions, 1967).

[46] Frank Stranges Interview https://youtu.be/tytnOJSNrqE (accessed 1/16/2022).

[47] Elena Danaan, *We Will Never Let You Down* (Independently published, 2021).

[48] Elena Danaan, *We Will Never Let You Down*, p. 93

[49] See "Kelly Johnson: The Man Behind Lockheed Skunk Works," https://internationalaviationhq.com/2020/08/12/kelly-johnson-skunk-works/ (accessed 3/6/2022).

[50] For detailed discussion of the flying saucer craft secretly stored and studied at Wright Patterson Air Force Base see Thomas Carey and Donald Schmitt, *UFO*

Secrets Inside Wright-Patterson: Eyewitness Accounts from the Real Area 51 (New Page Books, 2019).

[51] Cited from Michael Salla, "Eisenhower threatened to invade Area 51 former US Congress members hear testimony," https://exopolitics.org/eisenhower-threatened-to-invade-area-51-former-us-congress-members-hear-testimony/ (accessed 1/3/2021).

[52] For Stephen Lovekin's background and testimony, go to: "http://www.roswellproof.com/Lovekin.html (accessed 1/3/2021).

[53] See "Stephen Lovekin," http://www.roswellproof.com/Lovekin.html (accessed 3/12/2022).

[54] See "Stephen Lovekin," http://www.roswellproof.com/Lovekin.html (accessed 3/12/2022).

[55] "Transcript of President Dwight D. Eisenhower's Farewell Address (1961)," https://www.ourdocuments.gov/doc.php?flash=false&doc=90&page=transcript (accessed 1/3/2021).

[56] See Elena Danaan, *We Will Never Let You Down*, p. 93.

[57] "Exclusive - Ultra Top Secret Assessment of Situation/ Statement on Position on UFOs," https://www.darkmatter.radio/blogs/blog/exclusive-ultra-top-secret-assessment-situation-statement-position-ufos (accessed 1/3/2022).

[58] MUFON Journal articles are available for members at: https://mufon.com/mufon-journal/

[59] For example, see John Greenewald, "New Majestic-12 (MJ-12) Briefing Documents Released June 2017," https://www.theblackvault.com/casefiles/new-majestic-12-mj-12-briefing-documents-released-june-2017/ (accessed 1/3/2022).

[60] MUFON Journal articles are available for members at: https://mufon.com/mufon-journal/

[61] Linda Moulton Howe, "Leaked "ULTRA TOP SECRET "READ-AND-DESTROY Assessment of the Situation On Unidentified Flying Objects" https://www.earthfiles.com/2017/06/15/part-1-leaked-ultra-top-secret-read-and-destroy-assessment-of-the-situation-on-unidentified-flying-objects/ (accessed 1/3/2022).

[62] See Wikipedia entry on "William H. Webster," https://en.wikipedia.org/wiki/William_H._Webster (accessed 1/3/2022).

[63] DIA document can be downloaded at: http://wordpress-404679-1273906.cloudwaysapps.com/wp-content/uploads/2017/06/Ultra-Top-Secret-MITD.pdf (accessed 1/3/2022).

[64] DIA document can be downloaded at: http://wordpress-404679-1273906.cloudwaysapps.com/wp-content/uploads/2017/06/Ultra-Top-Secret-MITD.pdf (accessed 1/3/2022).

65 DIA document can be downloaded at: http://wordpress-404679-1273906.cloudwaysapps.com/wp-content/uploads/2017/06/Ultra-Top-Secret-MITD.pdf (accessed 1/3/2022).

66 DIA document can be downloaded at: http://wordpress-404679-1273906.cloudwaysapps.com/wp-content/uploads/2017/06/Ultra-Top-Secret-MITD.pdf (accessed 1/3/2022).

67 DIA document can be downloaded at: http://wordpress-404679-1273906.cloudwaysapps.com/wp-content/uploads/2017/06/Ultra-Top-Secret-MITD.pdf (accessed 1/3/2022).

68 Paul Blake Smith, *President Eisenhower's Close Encounters* (Foundations Book Publishing, 2020) p. 55.

69 DIA document can be downloaded at: http://wordpress-404679-1273906.cloudwaysapps.com/wp-content/uploads/2017/06/Ultra-Top-Secret-MITD.pdf (accessed 1/3/2022).

70 The membership process for countries wishing to join the European Union is available online at: https://ec.europa.eu/neighbourhood-enlargement/enlargement-policy/steps-towards-joining_en (accessed 11/29/2021).

71 Elena Danaan, *A Gift from the Stars* (Independently published, 2020) p. 65.

72 Cited in Michael Salla, *Space Force: Our Star Trek Future* (Exopolitics Consultants, 2021) p. 232.

73 See "Interview with Dr. Robert Wood – Chief Editor of Selected by Extraterrestrials Book 3," https://exopolitics.org/interview-with-dr-robert-wood/ (accessed 3/6/2022).

74 Elena Danaan, *We Will Never Let You Down*, p. 163.

75 Elena Danaan, *A Gift from the Stars* (Independently published, 2020) p. 78.

76 Alex Collier, "The Andromeda Council," *Defending Sacred Ground*," ch 1. For online quote, go to http://www.reptilianagenda.com/cont/co121099b.shtml (accessed 12/14/2021).

77 "The Galactic Federation of Worlds," https://farsight.org/FarsightPress/GFW_main_page.html (accessed 3/6/2022).

78 "The Galactic Federation of Worlds," https://farsight.org/FarsightPress/GFW_main_page.html (accessed 3/6/2022).

79 See Michael Salla, "Nazis and Reptilians in Antarctica – Uncovering the Truth through Remote Viewing," https://exopolitics.org/nazis-and-reptilians-in-antarctica/ (accessed 3/6/2022).

80 See Michael Salla, "Remote Viewing US Presidential Meetings with Extraterrestrials & Secret Agreements," https://exopolitics.org/remote-viewing-us-presidential-meetings-with-extraterrestrials/ (accessed 3/6/2022).

81 Dr. Courtney Brown's remarks can be found in the following video, "The Galactic Federation of Worlds,"

https://www.farsightprime.com/the-galactic-federation-of-worlds (accessed 3/6/2022).

[82] William Bramley, *The Gods of Eden* (Avon, 1993).

[83] Dr. Courtney Brown's remarks can be found in the following video, "The Galactic Federation of Worlds," https://www.farsightprime.com/the-galactic-federation-of-worlds (accessed 3/6/2022).

CHAPTER 3

[84] "Flying Saucer Club Blasts Earthlings for Doubts," *The York Dispatch* (York, Pennsylvania, July 13, 1959) p. 7.

[85] "Flying Saucer Club Blasts Earthlings for Doubts," *The York Dispatch* (York, Pennsylvania, July 13, 1959) p. 7.

[86] In the Wikipedia entry for Gabriel Green, the star system is instead referred to as Alpha Centauri, https://en.wikipedia.org/wiki/Gabriel_Green (accessed 11/6/2022).

[87] Robert Renaud, "The TerraKor Files," http://berkshire.net/~brenaud/HTML/Omegans.htm (accessed 12/13/2021)

[88] "Interview Transcript – US Navy Spies Learned of Nazi Alliance with Reptilian Extraterrestrials" https://exopolitics.org/interview-transcript-us-navy-spies-learned-of-nazi-alliance-with-reptilian-extraterrestrials/ (accessed 1/3/2022).

[89] Gabriel Green's questions to Robert Renaud and the Korendians are available at: http://berkshire.net/~brenaud/arkay/ArKay_to_Green.htm#19890910-5

[90] Robert Renaud, "The TerraKor Files," http://berkshire.net/~brenaud/HTML/Omegans.htm (accessed 12/13/2021)

[91] Robert Renaud, "The TerraKor Files," http://berkshire.net/~brenaud/HTML/Omegans.htm (accessed 12/13/2021)

[92] ArKay. In the News: 20090215-Galaxy Has 'billions of Earths'. TerraKor Alliance-Terran Communication Center. 2-15-2019. Retrieved 11-15-2019 from: http://berkshire.net/~brenaud/HTML/InTheNews1.htm#News3

[93] The articles Robert Renaud contributed to Gabriel Green's magazines are available online at: http://berkshire.net/~brenaud/ (accessed 12/13/2021).

[94] Gabriel Green's questions to Robert Renaud and the Korendians are available at: http://berkshire.net/~brenaud/arkay/ArKay_to_Green.htm#19890910-5 (accessed 1/3/2022).

[95] Gabriel Green's questions to Robert Renaud and the Korendians are available at: http://berkshire.net/~brenaud/arkay/ArKay_to_Green.htm#19890910-5

[96] Sixto Paz Wells, *The Invitation* (1st World Library, 2000) p. 59.

[97] Sixto Paz Wells, *The Invitation,* p. 73.

[98] Sixto Paz Wells, *The Invitation,* p. 54.

[99] See Martin Luther King, *Strength to Love* (Pocket, 1968) and Mohandas K. Gandhi, *The Story of My Experiments with Truth* (Beacon Press, 1948).

[100] See "The Latin Connection to Extraterrestrials," https://mothershipcafe.com/mission-rahma/ (accessed 1/3/2022).

[101] "Questions and Answers: A Guide to the Mission," http://www.exopoliticssouthafrica.org/download/mission_rahma_q_n_a.pdf (accessed 1/3/2022).

[102] Glossary, https://misionrahmaperu.org.pe/glosario/ (accessed 1/3/2022).

[103] Luis Fernando Mostajo Maertens, "Extraterrestrial Guides: The Great White Brotherhood in the Andes & Lake Titicaca," Exopolitics Journal 2:4 (2008). https://exopoliticsjournal.com/vol-2/vol-2-4-Fernando.htm

[104] Baird Spalding, *Life and Teachings of the Masters of the Far East,* Vol 1 (California Press, 1924).

[105] Luis Fernando Mostajo Maertens, "Extraterrestrial Guides: The Great White Brotherhood in the Andes & Lake Titicaca," Exopolitics Journal 2:4 (2008). https://exopoliticsjournal.com/vol-2/vol-2-4-Fernando.htm

[106] Enrique Castillo Rincon, *UFOs A Great New Dawn for Humanity* (Blue Dolphin Publishing, 1987) p. 184.

[107] Enrique Castillo Rincon, *UFOs A Great New Dawn for Humanity*, p. 185.

[108] Law of One, 6.24 https://www.lawofone.info/s/6#24 (accessed 1/3/2022).

[109] Law of One, 16.32 https://www.lawofone.info/s/16#32 (accessed 1/3/2022).

[110] Law of One, 11.31 https://www.lawofone.info/s/11#31 (accessed 1/3/2022).

CHAPTER 4

[111] Andrija Puharich, "A Critique of the Possible Usefulness of Extrasensory Perception in Psychological Warfare," paper presented to a Seminar on Psychological Warfare Department of Defense, Washington, D.C., November 23, 1952.

[112] H.G.M. Hermans, *Memories of a Maverick: Andrija Puharich M.D., LL.D.* (PI Publications, 1998) p. 56.

[113] See Wes Penre, "Galactic Federations and Councils" https://www.bibliotecapleyades.net/vida_alien/alien_galacticfederations43.htm (accessed 11/29/2021).

[114] See "Myth Nerd," https://mythnerd.com/ennead-gods-in-egyptian-mythology/ (accessed 11/29/2021).

[115] "Plan Nine from Outer Space," https://www.urigeller.com/plan-nine-outer-space/ (accessed 1/3/2022).

[116] H.G.M. Hermans, *Memories of a Maverick,* p. 58.

[117] H.G.M. Hermans, *Memories of a Maverick,* p. 60.

[118] "Plan Nine from Outer Space," https://www.urigeller.com/plan-nine-outer-space/ (accessed 1/3/2022).

[119] H.G.M. Hermans, *Memories of a Maverick,* pp. 112-13.

[120] H.G.M. Hermans, *Memories of a Maverick,* p. 114.

[121] H.G.M. Hermans, *Memories of a Maverick,* pp. 119-20.

[122] H.G.M. Hermans, *Memories of a Maverick,* p. 120.

[123] For more details on the CIA attempting to prevent publication of Puharich's book on the abuse of Tesla technology see H.G.M. Hermans, *Memories of a Maverick,* pp. 154-56.

[124] See H.G.M. Hermans, *Memories of a Maverick,* p. 179.

[125] Lynn Picknett and Clive Prince, *The Stargate Conspiracy: The Truth about Extraterrestrial life and the Mysteries of Ancient Egypt* (Berkley, 2001).

[126] "Plan Nine from Outer Space," https://www.urigeller.com/plan-nine-outer-space/ (accessed 1/3/2022).

[127] "Plan Nine from Outer Space," https://www.urigeller.com/plan-nine-outer-space/ (accessed 1/3/2022).

[128] For the complete list of publications and patents by Andrijia 'Henry K' Puharich, see H.G.M. Hermans, *Memories of a Maverick,* pp. 182-96.

[129] "Can Telepathy Penetrate the Iron Curtain," *Tomorrow,* vol 5, no. 2 (Winter 1957) pps 1-10

[130] See Stephen Kinzer, *Poisener in Chief, Sidney Gottlieb and the CIA Search for Mind Control* (Macmillan, 2019).

[131] Andrijia Puharich's research in psychedelic mushrooms is covered in his book, *The Sacred Mushroom* (Doubleday and Company, Inc, 1959).

[132] See H.G.M. Hermans, *Memories of a Maverick,* p. 168.

[133] For an example of how military officials would downplay the effectiveness of psychic abilities yet use these for intelligence gathering and other purposes, see Joseph McMoneagle, *The Stargate Chronicles: Memoirs of a Psychic Spy* (Crossroad Press, 2018).

[134] Stuart Holroyd, *The Nine: Briefing from Deep Space* (1978) p. 8.

[135] See Stuart Lynn Picknett and Clive Prince, *The Stargate Conspiracy,* p. 178.

[136] JJ. Hurtak, *An Introduction to the Keys of Enoch* (The Academy of Future Science, 1975) p. vii.

[137] Phyllis Schlemmer, *The Only Planet of Choice: Essential Briefings from Deep Space* (Gateway Books, 1993) p. 7

138 Source is BibleGateway,
https://www.biblegateway.com/passage/?search=Genesis%201&version=NOG
(accessed 1/3/2022).
139 Phyllis Schlemmer, *The Only Planet of Choice*, p. 11.
140 See Lynn Picknett and Clive Prince, *The Stargate Conspiracy,* p. 178.
141 "The Law of One," https://www.lawofone.info/s/7#9 (accessed 1/3/2022).
142 "The Law of One," https://www.lawofone.info/s/7#9 (accessed 1/3/2022).
143 Book of Revelation, New International Version, 4:4 & 4:9-10:
https://biblehub.com/niv/revelation/4.htm (accessed 1/4/2022).
144 JJ. Hurtak, *An Introduction to the Keys of Enoch*, p. 128.
145 "The Law of One," https://www.lawofone.info/s/7#10 (accessed 1/3/2022).
146 Phyllis Schlemmer, *The Only Planet of Choice*, p. viii.
147 Phyllis Schlemmer, *The Only Planet of Choice*, p. 33.

CHAPTER 5

148 Phyllis V. Schlemmer, *The Only Planet of Choice* (Old Kings Road Press, 2009
[1993]), pp. 34,35.
149 Phyllis V. Schlemmer, *The Only Planet of Choice*, pp. 70-71.
150 Phyllis V. Schlemmer, *The Only Planet of Choice*, p. 35.
151 Dolores Cannon, *Jesus and the Essenes* (Ozark Mountain Publishing, 1999).
152 Phyllis V. Schlemmer, *The Only Planet of Choice*, p.29.
153 The Free Dictionary, https://www.thefreedictionary.com/congress (accessed
12/7/2021).
154 Phyllis V. Schlemmer, *The Only Planet of Choice*, p. 46.
155 Phyllis V. Schlemmer, *The Only Planet of Choice*, p. 40.
156 Phyllis V. Schlemmer, *The Only Planet of Choice*, pp. 41-42.
157 Phyllis V. Schlemmer, *The Only Planet of Choice*, p. 64.
158 Phyllis V. Schlemmer, *The Only Planet of Choice*, p. 34.
159 Phyllis V. Schlemmer, *The Only Planet of Choice*, p. 78.
160 Phyllis V. Schlemmer, *The Only Planet of Choice*, p. 78.
161 Law of One, Session 17.32 (2/3/1981) https://www.lawofone.info/s/17#32
(accessed 3/7/2022).
162 Georges Metz, *Ovnis en France: Les enquêtes de Georges Metz* (Editions
Atlantes, 2011).
163 Georges Metz, *Ovnis en France: Les enquêtes de Georges Metz*, p. 180.
164 Sandeep Unnithan, "Mystery Sighting Spooks Soldiers," India Today
(11/2/2012): https://www.indiatoday.in/magazine/nation/story/20121112-
ufo-seen-in-ladakh-jammu-and-kashmir-by-indian-army-itbp-760402-2012-11-
02 (accessed 12/7/2021).
165 Georges Metz, *Ovnis en France: Les enquêtes de Georges Metz*, p. 180

[166] Zecharia Sitchin, *The 12th Planet* (Stein and Day, 1976).

[167] Alex Collier, *Defending Sacred Ground* (Leading Edge International Research Group, 1997) p. 32

[168] Alex Collier, Defending Sacred Ground, p. 48

[169] His 2002 lecture was transcribed and published as "An Andromedan Perspective on Galactic History," *Exopolitics Journal,* Vol 2:2 (2007): http://exopoliticsjournal.com/vol-2/vol-2-2-Collier.htm_(accessed 1/4/2022).

[170] Alex Collier, Defending Sacred Ground, p. 25.

[171] "Cosmic Disclosure," Gaia TV, Season 1, Episode 1, July 14, 2015. Transcript available at: https://tinyurl.com/yc5uhhy4 (accessed 1/4/2022).

[172] "Cosmic Disclosure," Gaia TV, Season 2, Episode 11, December 8, 2015.

[173] "Cosmic Disclosure," Gaia TV, Season 1, Episode 10, September 1, 2015.

[174] "Cosmic Disclosure," Gaia TV, Season 2, Episode 11, December 8, 2015.

ENDNOTES CHAPTER 6

[175] "Andromeda Constellation Facts, Stars, Map, Distance, Meteor Showers, Mythology and How to Find," https://www.universeguide.com/extrasolar/andromeda (accessed 12/13/2021).

[176] Wendelle Stevens, *UFO Contact from the Pleiades: A Preliminary Investigation Report* (UFO Photo Archives, 1982).

[177] Eduard Billy Meier, *Message from the Pleiades: The Contact Notes of Eduard Billy Meier (UFO Archives, 1988 -1995)* vols 1-4.

[178] Billy Meier, *Message From the Pleiades: The Contact Notes of Eduard Albert Meier*, Book 3. (UFO Photo Archives, 1993). Contact #70, Jan 6, 1977 http://www.futureofmankind.co.uk/meier/gaiaguys/Aryans.htm (accessed 12/13/2021).

[179] Published as Zitha Rodriquez Montiel & R. N. Hernandez, *UFO Contact from Andromeda: Extraterrestrial Prophesy*, tr. Wendelle Stevens (UFO Archives, 1989). Re-published in Robert Shapiro, *Ultimate UFO Series: Andromeda* (Light Technology, 2004). A chapter of his book is available online at: http://groups.yahoo.com/group/exopolitics/message/213 .

[180] Rodriquez and Hernandez, *UFO Contact From Andromeda*, in Shapiro, *Ultimate UFO Series,* 169-70.

[181] Rodriquez and Hernandez, *UFO Contact From Andromeda*, in Shapiro, *Ultimate UFO Series,* 239-40.

[182] Rodriquez and Hernandez, *UFO Contact From Andromeda*, in Shapiro, *Ultimate UFO Series,* 245.

[183] Rodriquez and Hernandez, *UFO Contact From Andromeda*, in Shapiro, *Ultimate UFO Series,* 294-95.

184 Letters from Andromeda,
https://www.bibliotecapleyades.net/andromeda/lfa/lfa.html (accessed
12/14/2021).
185 Available online at:
https://www.bibliotecapleyades.net/andromeda/esp_andromedacom_0.htm
(accessed 12/14/2021).
186 Alex Collier, "Let's Do Some Questions,"
http://www.reptilianagenda.com/cont/co121099f.shtml (accessed
12/14/2021).
187 Alex Collier, "The Andromeda Council," *Defending Sacred Ground*," ch 1.
For online quote, go to
http://www.reptilianagenda.com/cont/co121099b.shtml (accessed
12/14/2021).
188 Alex Collier, "The Andromeda Council," *Defending Sacred Ground*," ch 1.
For online quote, go to
http://www.reptilianagenda.com/cont/co121099b.shtml (accessed
12/14/2021).
189 Source: http://www.andromedacouncil.com/about.html (accessed
12/14/2021).
190 Tolec's website is http://www.andromedacouncil.com/ (accessed
12/14/2021).
191 Elena Danaan, *A Gift From the Stars* (Independently published, 2020), p. 78.
192 Elena Danaan, *A Gift From the Stars*, pp. 78,79.

CHAPTER 7

193 See "The Artemis Accords," https://www.nasa.gov/specials/artemis-
accords/index.html (accessed 12/24/2021).
194 Interview is available on YouTube at https://youtu.be/v-fBFXm3AyQ and
Rumble at https://rumble.com/vks7ou-update-on-galactic-federation-
intervention-on-earth-moon-mars-phobos-and-ju.html (accessed 1/5/2022).
195 See "The Artemis Accords: Principles for Cooperation in the Civil Exploration
and use of the Moon, Mars, Comets, and Asteroids for Peaceful Purposes,"
https://www.nasa.gov/specials/artemis-accords/img/Artemis-Accords-signed-
13Oct2020.pdf (accessed 12/24/2021).
196 See Joey Roulette, "'Star Trek, not Star Wars:' NASA releases basic principles
for moon exploration pact," https://www.reuters.com/article/us-space-
exploration-artemis/star-trek-not-star-wars-nasa-releases-basic-principles-for-
moon-exploration-pact-idUSKBN22R2Z9 (accessed 11/02/2020).
197 Sandra Erwin, "U.S. and France agree to expand cooperation on space
issues,"

https://spacenews.com/u-s-and-france-agree-to-expand-cooperation-on-space-issues/ (accessed 12/24/2021).

[198] See Pradeep Mohandas, Should India Sign the Artemis Accords? https://science.thewire.in/spaceflight/should-india-sign-the-artemis-accords/ (accessed 1/5/2022).

[199] I discuss the Artemis Accords and Safety Zones in *Space Force: Our Star Trek Future* (2021).

[200] The Artemis Accords Principles for Cooperation in the Civil Exploration and use of the Moon, Mars, Comets, and Asteroids for Peaceful Purposes, p. 5. https://www.nasa.gov/specials/artemis-accords/img/Artemis-Accords-signed-13Oct2020.pdf (accessed 12/01/2020).

[201] See Gareth Jennings, "UK to launch new Space Command," *Janes*, https://www.janes.com/defence-news/news-detail/uk-to-launch-new-space-command (accessed 1/5/2022).

[202] See Associated Press, "Germany launches 'space command' to protect infrastructure," https://phys.org/news/2021-07-germany-space-infrastructure.html (accessed 1/5/2022).

[203] See Giacomo Cavanna, "The italian Space Operations Command is getting ready," https://aresdifesa.it/the-italian-space-operations-command-is-getting-ready/ (accessed 1/5/2022).

[204] See Belinda Smith, "What is Australia's space division, and why is it in the military?" ABC News Australia, https://www.abc.net.au/news/science/2021-05-13/australia-space-division-military-satellites-air-force-commander/100127978 (accessed 1/5/2022).

[205] See "United States Space Command", Wikipedia, https://en.wikipedia.org/wiki/United_States_Space_Command (accessed 1/5/2022).

[206] See "French Space Command", https://en.wikipedia.org/wiki/French_Space_Command (accessed 1/5/2022).

[207] See "Russian Space Command", https://en.wikipedia.org/wiki/Russian_Space_Command (accessed 1/5/2022).

[208] See Elsa Kania, "China Has a 'Space Force.' What Are Its Lessons for the Pentagon?" https://www.defenseone.com/ideas/2018/09/china-has-space-force-what-are-its-lessons-pentagon/151665/ (accessed 1/5/2022).

[209] See "NATO Space Centre," https://shape.nato.int/about/aco-capabilities2/nato-space-centre (accessed 1/5/2022).

[210] US Space Command Public Affairs, "Combined Space Operations initiative welcomes France and Germany," https://www.spacecom.mil/MEDIA/NEWS-ARTICLES/Article/2083368/combined-space-operations-initiative-welcomes-france-and-germany/ (accessed 12/26/2021).

211 Sandra Erwin, "Japanese military strengthens ties with U.S. Space Command," *SpaceNews,* https://spacenews.com/japanese-military-strengthens-ties-with-u-s-space-command/ (accessed 12/26/2021).

212 "Israel Signs Artemis Accords," https://www.nasa.gov/feature/israel-signs-artemis-accords (accessed 3/8/2022).

213 Andrew E. Kramer and Steven Lee Myers, "Russia, Once a Space Superpower, Turns to China for Missions," *New York Times,* https://www.nytimes.com/2021/06/15/world/asia/china-russia-space.html

214 Christopher Newman, "Artemis Accords: why many countries are refusing to sign Moon exploration agreement," https://theconversation.com/artemis-accords-why-many-countries-are-refusing-to-sign-moon-exploration-agreement-148134 (accessed 1/5/2022).

215 See Voice of America, "US Intensifies Crackdown on China Intellectual Property Theft," https://www.voanews.com/a/usa_us-intensifies-crackdown-china-intellectual-property-theft/6189373.html (accessed 1/5/2022).

216 Michael Sheetz, "Richard Branson reaches space on Virgin Galactic flight," *CNBC News,* https://www.cnbc.com/2021/07/11/richard-branson-reaches-space-on-virgin-galactic-flight.html (accessed 1/5/2022).

217 Michael Sheetz, "Jeff Bezos reaches space on Blue Origin's first crewed launch," *CNBC News,* https://www.cnbc.com/2021/07/20/jeff-bezos-reaches-space-on-blue-origins-first-crewed-launch.html (accessed 1/5/2022).

218 "Core Secrets: NSA Saboteurs in China and Germany," https://firstlook.org/theintercept/2014/10/10/core-secrets/ (accessed 4/16/2022).

219 https://twitter.com/SpaceX/status/1418667693016711170 (accessed 1/5/2022).

220 Benjamin Fulford, "Nazis align with White Dragon as isolated Satanists continue their death throes," https://benjaminfulford.net/2018/02/05/nazis-align-white-dragon-isolated-satanists-continue-death-throes/ (accessed 1/5/2022).

221 See Michael Salla, Will Antarctic German Space Program Reveal Itself & Release Advanced Technologies? https://exopolitics.org/german-space-program-antarctica-to-reveal-itself/ (accessed 1/5/2022).

222 I had earlier discussed the possibility of a macronova in a number of articles such as: "Impending Solar Flash Event Supported by Scientific Studies & Insider Testimony," https://exopolitics.org/impending-solar-flash-event-supported-by-scientific-studies-insider-testimony/ (accessed 1/5/2022).

223 See Ben Davidson, "The Earth Disaster Documentary," https://youtu.be/ihwoIlxHI3Q (accessed 1/5/2022).

224 See "Preparing for Disclosure & Solar Flash Events – Corey Goode at Cosmic Waves," https://exopolitics.org/preparing-for-disclosure-solar-flash-events-corey-goode-at-cosmic-waves/ (accessed 1/5/2022).

225 First cited in Michael Salla, "Did Bezos, Branson & Musk secretly travel to Jupiter for negotiations with the Galactic Federation?" https://exopolitics.org/did-bezos-branson-musk-secretly-travel-to-jupiter-for-negotiations/ (accessed 1/5/2022).

226 First cited in Michael Salla,"Update on Jupiter Meetings with the Galactic Federation of Worlds," https://exopolitics.org/update-on-jupiter-meetings-with-the-galactic-federation/ (accessed 3/8/2022).

227 For discussion of the Council of Five, see Elena Danaan, *A Gift From the Stars*, (2020) p. 313.

228 First cited in Michael Salla, "Did Bezos, Branson & Musk secretly travel to Jupiter for negotiations with the Galactic Federation?" https://exopolitics.org/did-bezos-branson-musk-secretly-travel-to-jupiter-for-negotiations/ (accessed 1/5/2022).

229 See William Tompkins, *Selected by Extraterrestrials* (Createspace, 2015).

230 See "Combined Space Operations Initiative welcomes France and Germany," https://spacewatch.global/2020/02/combined-space-operations-initiative-welcomes-france-and-germany/ (accessed 1/5/2022).

231 See Brett Tingley, "The Secretive Inventor Of The Navy's Bizarre 'UFO Patents' Finally Talks," *The Drive*, https://www.thedrive.com/the-war-zone/31798/the-secretive-inventor-of-the-navys-bizarre-ufo-patents-finally-talks (accessed 1/5/2022).

232 See Michael Salla, "US Navy Disclosing Secret Space Program Technologies through Patents System," https://exopolitics.org/us-navy-disclosing-secret-space-program-technologies-through-patents-system/ (accessed 1/5/2022).

233 See David Vergun, "Spacecom attains initial operational capability, commander says," https://www.spacewar.com/reports/Spacecom_attains_initial_operational_capability_commander_says_999.html (accessed 1/5/2022).

CHAPTER 8

234 Richard Hoagland, *The Monuments of Mars: A City on the Edge of Forever* (North Atlantic Boos, 1992).

235 See Michael Salla, "CIA Used Remote Viewing to Learn about Mars Pyramids & Inhabitants," https://exopolitics.org/cia-used-remote-viewing-to-learn-about-mars-pyramids-inhabitants/ (accessed 3/8/2022).

[236] Dr. John Brandenburg, *Death on Mars: The Discovery of a Planetary Nuclear Massacre* (Adventures Unlimited Press, 2015).

[237] See Michael Salla, *Antarctica's Hidden History: Corporate Foundations of Secret Space Programs* (Exopolitics Consultants, 2018) pp. 295-309.

[238] For the history of the German Antarctica colony and agreements it reached with the Eisenhower administration, see Michael Salla, *Antarctica's Hidden History: Corporate Foundations of Secret Space Programs* (Exopolitics Consultants, 2018).

[239] For a summary of Corey Goode's statements on Mars and nuclear weapons see Michael Salla, "German Secret Societies Nuked Martians & Built Slave Colonies with U.S. Corporations," https://exopolitics.org/german-secret-societies-nuked-martians-built-slave-colonies-with-u-s-corporations/ (accessed 12/28/2021).

[240] See Michael Salla, "Alternative 3 & Global Consciousness," https://exopolitics.org/alternative-3-global-consciousness-repost/ (accessed 1/6/2022).

[241] See Michael Salla, "Insider Reveals UFO & Secret Space Program Disclosure War," https://exopolitics.org/insider-reveals-ufo-ssp-disclosure-war/ (accessed 1/6/2022).

[242] A transcript of my interview with Randy Cramer is available, "Mars Defense Force: Defending Human Colonies – Interview Transcript," https://exopolitics.org/mars-defense-force-defending-human-colonies-interview-transcript/ (accessed 1/6/2022).

[243] See Randy Cramer: Hybrid Soldier for the SSP (https://www.gaia.com/video/randy-cramer-hybrid-soldier-ssp (accessed 1/6/2022).

[244] The Mars Records are available online at: https://www.themarsrecords.com/wp/category/the-mars-records/ (accessed 12/28/2021).

[245] Cited in Michael Salla, "Part 2: Mars Defense Force: Defending Human Colonies – Interview Transcript," https://exopolitics.org/mars-defense-force-defending-human-colonies-interview-transcript-pt-2-2/ (accessed 1/6/2022).

[246] For a list of my interviews with Tony Rodrigues, see "13 Years on Ceres with the Dark Fleet – An Interview with Tony Rodrigues," https://exopolitics.org/13-years-on-ceres-with-dark-fleet/ (accessed 3/8/2022).

[247] An excellent summary of individuals claiming to have served with the Dark Fleet can be found in Len Kasten, *Dark Fleet: The Secret Nazi Space Program and the Battle for the Solar System* (Bear & Company, 2020).

[248] See Corey Goode, "Joint SSP, Sphere Alliance & ICC Leadership Conference & Tour of Mars Colony on 6.20.2015,"

https://spherebeingalliance.com/blog/joint-ssp-sphere-alliance-icc-leadership-conference-tour-of-mars-colony-on-6-20.html (accessed 1/6/2022).

[249] See Corey Goode, "Joint SSP, Sphere Alliance & ICC Leadership Conference & Tour of Mars Colony on 6.20.2015," https://spherebeingalliance.com/blog/joint-ssp-sphere-alliance-icc-leadership-conference-tour-of-mars-colony-on-6-20.html (accessed 1/6/2022).

[250] See Michael Salla, "Secret Mars Colonies Trade with up to 900 Extraterrestrial Civilizations https://exopolitics.org/secret-mars-colonies-trade-with-up-to-900-extraterrestrial-civilizations/ (accessed 1/6/2022).

[251] See Corey Goode, "Joint SSP, Sphere Alliance & ICC Leadership Conference & Tour of Mars Colony on 6.20.2015," https://spherebeingalliance.com/blog/joint-ssp-sphere-alliance-icc-leadership-conference-tour-of-mars-colony-on-6-20.html (accessed 1/6/2022).

[252] Elena Danaan, "Mars Wars - 30/04/2021," https://youtu.be/E4liNicY50I (accessed 1/6/2022).

[253] Elena Danaan, "Mars Wars - 30/04/2021", https://youtu.be/E4liNicY50I (accessed 1/6/2022).

[254] Elena Danaan, "Mars Wars - 30/04/2021", https://youtu.be/E4liNicY50I (accessed 1/6/2022).

[255] The Farsight Institute, "The Galactic Federation of Worlds," https://farsight.org/FarsightPress/GFW_main_page.html (accessed 1/6/2022).

[256] Elena Danaan, "Mars Wars - 30/04/2021", https://youtu.be/E4liNicY50I (accessed 1/6/2022).

[257] See Michael Salla, "Update on Galactic Federation attacks on Corporate Satellites & Mars Exodus," https://exopolitics.org/update-on-galactic-federation-attacks-on-corporate-satellites-mars-exodus/ (accessed 1/6/2022).

[258] Elena Danaan, "Mars Wars - 30/04/2021", https://youtu.be/E4liNicY50I (accessed 1/6/2022).

[259] For Corey Goode's comments about a solar system wide quarantine, see Michael Salla, "The Coming Solar Flash & the Galactic Federation – Q&A with Corey Goode," https://exopolitics.org/the-coming-solar-flash-the-galactic-federation-qa-with-corey-goode/ (accessed 1/6/2022).

[260] Elena Danaan, "Mars Wars - 30/04/2021", https://youtu.be/E4liNicY50I (accessed 1/6/2022).

[261] Elena Danaan, "Mars Wars - 30/04/2021", https://youtu.be/E4liNicY50I (accessed 1/6/2022).

[262] See "Seismic detection of the martian core," *Science* (Vol 373, Issue 6553) pp. 443-448. Available online at: https://www.science.org/doi/full/10.1126/science.abi7730 (accessed 12/28/2021).

[263] Marcia Dunn, "Marsquakes offer detailed look at red planet's interior," https://tinyurl.com/bdza8ma5 (accessed 1/6/2022).

[264] See "Cerberus Fossae," https://tinyurl.com/2p8c994a (accessed 1/6/2022).

[265] Email cited in Michael Salla, "Is Mars in the midst of a Planetary Liberation War?" https://exopolitics.org/is-mars-in-the-midst-of-a-planetary-liberation-war/ (accessed 1/6/2022).

[266] See Michael Salla, "Comparing Prime Directives of the Galactic Federation of Worlds and the Star Trek," https://exopolitics.org/comparing-prime-directives-of-the-galactic-federation-of-worlds-star-trek/ (accessed 1/6/2022).

[267] Cited in Michael Salla, "Is Mars in the midst of a Planetary Liberation War?" https://exopolitics.org/is-mars-in-the-midst-of-a-planetary-liberation-war/ (accessed 1/6/2022).

[268] I discuss this Temporal War in my May 22, 2021 webinar: "Antarctica, Dark Fleet, and Humanity's Liberation," https://vimeo.com/ondemand/antarcticadarkfleet (accessed 5/26/2022).

[269] Cited in Michael Salla, "Was Mars moon Phobos just liberated from hostile extraterrestrial control?" https://exopolitics.org/was-mars-moon-phobos-just-liberated-from-hostile-extraterrestrial-control/ (accessed 1/6/2022).

[270] See Nancy Atkinson, "Could Phobos Be Hollow?" Universe Today (3/5/2010) https://www.universetoday.com/58923/could-phobos-be-hollow/ (accessed 1/6/2022).

[271] See T.P. Andert, et. al., "Precise mass determination and the nature of Phobos," https://agupubs.onlinelibrary.wiley.com/doi/epdf/10.1029/2009GL041829 (accessed 1/6/2022).

[272] Cited in Michael Salla, "Was Mars moon Phobos just liberated from hostile extraterrestrial control?" https://exopolitics.org/was-mars-moon-phobos-just-liberated-from-hostile-extraterrestrial-control/ (accessed 1/6/2022).

[273] See "The Phobos II Incident, January 1989," https://www.ufocasebook.com/phobos2.html (accessed 1/6/2022).

[274] Cited in Michael Salla, "Was Mars moon Phobos just liberated from hostile extraterrestrial control?" https://exopolitics.org/was-mars-moon-phobos-just-liberated-from-hostile-extraterrestrial-control/ (accessed 1/6/2022).

[275] See Michael Salla, "Siemens Implicated in Tracking Forced Labor & Slaves in Space," https://exopolitics.org/siemens-implicated-in-tracking-forced-labor-slaves-in-space/ (accessed 1/6/2022).

CHAPTER 9

[276] First cited in Michael Salla, "Is the 4th Reich's Dark Fleet abandoning Antarctica?"
https://exopolitics.org/is-the-4th-reichs-dark-fleet-abandoning-antarctica/ (accessed 1/7/2022).

[277] First cited in Michael Salla, "Is the 4th Reich's Dark Fleet abandoning Antarctica?"
https://exopolitics.org/is-the-4th-reichs-dark-fleet-abandoning-antarctica/ (accessed 1/7/2022).

[278] For detailed discussion of Hitler and the Nazi's agreements with extraterrestrials see Michael Salla, *Antarctica's Hidden History: Corporate Foundations of Secret Space Programs* (Exopolitics Consultants, 2018).

[279] For discussion of Ceres as a major Dark Fleet base, see Michael Salla, "20 Years a Slave in Secret Space Programs – ExoNews TV Episodes 3-5," https://exopolitics.org/20-years-a-slave-in-secret-space-programs-exonews-tv-episodes-3-4/ (accessed 1/7/2022).

[280] First cited in Michael Salla, "Is the 4th Reich's Dark Fleet abandoning Antarctica?" https://exopolitics.org/is-the-4th-reichs-dark-fleet-abandoning-antarctica/ (accessed 1/7/2022).

[281] First cited in Michael Salla, "Is the 4th Reich's Dark Fleet abandoning Antarctica?" https://exopolitics.org/is-the-4th-reichs-dark-fleet-abandoning-antarctica/ (accessed 1/7/2022).

[282] First cited in Michael Salla, "Is the 4th Reich's Dark Fleet abandoning Antarctica?" https://exopolitics.org/is-the-4th-reichs-dark-fleet-abandoning-antarctica/ (accessed 1/7/2022).

[283] In May 2021, I updated my information about the Dark Fleet's history in a four-hour webinar that is available on Vimeo:
https://vimeo.com/ondemand/antarcticadarkfleet (accessed 1/7/2022).

[284] For discussion of Operation Highjump, see Michael Salla, *Antarctica's Hidden History*, pp. 91-103.

[285] For discussion of Operation Taberlan, see Britain's Secret War in Antarctica, "Britain's Secret War in Antarctica," https://plausiblefutures.com/britains-secret-war-in-antarctica/ (accessed 1/7/2022).

[286] See Michael Salla, *Insiders Reveal Secret Space Programs and Extraterrestrial Alliances* (Exopolitics Institute, 2015) pp. 179-88

[287] See Michael Salla, "Navy Insiders Confirm Multinational SSP with bases throughout Solar System & Beyond," https://exopolitics.org/navy-insiders-confirm-multinational-ssp-with-bases-throughout-solar-system-beyond/ (accessed 1/7/2022).

[288] See Michael Salla, "Illegal Military Research and Development in Antarctica," https://exopolitics.org/illegal-military-research-and-development-in-antarctica/ (accessed 1/7/2022).

289 See Michael Salla, "Secret Space Programs Battle over Antarctic Skies During Global Elite Exodus," https://exopolitics.org/secret-space-programs-battle-over-antarctic-skies-during-global-elite-exodus/ (accessed 1/7/2022).

290 Michael Wenger, "Turkey plans its own Antarctic Station", Polar Journal (2/25/2021) https://polarjournal.ch/en/2021/02/25/turkey-plans-its-own-antarctic-station/ (accessed 1/7/2022).

291 Craig Hooper, "With New Gear And Bases, China Is Beginning To Make A Play For Dominance In Antarctica", Forbers (12/23/2020) https://tinyurl.com/yw5vvd54 (accessed 1/7/2022).

292 Joseph P. Farrell, "More Antarctic Strangeness About Guess Who?" https://gizadeathstar.com/2021/12/more-antarctic-strangeness-about-guess-who/ (accessed 1/7/2022).

293 Benjamine Fulford, "Klaus Schwab and Christine Lagarde turned in major white hat victory," https://benjaminfulford.net/2021/12/13/78817/ (accessed 1/7/2022).

294 See The Void, "Did The Global Elite Meet In Antarctica?" https://www.thevoid.uk/void-post/did-the-global-elite-meet-in-antarctica-gossip/ (accessed 1/7/2022).

295 See Corey Goode update, "Antarctica – December Eclipse Ceremonies within ancient ruins beneath the ice", (12/22/2021) https://ascensionworks.tv/groups/corey-goode-updates/ (accessed 1/17/2022).

296 See Paul Seaburn, "Wikileaks Photos, John Kerry Visit and UFOs in Antarctica," Mysterious Universe (11/15/2016) https://mysteriousuniverse.org/2016/11/wikileaks-photos-john-kerry-visit-and-ufos-in-antarctica/ (accessed 1/7/2022).

297 First cited in Michael Salla, "Cabal leaders go to Antarctica to surrender to Extraterrestrials & Earth Alliance," https://exopolitics.org/cabal-leaders-go-to-antarctica-to-surrender-to-extraterrestrials-earth-alliance/ (accessed 1/7/2022).

298 See Nigel Matte, "The quantum financial system explained and updated in detail," https://nigelmattepost.wordpress.com/2021/07/02/the-quantum-financial-system-explained-and-updated-in-detail/ (accessed 1/7/2022).

299 For a breakdown of the total number of secrecy orders imposed on patents submitted to the US Patent and Trademark Office go to: https://sgp.fas.org/othergov/invention/stats.html (accessed 1/7/2022).

300 See Michael Salla, "Secret Presidential Memorandum issued to Declassify Anti-aging & Free Energy Technologies," https://exopolitics.org/secret-presidential-memo-anti-aging-free-energy/ (accessed 1/7/2022).

301 First cited in Michael Salla, "Cabal leaders go to Antarctica to surrender to Extraterrestrials & Earth Alliance,"

https://exopolitics.org/cabal-leaders-go-to-antarctica-to-surrender-to-extraterrestrials-earth-alliance/ (accessed 1/7/2022).

[302] See John Morse, "Astronomers Try To Explain Mysterious 'Photon Belt'", https://theeventchronicle.com/explain-mysterious-photon-belt/ (accessed 1/7/2022).

[303] See Noel Huntley, Ph.D., "The Photon Belt Encounter", https://www.bibliotecapleyades.net/universo/esp_cinturon_fotones_3a.htm (accessed 1/7/2022).

[304] Law of One, https://www.lawofone.info/s/33#20 (accessed 1/7/2022).

[305] For criticism of the Photon Belt hypothesis, see Rational Wiki, https://rationalwiki.org/wiki/Photon_belt (accessed 1/7/2022).

[306] First cited in Michael Salla, "Cabal leaders go to Antarctica to surrender to Extraterrestrials & Earth Alliance," https://exopolitics.org/cabal-leaders-go-to-antarctica-to-surrender-to-extraterrestrials-earth-alliance/ (accessed 1/7/2022).

[307] First cited in Michael Salla, "Cabal leaders go to Antarctica to surrender to Extraterrestrials & Earth Alliance," https://exopolitics.org/cabal-leaders-go-to-antarctica-to-surrender-to-extraterrestrials-earth-alliance/ (accessed 1/7/2022).

[308] Cited in Michael Salla, "QAnon on the Rothschilds & Satanism – Trump's Secret Alliance with Putin," https://exopolitics.org/qanon-rothschilds-satanism-trumps-alliance-putin/ (accessed 1/7/2022).

[309] Brad Olsen, *Beyond Esoteric: Escaping Prison Planet* (CCC Publishing, 2020) p. 55.

[310] First cited in Michael Salla, "Cabal leaders go to Antarctica to surrender to Extraterrestrials & Earth Alliance," https://exopolitics.org/cabal-leaders-go-to-antarctica-to-surrender-to-extraterrestrials-earth-alliance/ (accessed 1/7/2022).

[311] First cited in Michael Salla, "Part 2 - Cabal leaders go to Antarctica to surrender to Extraterrestrials & Earth Alliance," https://exopolitics.org/part-2-cabal-leaders-go-to-antarctica-to-surrender-to-extraterrestrials-earth-alliance/ (accessed 1/7/2022).

[312] Albert Pike, *Morals and Dogma of the Ancient and Accepted Scottish Rite of Freemasonry* (Supreme Council of the Thirty Third Degree for the Southern Jurisdiction of the United States, 1871) p. 321.

[313] Richard Hoagland and Mike Bara, *Dark Mission: The Secret History of NASA* (2007).

[314] Richard Hoagland and Mike Bara, *Dark Mission: The Secret History of NASA* (2007) Introduction.

[315] Alex Collier, *Defending Sacred Ground* (Leading Edge International Research Group, 1997) n.p.

[316] See Michael Salla, "Eisenhower's 1954 Meeting With Extraterrestrials: The Fiftieth Anniversary of First Contact?" https://exopolitics.net/Study-Paper-8.htm (accessed 1/7/2022).

[317] Alex Collier, *Defending Sacred Ground*, n.p.

[318] Alex Collier, *Defending Sacred Ground* (Leading Edge International Research Group, 1997) n.p.

[319] See Michael Salla, "French Contactee confirms Intergalactic Confederation is seeding human worlds," https://exopolitics.org/french-contactee-confirms-intergalactic-confederation-is-seeding-human-worlds/ (accessed 1/7/2022).

[320] Book of Enoch is available online at http://www.markfoster.net/rn/texts/AllBooksOfEnoch.pdf (accessed 1/7/2022).

[321] For discussion of the end of Apartheid in South Africa, see Office of the Historian, "The End of Apartheid," https://history.state.gov/milestones/1989-1992/apartheid (accessed 3/9/2022).

[322] For discussion of military juntas in South America and their end in 1990, see Roberto Malta, https://www.risetopeace.org/2018/09/14/latin-american-military-dictatorships/rmalta/ (accessed 3/9/2022).

[323] Cited on the blogsite of Nigel Matte, https://nigelmattepost.wordpress.com/2021/07/02/the-quantum-financial-system-explained-and-updated-in-detail/ (accessed 1/7/2022).

CHAPTER 10

[324] See Alan Martin, "Scientists have found the perfect spot to set up camp on the moon," https://www.alphr.com/space/1007415/scientists-have-found-the-perfect-spot-to-set-up-camp-on-the-moon/ (accessed 1/9/2022).

[325] Frank Tavares, "Ice Confirmed at the Moon's Poles," NASA (/20/2022) https://www.nasa.gov/feature/ames/ice-confirmed-at-the-moon-s-poles (accessed 1/9/2022).

[326] John Grant, "The Moon's Surface Has Enough Oxygen to Sustain 8 Billion People for 100,000 Years," https://singularityhub.com/2021/11/14/the-moons-surface-has-enough-oxygen-to-sustain-8-billion-people-for-100000-years/ (accessed 1/9/2022).

[327] For discussion of these secret agreements, see Michael Salla, US Air Force Secret Space Program: Shifting Extraterrestrial Alliances & Space Force (Exopolitics Consultants, 2019): pp. 167-86.

[328] I first discussed the "Interplanetary Corporate Conglomerate" in "Secret Space Programs More Complex than previously revealed (4/17/2015): https://exopolitics.org/secret-space-programs-more-complex-than-previously-revealed/ (accessed 1/9/2022).

[329] For discussion of this corporate infiltration, see Michael Salla, *Antarctica's Hidden History: Corporate Foundations of Secret Space Programs* (Exopolitics Consultants, 2018).

[330] See "Audio – Supersoldiers and Project Moon Shadow - Full Interview with Captain K. Part 1," https://youtu.be/9vj4N2RHYc0 (accessed 1/9/2022).

[331] See "Mars Defense Force: Defending Human Colonies - Part 2 Capt K Interviews," https://youtu.be/ZJ6OpdyNHIQ (accessed 1/9/2022).

[332] See "Full Audio - Capt K Interviews Part 4 - Physical age regression & regaining wiped memories" https://youtu.be/WwinDEomGvM (accessed 1/9/2022).

[333] See Michael Salla, "Comparative Analysis: Corey/GoodETxSG & Randy Cramer/Capt Kaye," https://exopolitics.org/recruitment-covert-service-for-secret-space-programs/#Comparison (accessed 1/9/2022).

[334] See Michael Salla, *Insiders Reveal Secret Space Programs and Extraterrestrial Alliances* (Exopolitics Institute, 2015) pp. 309-344.

[335] See "Moon Training & Suicide Missions on Mars – 20 Years a Slave in Secret Space Programs – Pt2" https://exopolitics.org/moon-training-suicide-missions-on-mars-20-years-a-slave-in-secret-space-programs-pt2/ (accessed 1/9/2022).

[336] Niara Isley, *Facing the Shadow, Embracing the Light* (Createspace, 2013) p. 271.

[337] "We Were Never Alone with David Wilcock and Corey Goode, *Cosmic Disclosure*, Season 2, Episode 6 (11/3/2015).

[338] See Tony Rodrigues, Ceres Colony Cavalier (Independently Published, 2022)

[339] Elena Danaan, *We Will Never Let You Down* (Independently Published, 2021) p. 125.

[340] NASA, https://www.nasa.gov/specials/artemis/ (accessed 3/9/2022).

[341] The Artemis Plan is available at: https://www.nasa.gov/sites/default/files/atoms/files/artemis_plan-20200921.pdf (accessed 3/9/2022).

[342] Stuart Clark, "Russia and China team up to build a moon base," https://www.theguardian.com/science/2021/jun/25/russia-china-team-up-build-moon-base (accessed 3/9/2022).

[343] For articles, photos and videos concerning JP, go to: https://exopolitics.org/jp-articles-photos-videos/ (accessed 1/11/2022).

[344] See Michael Salla, "Covert Disclosure of Antigravity Rectangle Weapons Platforms by USAF Special Operations,"
  https://exopolitics.org/covert-disclosure-rectangle-craft-usaf-spec-ops/ (accessed 1/11/2022).

[345] See US Army, "Quartermaster and Chemical Equipment Repairer," https://tinyurl.com/5ckv5s24 (accessed 1/11/2022).

346 See Michael Salla, "Contact with Nordic Alien in USAF Uniform whose Spacecraft was Photographed," https://exopolitics.org/contact-with-nordic-alien-in-usaf-uniform-whose-spacecraft-was-photographed/ (accessed 1/8/2022).

347 Cited in Michael Salla, "Galactic Federation is helping humanity build a Starfleet for Planetary Defense," https://exopolitics.org/galactic-federation-is-helping-humanity-build-a-starfleet-for-planetary-defense/ (accessed 1/17/2022).

348 The Galactic Federation's Prime Directive is available online at: "Did the Galactic Federation just release its Prime Directive," https://exopolitics.org/did-the-galactic-federation-just-release-its-prime-directive/ (accessed 1/10/2022).

349 For a breakdown of the total number of secrecy orders imposed on patents submitted to the US Patent and Trademark Office go to: https://sgp.fas.org/othergov/invention/stats.html (accessed 1/7/2022).

350 "Cislunar Highway Patrol System (CHPS)": https://afresearchlab.com/technology/cislunar-highway-patrol-system-chps/ (accessed 3/12/2022).

351 See "NASA Funds Research for Moon Infrastructure Construction," https://www.governing.com/next/nasa-funds-research-for-moon-infrastructure-construction (accessed 3/12/2022).

CHAPTER 11

352 See NASA, https://www.nasa.gov/specials/artemis-accords/index.html (accessed 1/11/2022).

353 See David Vergun, "Spacecom attains initial operational capability, commander says," https://www.spacewar.com/reports/Spacecom_attains_initial_operational_capability_commander_says_999.html (accessed 1/5/2022).

354 This was first cited in Michael Salla, "Did Bezos, Branson & Musk secretly travel to Jupiter for negotiations with the Galactic Federation?" https://exopolitics.org/did-bezos-branson-musk-secretly-travel-to-jupiter-for-negotiations/ (accessed 1/5/2022).

355 See Air Force Space Command, "The Future of Space 2060 and implications for US Strategy: Report on the Space Futures Workshop," https://tinyurl.com/4htrh793 (accessed 1/11/2022).

356 See Michael Salla, "Trump signs Space Force Act – Stage Set for Secret Space Program Disclosure," https://exopolitics.org/trump-signs-space-force-act/ (accessed 1/8/2022).

357 See Michael Salla, "Contact with Nordic Alien in USAF Uniform whose Spacecraft was Photographed," https://exopolitics.org/contact-with-nordic-

alien-in-usaf-uniform-whose-spacecraft-was-photographed/ (accessed 1/8/2022).

[358] For JP's discussion of these autonomous shuttle spacecraft, see Michael Salla, "Galactic Federation is helping humanity build a Starfleet for Planetary Defense," https://exopolitics.org/galactic-federation-is-helping-humanity-build-a-starfleet-for-planetary-defense/ (accessed 3/15/2021)

[359] See US Army, "Quartermaster and Chemical Equipment Repairer," https://tinyurl.com/5ckv5s24 (accessed 1/11/2022).

[360] See Air Force Space Command, "The Future of Space 2060 and implications for US Strategy: Report on the Space Futures Workshop," https://tinyurl.com/4htrh793 (accessed 1/11/2022).

[361] See Michael Salla, "French SSP Insiders Speak Out," https://exopolitics.org/french-ssp-insiders-speak-out/ (accessed 1/8/2022).

[362] David Rousseau has chronicled his experiences in two books published in French, the first of which is available in English. His website with information about his books is https://davidrousseau.net/

CHAPTER 12

[363] See Richard Luscombe, "William Shatner in tears after historic space flight: 'I'm so filled with emotion' https://www.theguardian.com/science/2021/oct/13/william-shatner-jeff-bezos-rocket-blue-origin (accessed 3/10/2022)

[364] JP's information about the Moon base construction was first published in Michael Salla, "Galactic Federation is helping humanity build a Starfleet for Planetary Defense," https://exopolitics.org/galactic-federation-is-helping-humanity-build-a-starfleet-for-planetary-defense/ (accessed 1/12/2022).

[365] First cited in Michael Salla, "Earth Alliance Mission to Ganymede to greet ET visitors & inaugurate a Star Trek Future," https://exopolitics.org/earth-alliance-mission-to-ganymede-to-greet-et-visitors-inaugurate-a-star-trek-future/ (accessed 1/12/2022).

[366] See Michael Salla, "Did Bezos, Branson & Musk secretly travel to Jupiter for negotiations with the Galactic Federation? https://exopolitics.org/did-bezos-branson-musk-secretly-travel-to-jupiter-for-negotiations/ (accessed 1/12/2022).

[367] See Michael Salla, "SpaceX to launch the Europa Clipper mission for a bargain price," https://arstechnica.com/science/2021/07/spacex-to-launch-the-europa-clipper-mission-for-a-bargain-price/

[368] See Michael Salla, "Contact with Nordic Alien in USAF Uniform whose Spacecraft was Photographed,"

https://exopolitics.org/contact-with-nordic-alien-in-usaf-uniform-whose-spacecraft-was-photographed/ (accessed 3/10/2022)

[369] A series of articles analyzing photos and videos shared by JP are available online at: https://exopolitics.org/jp-articles-photos-videos/ (accessed 1/12/2022).

[370] First cited in Michael Salla, "Earth Alliance Mission to Ganymede to greet ET visitors & inaugurate a Star Trek Future," https://exopolitics.org/earth-alliance-mission-to-ganymede-to-greet-et-visitors-inaugurate-a-star-trek-future/ (accessed 1/12/2022).

[371] First cited in Michael Salla, "Earth Alliance Mission to Ganymede to greet ET visitors & inaugurate a Star Trek Future," https://exopolitics.org/earth-alliance-mission-to-ganymede-to-greet-et-visitors-inaugurate-a-star-trek-future/ (accessed 1/12/2022).

[372] First cited in Michael Salla, "Earth Alliance Mission to Ganymede to greet ET visitors & inaugurate a Star Trek Future," https://exopolitics.org/earth-alliance-mission-to-ganymede-to-greet-et-visitors-inaugurate-a-star-trek-future/ (accessed 1/12/2022).

[373] See Arthur Horn, Ph.D., *Humanity's Extraterrestrial Origins* (Silberschnur, 1997).

[374] See Jason Horne, "The Biblical Elohim were a Race of Extraterrestrial Extradimensional Aliens," https://discover.hubpages.com/religion-philosophy/elohim-race-et (accessed 3/10/2022).

[375] Alex Collier, *Defending Sacred Ground* (Leading Edge, 1997) n.p.

[376] First cited in Michael Salla, "Earth Alliance Mission to Ganymede to greet ET visitors & inaugurate a Star Trek Future," https://exopolitics.org/earth-alliance-mission-to-ganymede-to-greet-et-visitors-inaugurate-a-star-trek-future/ (accessed 1/12/2022).

[377] Phyllis Schlemmer, *The Only Planet of Choice* (Gateway Books, 1993).

[378] First cited in Michael Salla, "Earth Alliance Mission to Ganymede to greet ET visitors & inaugurate a Star Trek Future," https://exopolitics.org/earth-alliance-mission-to-ganymede-to-greet-et-visitors-inaugurate-a-star-trek-future/ (accessed 1/12/2022).

[379] Elena Danaan, *We Will Never Let You Down: Encounters with Val Thor and journeys beyond Earth* (Independently Published, 2021).

[380] See US Department of Defense, "Space Force Personnel To Be Called Guardians," https://www.defense.gov/News/News-Stories/Article/Article/2452910/space-force-personnel-to-be-called-guardians/ (12/19/2020).

[381] Alex Collier, *Defending Sacred Ground* (1996): https://www.alexcollier.org/alex-collier-defending-sacred-ground-1996/ (accessed 3/10/2022).

[382] Alex Collier on the Andromeda Council and Human Liberation, https://youtu.be/x1gpEGdiMaY?t=2702 (accessed 3/10/2022).

[383] James Gilliland's three books are listed on Amazon.com at: https://tinyurl.com/z8cscfb5 (accessed 1/18/2022).

[384] "Extraterrestrial Fleet arrives to watch humanity's liberation - Interview with James Gilliland," https://youtu.be/l_WS-m5ZZyI?t=1692 (accessed 1/18/2022).

[385] See "French SSP Insiders Speak Out," https://exopolitics.org/french-ssp-insiders-speak-out/ (accessed 3/16/2022).

[386] "French SSP Insiders Speak Out," https://exopolitics.org/french-ssp-insiders-speak-out/ (accessed 3/16/2022).

[387] "French SSP Insiders Speak Out," https://exopolitics.org/french-ssp-insiders-speak-out/ (accessed 3/16/2022).

[388] "French SSP Insiders Speak Out," https://exopolitics.org/french-ssp-insiders-speak-out/ (accessed 3/16/2022).

[389] William Harwood, "William Shatner sets record in space with Blue Origin spaceflight," CBS News (10/13/2021) https://www.cbsnews.com/live-updates/william-shatner-blue-origin-space-flight/ (accessed 12/30/2021).

[390] See Michael Salla, "Are Secret Moon Construction Projects causing Worldwide Labor Shortage?" https://exopolitics.org/are-secret-moon-construction-projects-causing-a-worldwide-labor-shortage/ (accessed 1/12/2022).

[391] First cited in https://exopolitics.org/contact-with-the-council-of-nine-roddenberrys-star-trek-future/ (accessed 3/10/2022).

[392] Phyllis Schlemmer, *The Only Planet of Choice* (Gateway Books, 1993) p. 9.

[393] "The Law of One, 7.9," https://www.lawofone.info/s/7#9 (accessed 1/12/2022).

[394] "The Law of One, 7.9," https://www.lawofone.info/s/6#8 (accessed 1/12/2022).

[395] Wes Penre, "Galactic Federations and Councils," https://www.bibliotecapleyades.net/vida_alien/alien_galacticfederations43.htm (accessed 1/12/2022).

[396] Chris Knowles, Secret Star Trek: "Not Entirely Real", https://secretsun.blogspot.com/2013/06/secret-star-trek-part-3-stranger-than.html (accessed 1/12/2022).

[397] First cited in https://exopolitics.org/contact-with-the-council-of-nine-roddenberrys-star-trek-future/ (accessed 3/10/2022).

[398] See "Interview with Dr. Robert Wood – Chief Editor of Selected by Extraterrestrials Book 3," https://exopolitics.org/interview-with-dr-robert-wood/ (accessed 3/10/2022).

[399] See Air Force Space Command, "The Future of Space 2060 and Implications for U.S. Strategy: Report on the Space Futures Workshop", https://tinyurl.com/2p87rfn8 (accessed 1/12/2022).

[400] See my interview, "French Secret Space Program Insiders Speak Out": https://youtu.be/la4Npl3dkfA?t=3445 (accessed 3/12/2022).

[401] For a comparison of the story of Noah's Ark and the Epic of Gilgamesh, see Hannah Bird, "Noah's Ark and the Epic of Gilgamesh: A Comparison," https://fellowshipandfairydust.com/2015/05/27/noahs-ark-and-the-epic-of-gilgamesh-a-comparison/ (accessed 3/16/2022).

[402] Courtney Brown, "Noah's Ark," https://www.farsightprime.com/noah-s-ark/videos/noahs-ark (accessed 3/12/2022).

[403] See Andrew Jones, "China's Yutu 2 rover spots cube-shaped 'mystery hut' on far side of the moon," https://www.space.com/china-yutu-2-moon-rover-cube-shaped-object-photos (accessed 1/12/2021).

[404] See Michael Salla, "Earth Alliance Mission to Ganymede to greet ET visitors & inaugurate a Star Trek Future," https://exopolitics.org/earth-alliance-mission-to-ganymede-to-greet-et-visitors-inaugurate-a-star-trek-future/ (accessed 1/12/2021).

[405] I first wrote about JP's mission to the Atlantic ark in "Joint US China Mission to Giant ET Space Ark under Atlantic Ocean," https://exopolitics.org/giant-et-space-ark-under-atlantic (accessed 1/12/2021).

[406] See my interview with JP, "Atlantic Space Ark Rescue Mission," https://exopolitics.org/atlantic-space-ark-rescue-mission/ (accessed 2/2/2022).

[407] For my report on JP's Moon Mission, see "Joint US China missions sent to crashed alien spacecraft discovered by Yutu 2," https://exopolitics.org/china-us-explore-crashed-alien-spacecraft-found-by-yutu-2/ (accessed 1/12/2021).

[408] See Michael Salla, "Covert Disclosure of Antigravity Rectangles by USAF Special Operations" https://exopolitics.org/covert-disclosure-of-antigravity-rectangles-by-usaf-special-operations/ (accessed 1/13/2022).

[409] Cited in "Ancient Space Arks Activate with arrival of Intergalactic Confederation Fleet," https://exopolitics.org/ancient-space-arks-activate/ (accessed 3/10/2022).

[410] Cited in "Ancient Space Arks Activate with arrival of Intergalactic Confederation Fleet," https://exopolitics.org/ancient-space-arks-activate/ (accessed 3/10/2022).

[411] Cited in "Ancient Space Arks Activate with arrival of Intergalactic Confederation Fleet," https://exopolitics.org/ancient-space-arks-activate/ (accessed 3/10/2022).

[412] Cited in "Ancient Space Arks Activate with arrival of Intergalactic Confederation Fleet," https://exopolitics.org/ancient-space-arks-activate/ (accessed 3/10/2022).

413 The coordinates along with my analysis are discussed in Michael Salla, "USAF Colonel leaks coordinates of ancient Antarctic Ruins," https://exopolitics.org/usaf-colonel-leaks-coordinates-of-antarctic-ruins/ (accessed 3/10/2022).

414 Jason Samenow & Kasha Patel, "It's 70 degrees warmer than normal in eastern Antarctica. Scientists are flabbergasted," *Washington Post* (3/18/2022) https://www.washingtonpost.com/weather/2022/03/18/antarctica-heat-wave-climate-change/ (accessed 4/30/2022).

415 Jason Samenow & Kasha Patel, "It's 70 degrees warmer than normal in eastern Antarctica. Scientists are flabbergasted," *Washington Post* (3/18/2022) https://www.washingtonpost.com/weather/2022/03/18/antarctica-heat-wave-climate-change/ (accessed 4/30/2022).

416 Kristan Hutchison Sabbatini, "Soaring below Vostok," https://antarcticsun.usap.gov/pastIssues/2000-2001/2001_02_04.pdf (accessed 4/30/2022).

417 Richard Hoagland and Mike Bara, "What is Happening at the South Pole?" https://web.archive.org/web/20120103015714/https:/enterprisemission.com/antarctica.htm (accessed 4/30/2022).

418 See Michael Salla, "Possible New Source on Discovery of Frozen City under Antarctic Ice," https://exopolitics.org/possible-new-source-on-discovery-of-frozen-city-under-antarctic-ice/ (accessed 4/30/2022).

419 First cited in Michael Salla, "Is an Ancient Space Ark at Lake Vostok heating up Antarctica?" https://exopolitics.org/is-an-ancient-space-ark-at-lake-vostok-heating-up-antarctica/ (accessed 4/30/2022).

420 Interview with Jean Charles Moyen and Elena Danaan, "Space Arks & Halls of Records in Antarctica, Giza, Tibet & Bahamas" https://exopolitics.org/space-arks-halls-of-records-in-antarctica-giza-tibet-bahamas/ (accessed 4/30/2022).

421 First cited in Michael Salla, "Is an Ancient Space Ark at Lake Vostok heating up Antarctica?" https://exopolitics.org/is-an-ancient-space-ark-at-lake-vostok-heating-up-antarctica/ (accessed 4/30/2022)

422 Michael Salla, "Cabal leaders go to Antarctica to surrender to Extraterrestrials & Earth Alliance," https://exopolitics.org/cabal-leaders-go-to-antarctica-to-surrender-to-extraterrestrials-earth-alliance/ (accessed 4/30/2022).

423 Michael Salla, "Cabal leaders go to Antarctica to surrender to Extraterrestrials & Earth Alliance," https://exopolitics.org/cabal-leaders-go-to-antarctica-to-surrender-to-extraterrestrials-earth-alliance/ (accessed 4/30/2022).

424 See Michael Salla, "Atlantic Space Ark Rescue Mission," https://exopolitics.org/atlantic-space-ark-rescue-mission/ (accessed 4/30/2022).

https://exopolitics.org/atlantic-space-ark-rescue-mission/ (accessed 4/30/2022).

425 First cited in Michael Salla, "Is an Ancient Space Ark at Lake Vostok heating up Antarctica?" https://exopolitics.org/is-an-ancient-space-ark-at-lake-vostok-heating-up-antarctica/ (accessed 4/30/2022).

426 See Michael Salla, "Joint US China Mission to Giant ET Space Ark under Atlantic Ocean," https://exopolitics.org/giant-et-space-ark-under-atlantic/ (accessed 4/30/2022).

427 Interview with Jean Charles Moyen and Elena Danaan, "Space Arks & Halls of Records in Antarctica, Giza, Tibet & Bahamas" https://exopolitics.org/space-arks-halls-of-records-in-antarctica-giza-tibet-bahamas/ (accessed 4/30/2022).

428 In a 2015 article, I discussed Corey Goode's secret space program testimony about giants being found in stasis chambers around the world. "Sleeping giants in stasis chambers ready to awaken whistleblower claims," https://exopolitics.org/sleeping-giants-in-stasis-chambers-ready-to-awaken-whistleblower-claims/ (accessed 4/30/2022).

429 Cited in Michael Salla, "Navy Seal Reveals Secret Mission to Ancient Buried Structure in Antarctica," https://exopolitics.org/navy-seal-reveals-secret-mission-to-ancient-buried-structure-in-antarctica/ (accessed 1/13/2022).

430 See "Oleshky Sands," https://earthobservatory.nasa.gov/images/145801/oleshky-sands (accessed 3/11/2022).

431 First cited in Michael Salla, "Buried Ukraine space ark in Kherson activates so Russia takes over," https://exopolitics.org/buried-ukraine-space-ark-in-kherson-activates/ (accessed 3/11/2022).

432 See Michael Salla, "Were US Special Forces trapped in Ukraine Space Ark Now Controlled by Russia?" https://exopolitics.org/were-us-special-forces-trapped-in-ukraine-space-ark-now-controlled-by-russia/ (accessed 3/11/2022).

433 See Michael Salla, "What's Coming in 2022 and Beyond: The Exopolitics Paradigm Shift," available at: https://vimeo.com/ondemand/whatscomingin2022 (accessed 3/11/2022).

434 First cited in Michael Salla, "Buried Ukraine space ark in Kherson activates so Russia takes over," https://exopolitics.org/buried-ukraine-space-ark-in-kherson-activates/ (accessed 3/11/2022).

435 First cited in Michael Salla, "Buried Ukraine space ark in Kherson activates so Russia takes over," https://exopolitics.org/buried-ukraine-space-ark-in-kherson-activates/ (accessed 3/11/2022).

[436] For an excellent analysis of the causes of the Ukraine Civil War, see John Mearsheimer, "Why is Ukraine the West's Fault", University of Chicago https://youtu.be/JrMiSQAGOS4 (accessed 3/11/2022).

[437] The Minsk agreement is available online at: https://www.unian.info/politics/1043394-minsk-agreement-full-text-in-english.html (accessed 3/11/2022).

[438] Greg Butterfield, 'Washington is pushing Ukraine to attack Donbass,'https://www.struggle-la-lucha.org/2022/02/05/washington-is-pushing-ukraine-to-attack-donbass/ (accessed 3/11/2022).

[439] "Operation Storm — The Battle for Croatia, 1995", https://adst.org/2016/08/operation-storm-the-battle-croatia-1995/ (accessed 3/11/2022).

[440] *Greanville Post*, "Russia claims to have discovered Ukrainian Donbass attack plan," https://www.greanvillepost.com/2022/03/09/russia-claims-to-have-discovered-ukrainian-donbass-attack-plan/ (accessed 3/11/2022).

[441] Veterans Today, "US Bioweapon Labs in Ukraine, What will Russia Find?" https://www.veteranstoday.com/2022/02/24/us-bioweapons-labs-in-ukraine-what-will-russia-find-in-the-labs/ (accessed 3/11/2022).

[442] U.S. Embassy in Ukraine, "Biological Threat Reduction Program," https://ua.usembassy.gov/embassy/kyiv/sections-offices/defense-threat-reduction-office/biological-threat-reduction-program/ (accessed 3/11/2022).

[443] Reuters, "U.S. dismisses Russian claims of biowarfare labs in Ukraine,"https://www.reuters.com/world/russia-demands-us-explain-biological-programme-ukraine-2022-03-09/ (accessed 3/11/2022).

[444] Odishatv, "Russia Reveals Documents Of Labs Developing Biological Weapons In Ukraine Funded By The US," https://odishatv.in/news/international/russia-reveals-documents-of-labs-developing-biological-weapons-in-ukraine-funded-by-the-us-172144 (accessed 3/11/2022).

[445] See Michael Salla, "Were US Special Forces trapped in Ukraine Space Ark Now Controlled by Russia?" https://exopolitics.org/were-us-special-forces-trapped-in-ukraine-space-ark-now-controlled-by-russia/ (accessed 3/11/2022).

CHAPTER 14

[446] See Samuel Chamberlain and Bruce Golding, "Truth is in here: $770B defense bill includes agency to investigate UFOs", New York Post (12/15/2021) https://nypost.com/2021/12/15/770b-defense-bill-includes-agency-to-investigate-ufos/ (accessed 1/14/2022).

[447] Department of Defense, "DoD Announces the Establishment of the Airborne Object Identification and Management Synchronization Group (AOIMSG)," https://tinyurl.com/2x8pdz7u (accessed 1/14/2022).

[448] https://www.thetimes.co.uk/article/heavens-above-nasa-hires-priest-to-prepare-for-an-alien-discovery-sdczvwgqm (accessed 1/14/2022).

[449] See NASA, "NASA's Webb Telescope Launches to See First Galaxies, Distant Worlds," https://www.nasa.gov/press-release/nasas-webb-telescope-launches-to-see-first-galaxies-distant-worlds (accessed 1/14/2022).

[450] At time of writing there were 4903 exoplanets that were confirmed using data from Hubble and Kepler space satellites, see NASA, Exoplanet Exploration, https://exoplanets.nasa.gov/ (accessed 1/14/2022).

[451] Brookings Institute, *Proposed Studies on the Implications of Peaceful Space Activities for Human Affairs*, (Brookings Institute, 1960) p. 215.

[452] Brookings Report, p. 215.

[453] Brookings Report, p. 215.

[454] Brookings Report, p. 225.

[455] This suppression has been well documented in many UFO books. The earliest of these was Donald Keyhoe's, *The Flying Saucer Conspiracy* (Holt, 1955).

[456] Cited from online version of Robertson Panel at: http://www.cufon.org/cufon/robertdod.htm (accessed 1/14/2022).

[457] Wes Penre, "Galactic Federations and Councils," https://wespenre.com/2019/02/02/third-level-of-learning-paper-8-galactic-federations-and-councils/ (accessed 1/14/2022).

[458] See Elena Danaan, *We Will Never Let You Down* (Independently Published, 2021) p. 300.

INDEX

Ingram Content Group UK Ltd.
Milton Keynes UK
UKHW020629100323
418360UK00012B/1043

9 780998 603889